THE ALLYN & BACON

SOCIAL ATLAS

of the

UNITED STATES

THE ALLYN & BACON
SOCIAL ATLAS
of the
UNITED STATES

WILLIAM H. FREY
with Amy Beth Anspach, John Paul DeWitt,
and staff members of the Social Science Data Analysis Network

Boston   New York   San Francisco
Mexico City   Montreal   Toronto   London   Madrid   Munich   Paris
Hong Kong   Singapore   Tokyo   Cape Town   Sydney

Executive Editor: Jeff Lasser
Series Editorial Assistant: Lauren Houlihan
Senior Marketing Manager: Kelly May
Production Editor: Judy Fiske
Editorial Production Service: Lisa Torri (Precision Graphics)
Composition Buyer: Linda Cox
Manufacturing Buyer: Megan Cochran
Electronic Composition: Precision Graphics
Interior Design: Precision Graphics
Photo Researcher: Precision Graphics
Cover Designer: Joel Gendron

For related titles and support materials, visit our online catalog at www.ablongman.com

Between the time website information is gathered and then published, it is not unusual for some sites to have closed. Also, the transcription of URLs can result in typographical errors. The publisher would appreciate notification where these errors occur so they may be corrected in subsequent editions.

ISBN-13: 978-0-205-43917-1   ISBN-10: 0-205-43917-9

CIP data not available at time of publication

Printed in the United States of America
10 9 8 7 6 5 4 3 2 1 RRD-OH 11 10 09 08 07

Photo credits: Chapter 1, Pixland/Jupiterimages; Chapter 2, Mike Watson Images/SuperStock; Chapter 3, © Darren Greenwood/Design Pics/Corbis; Chapter 4, Corbis; Chapter 5, Glowimages/Getty Images; Chapter 6, Brand X/SuperStock; Chapter 7, Image Source/SuperStock; Chapters 8 and 9, Digital Vision Ltd./SuperStock

CONTENTS

CHAPTER 8
NATURAL RESOURCES AND THE ENVIRONMENT

CHAPTER 9
MODERN AMERICA

MAPPING A CHANGING AMERICA

As we move onward into the twenty-first century, America continues to be a major player in the new global economy. With technological advances undreamed of 20 years ago, and new immigration flows to our shores, we are a vital, vibrant nation facing new opportunities and challenges. Yet this new richness and vibrancy is not evenly spread across the country. Any national snapshot belies considerable geographic variation in the social structure that is evolving across states, regions, and urban and rural areas.

We are a nation constantly in flux. It is this dynamic picture of our social change that is graphically portrayed in *The Allyn & Bacon Social Atlas of the United States*. In the pages that follow, we identify the most salient trends in the fields of demographics, economics, health, politics, criminal justice, and the environment. We illustrate these trends in bold relief through eye-catching charts and vivid maps. And, in addition to these mega-trends, we present some less well known—often countering conventional wisdoms—selected to provide insights into the myriad changes our society is undergoing.

What follows is a brief description of each of the chapters in the *Atlas*.

Our Dynamic Populace

The *Atlas* begins with a chapter on our dynamic populace, framing other changes to come. It points out that most of our population, now over 300 million strong, is concentrated in the 10 biggest states, largely in urban areas on the coasts, and still in the industrial heartland. Yet there has been a flurry of movement in recent decades, out of the Great Plains toward the far West and Southeast, and out of older cities to booming, far out suburbs. New waves of immigrants have begun to fill in all parts of the country, while native born migration has slowed down.

We see the gradual aging of the huge baby boom generation, at the same time that younger GenXers and GenYers prepare to take their place. The aging of America is uneven, however, showing central and northern regional concentrations of older, age 65+ residents, as well as very old, age 85+, residents. At the same time, the higher fertility of minorities, Hispanics especially, serves to decelerate the aging process in large parts of the South and West.

Intimate relations within the population have also changed. Late marriage, more frequent divorce, and remarriage characterize generations from the baby boomers onwards. Here again, there are geographic variations. Divorce rates are higher in large swaths of the West, but family size is also highest in parts of this region.

Race, Ethnicity, and Minority Status

In the chapter on race, ethnicity, and minority status we literally map how America's new racial geography is transforming our national landscape. No longer confined to simple categories, America's racial and ethnic groups are a kaleidoscope of hues, nationalities, and cultural backgrounds. They are also clustered in different parts of the country: blacks in the South, Hispanics in the South and West, Asians in selected metropolitan areas. Even whites can be viewed according to ancestries that form communties in different parts of the country, including Italians in the Northeast, French in Louisiana, and Norwegians in Minnesota.

Yet the clustering of race and ethnic groups is also accompanied by challenges of the immigrant assimilation of Hispanics and Asians, concentrated poverty for blacks, and continued levels of residential segregation. As different parts of the country evolve into their own "melting pots," a new America is bubbling up from the younger generations, bringing with them new issues and hopes.

Wealth, Income, and Opportunity

These hopes and fears are taken up more explicitly in the chapter on wealth, income, and opportunity. Here we document success stories of minorities and immigrants achieving the American Dream though ownership of homes and small businesses, and financial success. We also address the other side of the coin—the rise of consumer debt, as well as the ebbs and flows of poverty in America. Educational attainment is an important means to achieving life goals. We portray the successes and failures of different groups in receiving higher education, as well as high school and college dropouts. The increasing number of students enrolled in alternatives to public schools, both homeschooled and private, reflects a significant new trend that shows considerable regional variation.

The Economy and Workplace

Matters associated with work are presented in the chapter on the economy and the workplace. The link between the types of jobs people hold and the earnings they receive has changed dramatically in our postindustrial economy. Still, there are wide variations across industry and region in pay, working conditions, and benefits. Union membership, while declining, helps to account for most of these variations. At the same time, the labor force has become increasingly diverse in terms of its racial, ethnic, and gender make up. And while legislation, originating with the Civil Rights movement, has reduced discrimination and earnings differences between groups, gaps are still evident in different parts of the country.

Health and Wellness

An important dimension of a society's well-being is the state of its health, a topic that is taken up in the chapter on health and wellness. Despite medical advances, there is differential access to health care in our country, related to such factors as income, education, and immigrant status, as well as geographic area. Behavior with health risks, such as smoking, alcohol consumption, poor diet, and lack of physical activity, also shows wide variation. The chapter also depicts how regions of the country differ in the incidence of cancer, sexually transmitted diseases, and pandemics such as the West Nile virus, as well as the geography of persons with disabilities.

Politics and Government

In the chapter on politics and government we take a look at government spending at the federal and local level. We also examine voting in America. The question of who does or does not vote—along with when and where—are important issues in national and local elections. For example, as more immigrants and Hispanics become citizens, their voting participation will become crucial in deciding close elections. We also examine the impact of the increased presence of minorities among elected officials and among members of the military.

Crime and Law Enforcement

The chapter on crime and law enforcement takes up several important topics involving criminal justice in America. We track the downturn in violent crime commencing in the 1990s, and plot geographic variations in crime in this decade. At the same time, prison incarceration rates have risen, and inmates continue to be disproportionately black males. The chapter also discusses variations in alcohol, drug abuse, and gambling, with special emphasis on how it affects children. This leads to a focus on juvenile delinquency and the recent decrease in juvenile crimes. The chapter ends with a discussion of children as victims of abuse and neglect, and its variations across regions of the country.

Natural Resources and the Environment

The chapter on natural resources and the environment focuses on some of the most of important issues facing the nation, including the impact of Hurricane Katrina and the concern about climate change. The chapter covers topics related to land use trends in farmlands, parks, and forests. It addresses, as well, alternative sources of energy and geographic variation in energy consumption. Environmental degradation, focusing on solid waste, acid rain, and greenhouse-effect emissions, is discussed, with a special emphasis on natural disasters.

Modern America

In the chapter on modern America we take a look the new challenges of connecting with each other given technological advances in transportation and communication. The urban sprawl that envelops much of America has increased congestion to record levels, leaving open the question of how well can public transportation fill the void. Increasingly, the Internet is taking over both workplace and social functions that required personal travel, or more traditional ways of communication. Yet not all parts of the population have access to the Internet. And in the new era of communications, even mass media is changing. With the advent of digital satellite television, digital video recorders (DVRs), and digital music players, the three or four broadcast networks are no longer satisfying the prime audience needs for information and entertainment.

It is our hope that in perusing the topics in this *Atlas,* you will come away with an appreciation for the dynamic change and regional differences that are underway in twenty-first century America. The statistics we present here are just the "tip of the iceberg" of those available from the variety of sources we have mined. But by laying out these broad themes of American society, we hope to whet your appetite for their further investigation.

ACKNOWLEDGEMENTS

This *Atlas* is intended to illuminate broad social patterns in American society, based on recent statistics and with an eye toward future trends. It reflects an extensive mining of large databases from a variety of government, nonprofit, and university sources, in an effort to present the most salient aspects of social change in America

As such, this *Atlas* fits in well with other activities of the Social Science Data Analysis Network (SSDAN)—a university-based organization that creates demographic media including printed publications, interactive websites, and web-based classroom materials. SSDAN's goal is to make information on social and demographic trends available in lively, engaging, and accessible formats to a broad audience of educators, policy makers, and informed citizens. An overview can be found at http://www.ssdan.net.

SSDAN is directed by demographer, Dr. William H. Frey, at the University of Michigan's Institute for Social Research and involves a network of student and staff associates affiliated with the University. The authors are appreciative of the contributions of SSDAN associates, Peter Acuff, Megan Esseltine, Melanie Mason, Emily Beam, Rachel Burrage, and Tamara Livshiz, as well as the efforts of senior programmer Cathy Sun.

We also appreciate the guidance and data provided by Jennifer Lehman of the CDC's Division of Vector-Borne Infectious Diseases.

We are especially indebted to Jeff Lasser, editor at Allyn & Bacon, who was the guiding spirit behind this project. The encouragement and efforts of Jeff and the editorial team, including Judy Fiske and Lisa Torri, were essential in bringing this *Atlas* to life and made this project a valuable and enjoyable experience for all involved.

William H. Frey
Amy B. Anspach
John P. DeWitt

THE ALLYN & BACON

SOCIAL ATLAS

of the

UNITED STATES

1 OUR DYNAMIC POPULACE

- **Adding and Subtracting: Regional Population Change**

- **The Newest Americans: Immigration**

- **Pulling Up Stakes: Migration and Mobility**

- **Generations: Young and Old**

- **The Baby Factor: Fertility and Birth Rates**

- **Witnesses to a Century: Americans 65 and Older**

- **Life Expectancy and Mortality**

- **Urban and Rural Living**

- **Marriage and Divorce**

- **Blood, Marriage, or Adoption: Family Structure**

Adding and Subtracting: Regional Population Change

In 2005, the population of the United States was concentrated in three distinct regions: the Pacific Coast and Arizona, the Frost Belt (Great Lakes states and New England), and Florida. There were also a few clusters of population near major cities.

As of 2005, eight states had populations greater than 10 million people; seven states and the District of Columbia had fewer than 1 million people. California, with a population of 36,132,147, led the nation by a margin of 13 million people. Wyoming was the least populated state, with only 509,294 people.

The Great Plains, from western Texas through Montana, have the lowest county populations, and experienced the heaviest population decline from 1990 to 2005. The county with the greatest population is Los Angeles County, California (9,935,475), which is slightly less than the population of the entire state of Michigan, but more populated than the entire state of Georgia. Thirty-eight counties had populations greater than 1 million.

Americans seem to be drawn to water. In spite of the nation's geographic size, approximately 153 million people (53 percent of the population) lived in a coastal county in 2003. In fact, 23 of the 25 most densely populated counties were coastal. Tennessee was the most populated state (ranked 16th, with 5,962,959 people in 2005) not on an ocean, Great Lake, or the Gulf of Mexico.

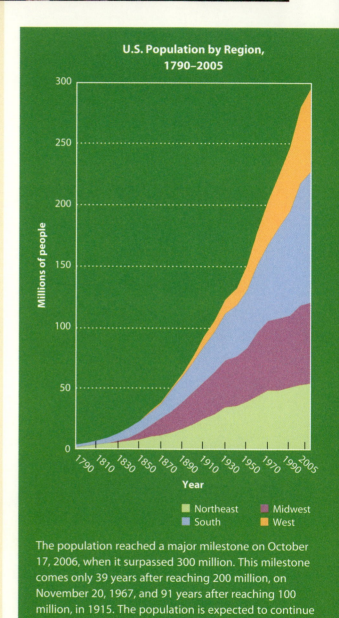

U.S. Population by Region, 1790–2005

Legend: Northeast, Midwest, South, West

The population reached a major milestone on October 17, 2006, when it surpassed 300 million. This milestone comes only 39 years after reaching 200 million, on November 20, 1967, and 91 years after reaching 100 million, in 1915. The population is expected to continue its rapid growth and it is estimated it will reach 400 million sometime around 2043.

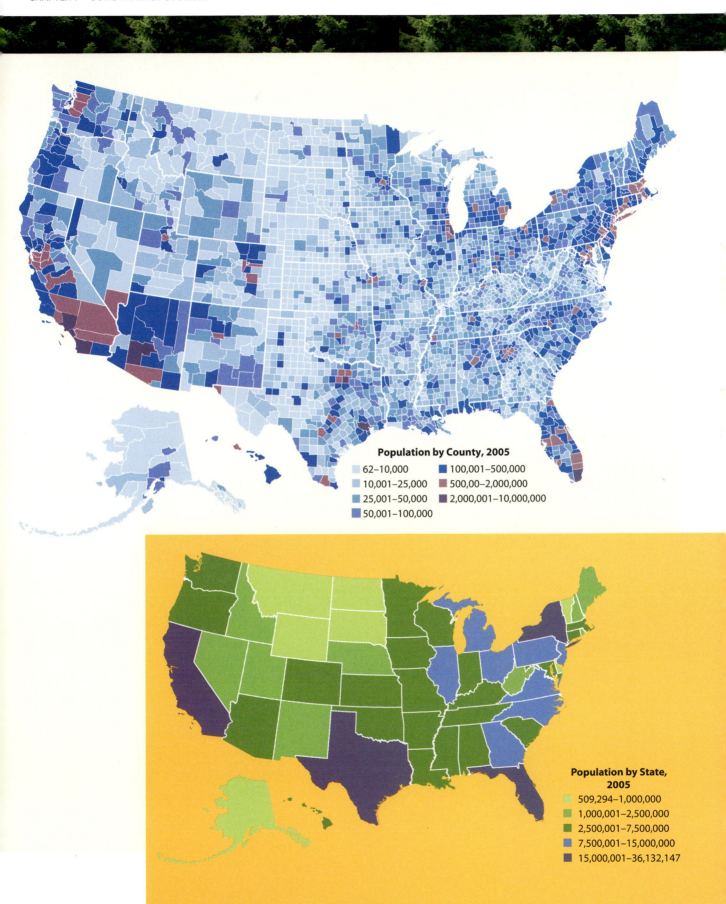

Population by County, 2005

- 62–10,000
- 10,001–25,000
- 25,001–50,000
- 50,001–100,000
- 100,001–500,000
- 500,00–2,000,000
- 2,000,001–10,000,000

Population by State, 2005

- 509,294–1,000,000
- 1,000,001–2,500,000
- 2,500,001–7,500,000
- 7,500,001–15,000,000
- 15,000,001–36,132,147

Adding and Subtracting: Regional Population Change

From 1990 to 2005, the most noticeable trend in U.S. population change was a drop in the Great Plains region. County populations doubled near Denver, Dallas, Atlanta, Washington, Salt Lake City, Boise, and San Antonio. Overall, Nevada, Arizona and Florida had very high growth rates.

Almost all counties having negative growth from 1990 to 2005 were both inland and rural. Counties near a coast or in a metropolitan area typically grew in population.

Of particular note are the "suburban rings" that show up around several major cities including Dallas–Fort Worth, Minneapolis–St. Paul, and Atlanta. The counties surrounding these cities show distinctly higher rates of population growth than do the cities themselves, suggesting an increase in suburbanization.

Dallas–Fort Worth "suburban ring"

Florida is the only state east of the Mississippi that grew by more than 400 percent during the last century

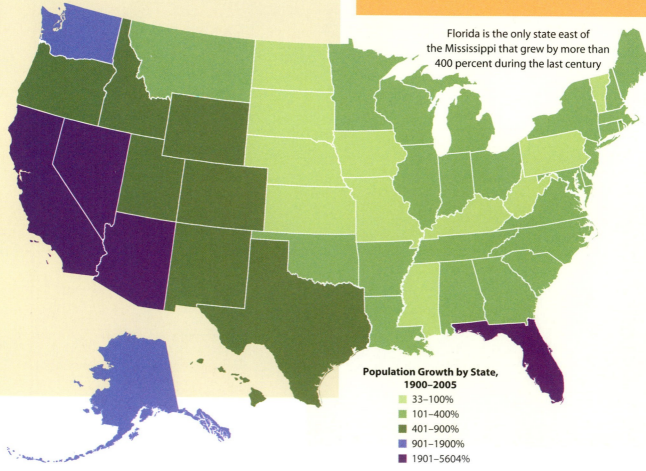

Population Growth by State, 1900–2005

- 33–100%
- 101–400%
- 401–900%
- 901–1900%
- 1901–5604%

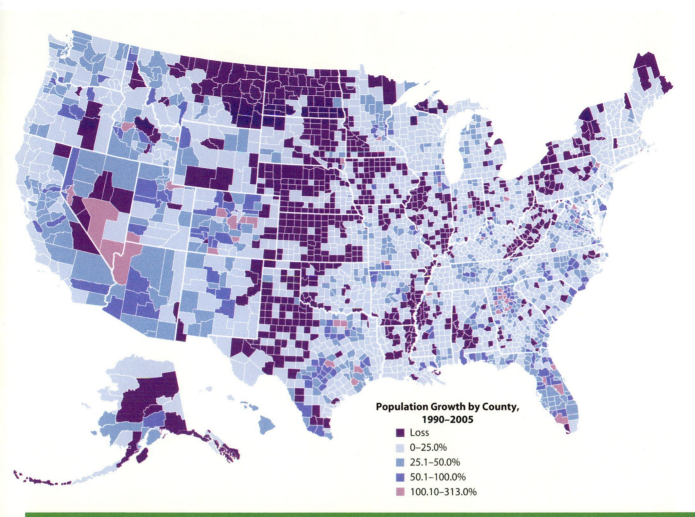

**Population Growth by County,
1990–2005**

- Loss
- 0–25.0%
- 25.1–50.0%
- 50.1–100.0%
- 100.10–313.0%

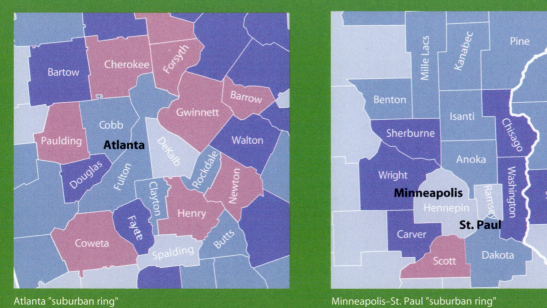

Atlanta "suburban ring"   Minneapolis–St. Paul "suburban ring"

The Newest Americans: Immigration

America's foreign-born population has played an important role throughout its history. In 2005, immigrants made up about 12 percent of the population.

While Europeans were traditionally the largest group of immigrants, Latin Americans and Asians composed nearly 70 percent of the arriving immigrant population in 2000. There are large differences in education level and income depending on region of origin. For example, 50 percent of Asian immigrants have a bachelor's degree or higher, compared with 12 percent of those from Latin America.

Nearly 95 percent of all immigrants move to metropolitan areas. Almost one in every five immigrants heads to New York City or Los Angeles upon arrival, and over 50 percent of the Miami County population is foreign born. California has the greatest proportion of foreign-born residents (26 percent), followed by New York (20 percent).

Many immigrants to the United States are married, young, and in their reproductive years. Of the immigrants naturalized in 2004, 65 percent were married and 64.4 percent were age 20 to 44. Also notable is that in 2006, the median age of people of Mexican descent was 25.3 years, compared with 36.2 for the United States as a whole.

Today the United States struggles with the problem of illegal immigration; approximately 12 million undocumented immigrants lived in the United States in mid 2006, with roughly one-quarter residing in California.

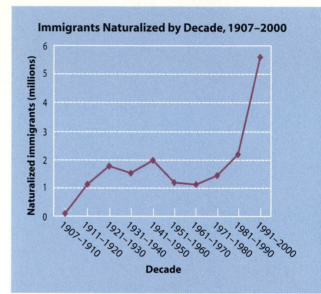

Immigrants Naturalized by Decade, 1907–2000

Top 10 Countries of Origin and Number of Immigrants

Country	2004	1921–1930 (avg/yr)	Country
Mexico	173,644	92,452	Canada
India	65,472	45,929	Mexico
Philippines	54,632	45,532	Italy
China	45,942	41,220	Germany
Former USSR	36,646	33,957	United Kingdom
Vietnam	30,064	22,773	Poland
Dom. Republic	30,049	21,123	Ireland[1]
El Salvador	29,285	10,219	Czechoslovakia
Canada	22,437	9,725	Sweden
Korea	19,441	6,853	Norway

[1] Prior to 1926, data for Northern Ireland included in Ireland.

Immigrants from Asia and Europe have lower poverty rates than native-born Americans, although the rate for immigrants as a whole is higher.

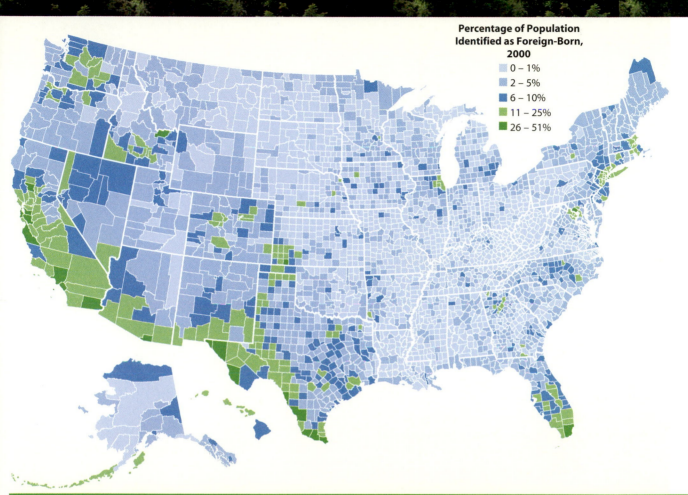

Percentage of Population Identified as Foreign-Born, 2000

- 0 – 1%
- 2 – 5%
- 6 – 10%
- 11 – 25%
- 26 – 51%

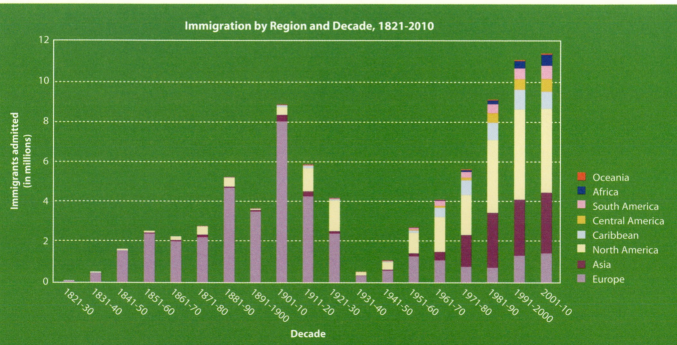

Immigration by Region and Decade, 1821-2010

- Oceania
- Africa
- South America
- Central America
- Caribbean
- North America
- Asia
- Europe

The last category, 2001–10, is projected using data from 2001–04.

The Newest Americans: Immigration

Foreign citizens may request asylum or refugee status to obtain residence in the United States. In 2004, the U.S. government granted asylum to 14,359 individuals (down from 22,852 in 2000 and 28,677 in 2001). The two most common regions of origin in 2004 were Africa and South America, where 3,857 and 4,288, respectively, were granted asylum. The federal government granted asylum to more individuals from Colombia (2,930) in 2004 than any other nation.

Immigrants need not be adults or moving with their families. In 2005, there were 22,710 immigrant orphans adopted by U.S. citizens. Although China remained the most common country of origin for immigrant adoptees, 95.0 percent of adoptees from China are female. The lopsided figure for China contrasts with the fairly balanced rate for all other countries, where 50.3 percent of adoptees are female.

The term "foreign-born" includes several groups: naturalized immigrants (those who have obtained U.S. citizenship), lawful permanent residents, temporary migrants (such as students), humanitarian migrants (such as refugees), and persons illegally present in the United States. Although there was a lull in immigration overall from the late 1920s until the 1960s, naturalizations were not as drastically reduced.

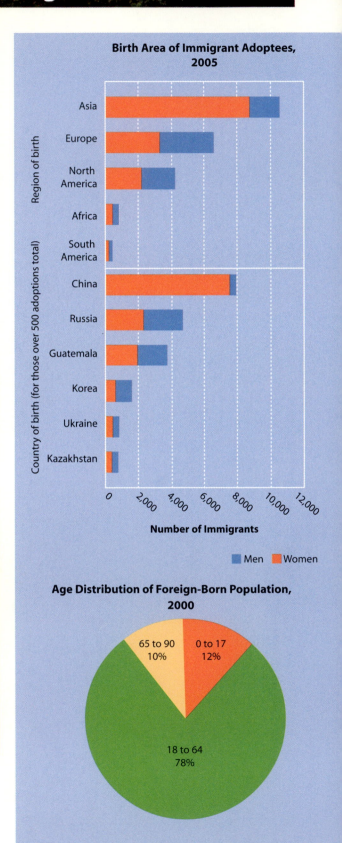

Birth Area of Immigrant Adoptees, 2005

Region of birth

Country of birth (for those over 500 adoptions total)

Number of Immigrants

■ Men   ■ Women

Age Distribution of Foreign-Born Population, 2000

65 to 90
10%

0 to 17
12%

18 to 64
78%

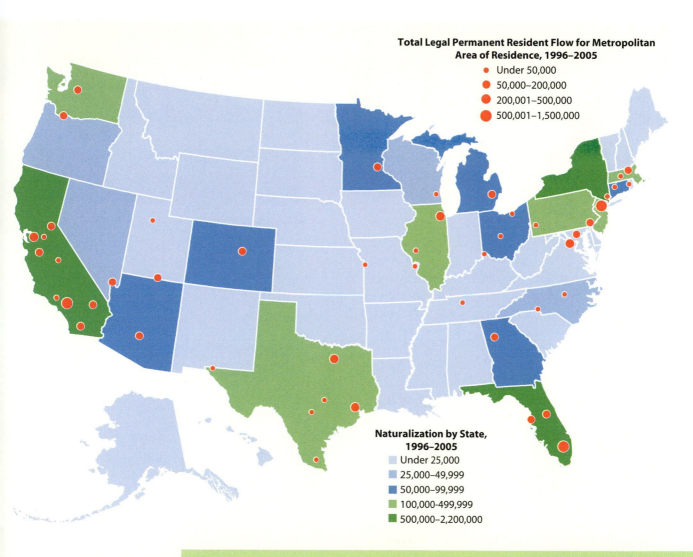

Total Legal Permanent Resident Flow for Metropolitan Area of Residence, 1996–2005

- Under 50,000
- 50,000–200,000
- 200,001–500,000
- 500,001–1,500,000

Naturalization by State, 1996–2005

- Under 25,000
- 25,000–49,999
- 50,000–99,999
- 100,000-499,999
- 500,000–2,200,000

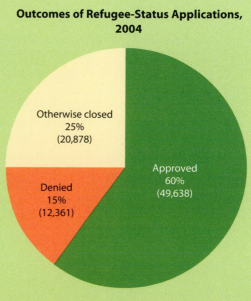

In 2004, 75,537 individuals applied for refugee status in order to enter or remain in the country. During that year, 49,638 applications were approved, and 12,361 applications were denied. An additional 20,878 applications were closed prior to a decision. According to U.S. Citizenship and Immigration Services, 80 percent of applications for refugee status that received a decision were approved in 2004.

Outcomes of Refugee-Status Applications, 2004

- Otherwise closed 25% (20,878)
- Denied 15% (12,361)
- Approved 60% (49,638)

Pulling Up Stakes: Migration and Mobility

Although Americans may feel nostalgic, they cherish the freedom that allows them to move about the country. We move around for various reasons: school, work, family needs, better weather, and sometimes just for a change of pace. Others change residences but move only minutes away. These cross-town moves commonly involve an improved living situation (especially for recent increases in family size), transient lifestyle (such as for college students), or simple matter of convenience.

Americans are moving less now than in previous decades. During the 1950s and 1960s, approximately one-fifth of the population relocated each year. Since then, the rate steadily dropped to just over 14 percent annually during the early 2000s. Although 40 million Americans moved each year from 2000 to 2003, fewer than 20 million moved to a different county.

Intracounty moves are most common among young children (who likely move as their parents accommodate the increased family size) and 20-somethings. In fact, although 20-somethings made up only 14 percent of the population in 2004, they accounted for 28 percent of all intracounty relocations during the previous year.

The distance of moves varies greatly, but most moves are not far. For intercounty moves, people are slightly more likely to move under 50 miles away, than to move 500 miles away or greater from their previous residence.

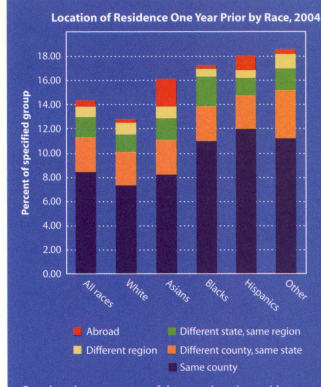

Based on the percentage of the race changing residence, whites were least mobile, and those belonging to races not specified were most mobile. As the graph shows, for all races, most moves were within the state. Also, over two percent of Asians had lived abroad the previous year, which is five times the average.

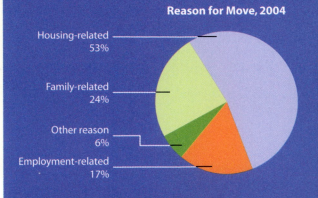

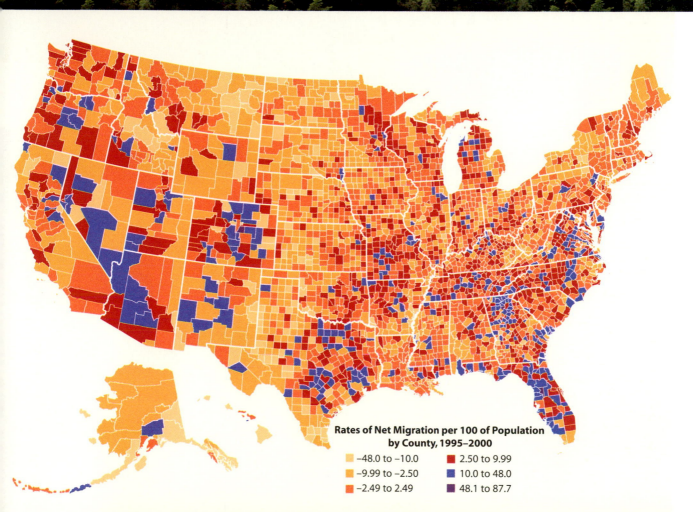

Rates of Net Migration per 100 of Population by County, 1995–2000

- −48.0 to −10.0
- −9.99 to −2.50
- −2.49 to 2.49
- 2.50 to 9.99
- 10.0 to 48.0
- 48.1 to 87.7

Many of the metropolitan areas having the highest rates of in- and outmigration contain either a large college/university or a military base. Although these communities are highly mobile, the migration in and migration out cancel each other out. Numbers do not include the number of people who moved but stayed within the metropolitan area.

Migration Rates in the Top 10 Metropolitan Areas[1] (per 100 of Population)

Migration In		Migration Out		Net Migration[2]	
Metropolitan Area		Metropolitan Area		Metropolitan Area	
Jacksonville, NC	42.26	Jacksonville, NC	41.99	Las Vegas, NV	15.54
Bryan-College Station, TX	39.88	Fayetteville, NC	34.60	Punta Gorda, FL	14.11
Bloomington, IN	35.34	Killeen-Temple, TX	34.51	Naples, FL	13.48
Iowa City, IA	33.94	Lawton, OK	34.39	Myrtle Beach, SC	12.39
Auburn-Opelika, AL	33.70	Bryan-College Station, TX	32.59	Fort Myers-Cape Coral, FL	11.01
Gainesville, FL	33.34	Iowa City, IA	31.24	Ocala, FL	10.68
Killeen-Temple, TX	32.48	Flagstaff, AZ-UT	29.96	State College, PA	9.84
State College, PA	32.15	Anchorage, AK	29.60	Sarasota-Bradenton, FL	9.14
Athens, GA	31.89	Bloomington, IN	29.39	Austin-San Marcos, TX	9.01
Boulder-Longmont, CO	31.03	Clarksville-Hopkinsville, TN-KY	28.61	Wilmington, NC	8.82

[1] Using Metropolitan Statistical Areas (MSAs) and Primary Metropolitan Statistical Areas (PMSAs) having population greater than 100,000
[2] Calculated as rate of immigration – outmigration.

Generations: Young and Old

The U.S. population quadrupled during the 20th century, from 75.7 million in 1900 to 281.4 million in 2000. In 2000, 35 percent of the population was below the age of 25. Fifty-two percent of the population was between the ages of 25 and 64. People 65 and over accounted for over 12 percent of the population.

The Greatest Generation is remembered for having lived out their formative years in the midst of the Great Depression and World War II. The persons in the Lucky Generation, many too young to have remembered the difficult times their parents' generation struggled through, experienced adolescence in the prosperous postwar economic "boom."

During the boom that followed the war, a population explosion, coupled with both an increase in homeownership and economic security, defined the name for the next two generations: the Early and Late Baby Boomers. Baby Boomers accounted for 28 percent of the population in 2000.

Generation X arrived to experience the Me Decade of the 1980s and life in the shadows of the Boomers. This generation was followed by the equally vaguely defined Generation Y. Americans born between 1986 and 1995 have been given a number of potential labels, including Generation Z and the iGeneration, but there is no consensus yet on just what defines the upcoming generation of young adults.

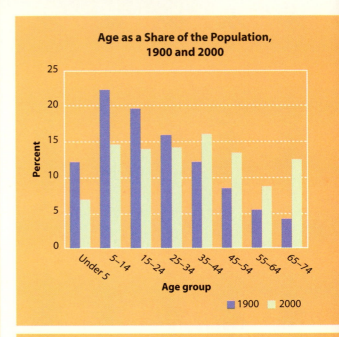

Age as a Share of the Population, 1900 and 2000

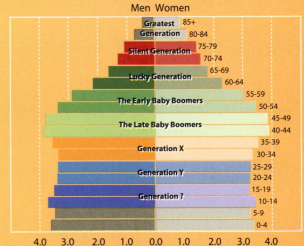

Age Distribution, 2005

Advances in medicine and improved standards of living contributed to an increase in life expectancy. Compared to 1900, the population a century later is now more evenly dispersed across age groups. In 1900, only four percent of the population was reported to be 65 years or older.

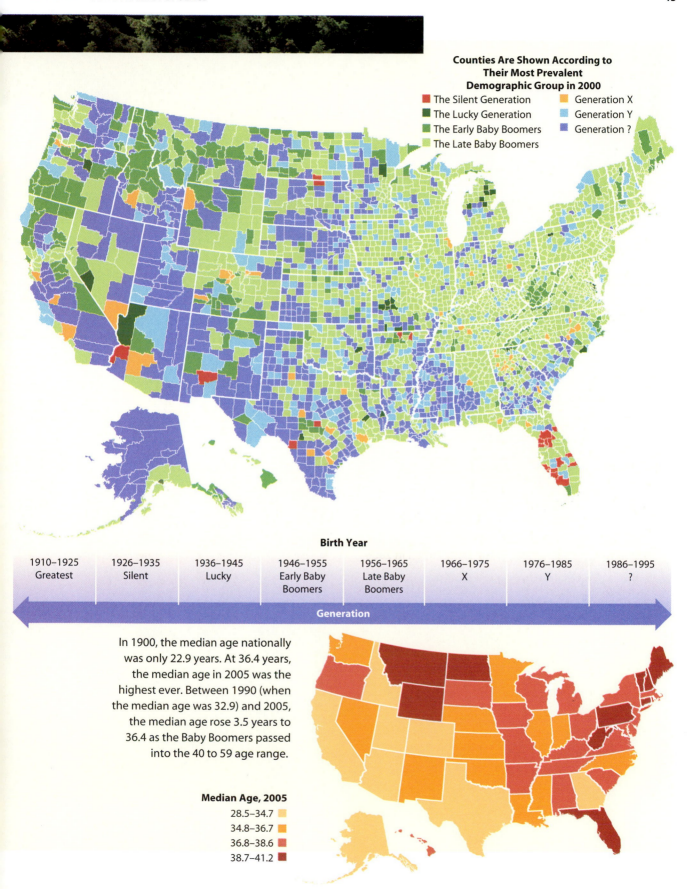

**Counties Are Shown According to
Their Most Prevalent
Demographic Group in 2000**

- ■ The Silent Generation
- ■ The Lucky Generation
- ■ The Early Baby Boomers
- ■ The Late Baby Boomers
- ■ Generation X
- ■ Generation Y
- ■ Generation ?

Birth Year

| 1910–1925 Greatest | 1926–1935 Silent | 1936–1945 Lucky | 1946–1955 Early Baby Boomers | 1956–1965 Late Baby Boomers | 1966–1975 X | 1976–1985 Y | 1986–1995 ? |

Generation

In 1900, the median age nationally was only 22.9 years. At 36.4 years, the median age in 2005 was the highest ever. Between 1990 (when the median age was 32.9) and 2005, the median age rose 3.5 years to 36.4 as the Baby Boomers passed into the 40 to 59 age range.

Median Age, 2005

- 28.5–34.7
- 34.8–36.7
- 36.8–38.6
- 38.7–41.2

The Baby Factor: Fertility and Birth Rates

Population structure and overall population growth are influenced by fluctuations in birth rate. While small changes in birth rate are expected, inability to predict large and lasting changes can lead to many social challenges. High birth rates such as those occurring during the Baby Boom can place strains on school systems with inadequate classroom capacity. Low birth rates following times of high birth rates, as in the decades after the Baby Boom, create a disproportionately large older population, which will challenge the Social Security system.

In 2003, there were over four million births in the United States. That's 14.1 births for every 1,000 persons in the total population, down from 24 births for every 1,000 persons in 1950. The birth rate remained fairly steady from 1995 through 2003.

Geographically, the southwestern states had the highest birth rate in 2003. Utah stood out among the others with a birth rate of 21.2 per 1,000 persons. The Northeast tends to have the lowest birth rates. Vermont and Maine tied for the lowest birth rate of 10.6 per 1,000.

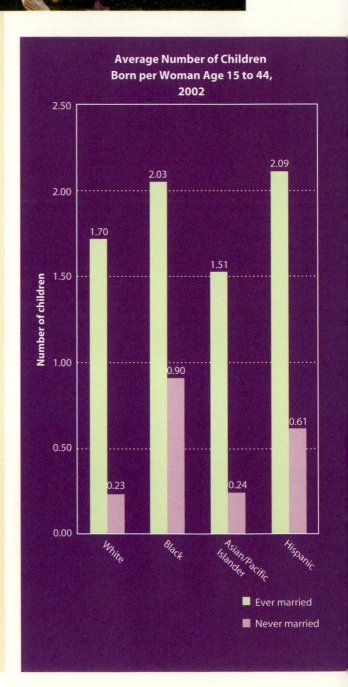

Average Number of Children Born per Woman Age 15 to 44, 2002

Number of children

	White	Black	Asian/Pacific Islander	Hispanic
Ever married	1.70	2.03	1.51	2.09
Never married	0.23	0.90	0.24	0.61

■ Ever married
■ Never married

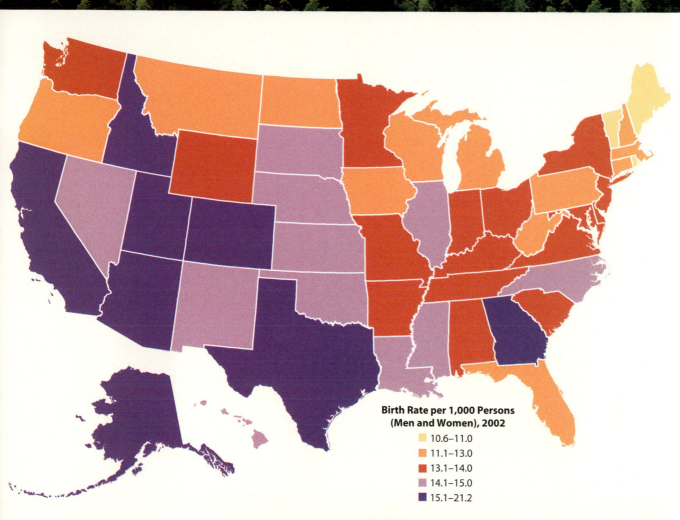

Birth Rate per 1,000 Persons (Men and Women), 2002

- 10.6–11.0
- 11.1–13.0
- 13.1–14.0
- 14.1–15.0
- 15.1–21.2

In spite of a reduction in the overall birth rate, births to single mothers have tripled since 1970. In 2003, 34.6 percent of all births were to unmarried women. In 1970 women under the age of 20 accounted for half of out-of-wedlock births. Since then, the age of single mothers at delivery has increased: women under age 20 accounted for only 24.3 percent of births to single mothers in 2003 while women age 25 and over accounted for 37 percent of births to single mothers.

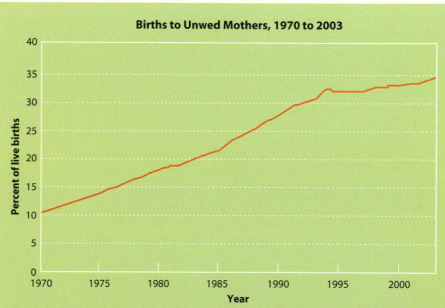

Births to Unwed Mothers, 1970 to 2003

The Baby Factor: Fertility and Birth Rates

Americans are not just having fewer children; they're also waiting longer to have them. The average age of a woman at the birth of her first child in 2003 was at an historical high of 25.2 years. In 2003 birth rates for women between 30 and 44 reached the highest levels since the 1960s.

The birth rate for teenage mothers has declined since the 1991 peak of 61.8 births per every 1,000 women age 15 to 19. In 2003, the birth rate of 41.6 births per 1,000 women 15 to 19 represented a decrease by one-third, and a drop from highest to lowest birth rate among teens in only 12 years. Teenage birth rates are higher in the South than the North, with the highest rates in Texas and Mississippi and the lowest in New Hampshire and Vermont.

In 2003, births to teen mothers were highest among Hispanics, at more than twice the national rate. Between 1991 and 2000, the birth rate for African American teens decreased from 118 to 68 births per 1,000 females age 15 to 19.

Multiple births have become increasingly common, perhaps due to an increase in the use of fertility drugs (most commonly used by older women) and a rise in the average age of women giving birth. Incidence of twin births has increased to 31 per 1,000 births, a 65 percent increase since 1980.

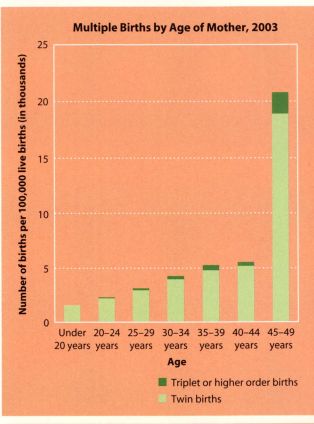

Multiple Births by Age of Mother, 2003

(Y-axis: Number of births per 100,000 live births (in thousands); X-axis: Age — Under 20 years, 20–24 years, 25–29 years, 30–34 years, 35–39 years, 40–44 years, 45–49 years)

■ Triplet or higher order births
■ Twin births

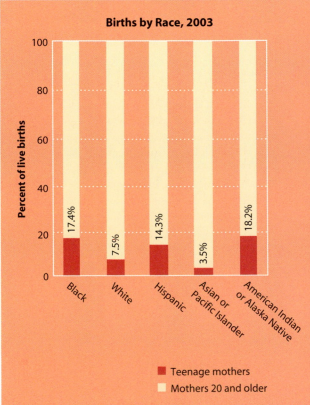

Births by Race, 2003

(Y-axis: Percent of live births; X-axis: Black 17.4%, White 7.5%, Hispanic 14.3%, Asian or Pacific Islander 3.5%, American Indian or Alaska Native 18.2%)

■ Teenage mothers
□ Mothers 20 and older

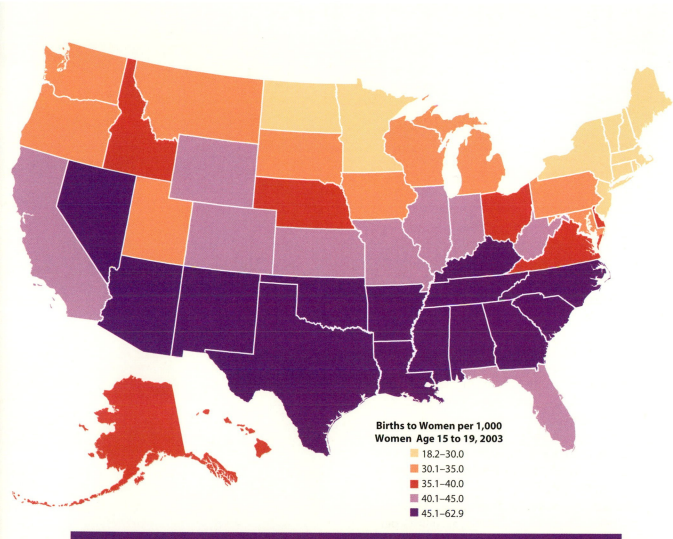

Births to Women per 1,000 Women Age 15 to 19, 2003

- 18.2–30.0
- 30.1–35.0
- 35.1–40.0
- 40.1–45.0
- 45.1–62.9

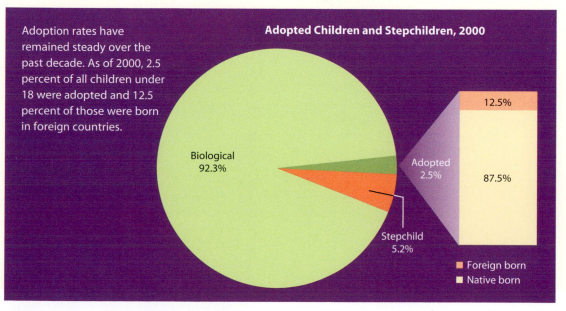

Adoption rates have remained steady over the past decade. As of 2000, 2.5 percent of all children under 18 were adopted and 12.5 percent of those were born in foreign countries.

Adopted Children and Stepchildren, 2000

Biological 92.3%

Stepchild 5.2%

Adopted 2.5%

12.5%

87.5%

- Foreign born
- Native born

Witnesses to a Century: Americans 65 and Older

With the exception of the 1990s, the population of those age 65 and over grew at a greater rate than the rest of the population throughout the twentieth century. The older (65+) population grew from 3.1 million in 1900 to over 36.8 million in 2005. Of those in 2005, 18.6 million were age 65 to 74, 13.1 million were age 75 to 84, and 5.1 million were age 85 or older. In 2000, the oldest-old (85+) population was 34 times the size of the group's population in 1900. The population age 65 to 84 multiplied its size in 1900 by 11. The population as a whole was just under four times as large in 2000 as in 1900. Around 2030, the oldest-old population is expected to grow more rapidly as Baby Boomers join this group.

The experiences of today's older population differ from the experiences of the remainder of the population. This segment of the population lived during periods of the Great Depression, World War II, the Holocaust, and the full length of the Cold War. Some even grew up during World War I. In 2000, 61.9 percent of the male population age 65 to 74 were veterans, as were 73.5 percent of the male population age 75 to 84. In contrast, by 2020, veterans are projected to comprise 31 percent of the population age 65 and older. The women of the older population made great contributions to society, including fighting for (and expanding) civil rights and paving the way for women in future years to enter the work force.

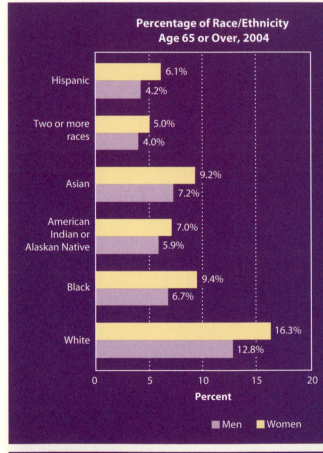

Percentage of Race/Ethnicity Age 65 or Over, 2004

- Hispanic: 6.1% (Women), 4.2% (Men)
- Two or more races: 5.0% (Women), 4.0% (Men)
- Asian: 9.2% (Women), 7.2% (Men)
- American Indian or Alaskan Native: 7.0% (Women), 5.9% (Men)
- Black: 9.4% (Women), 6.7% (Men)
- White: 16.3% (Women), 12.8% (Men)

Percent

■ Men ■ Women

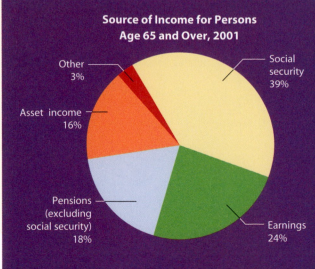

Source of Income for Persons Age 65 and Over, 2001

- Social security 39%
- Earnings 24%
- Pensions (excluding social security) 18%
- Asset income 16%
- Other 3%

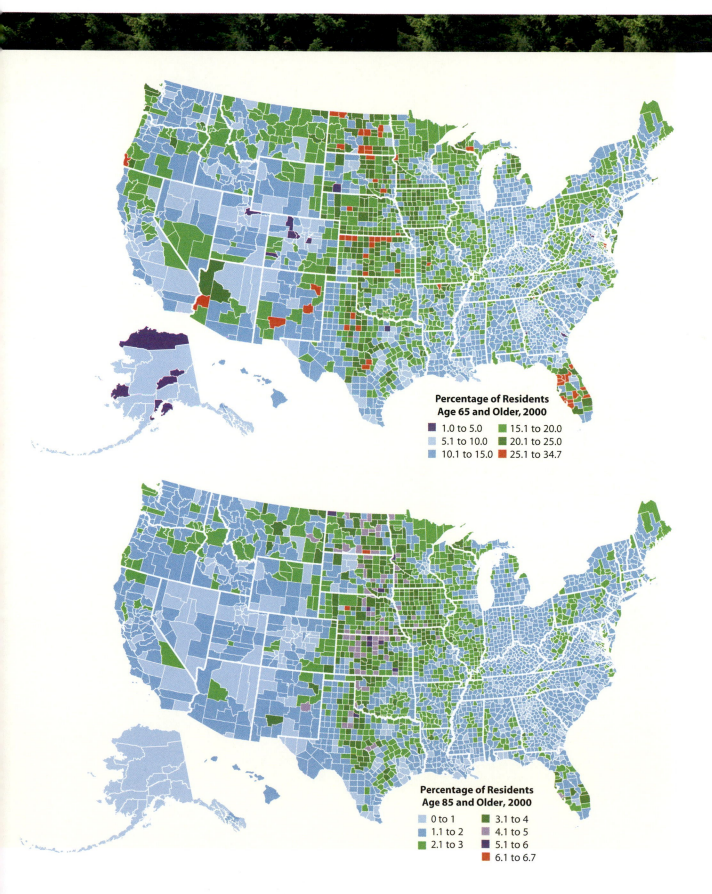

**Percentage of Residents
Age 65 and Older, 2000**

- 1.0 to 5.0
- 5.1 to 10.0
- 10.1 to 15.0
- 15.1 to 20.0
- 20.1 to 25.0
- 25.1 to 34.7

**Percentage of Residents
Age 85 and Older, 2000**

- 0 to 1
- 1.1 to 2
- 2.1 to 3
- 3.1 to 4
- 4.1 to 5
- 5.1 to 6
- 6.1 to 6.7

Witnesses to a Century: Americans 65 and Older

Health issues become more common as age increases. About 80 percent of the population age 65 and over had at least one chronic health condition in 2000. In addition, about 14 million individuals belonging to this age group reported a disability. Some of the most common conditions limiting activity among older people include arthritis, hypertension, heart disease, and respiratory disorders.

Rates of participation in the labor force dropped dramatically for older men during the last half of the twentieth century. In 1950, 46 percent of older men were in the labor force, but by 2003, that figure had dropped to 19 percent. The rates for older women increased minimally from 10 percent to 11 percent during the same period.

Although a smaller fraction of the older population is working than in past decades, the poverty rate has decreased dramatically. In 2003, 10 percent of the population age 65 and over lived below the poverty line, down from 35 percent in 1959. Though commonly seen as a popular seasonal or extended destination for the older population, individuals age 75 and over are more likely to move out of the South rather than into it. Interestingly, for the older population in 2003, net migration into the Midwest nearly matched net migration into the South. The migration data suggest that while many seniors do move to the South, migrants may return home or head elsewhere for reasons such as declining health, loss of a spouse, or reduced physical mobility. Perhaps most surprising is the extent of the migration out of the Northeast and lack of returning residents.

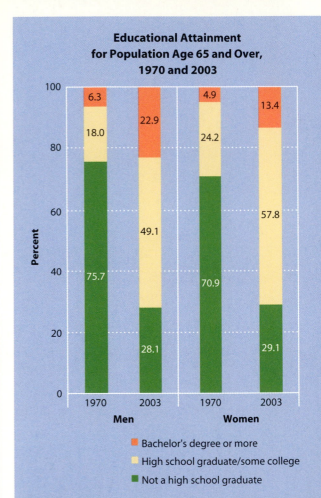

Educational Attainment for Population Age 65 and Over, 1970 and 2003

- Bachelor's degree or more
- High school graduate/some college
- Not a high school graduate

Older Americans are more highly educated than ever. In 1950, only 17 percent of the population age 65 and over had graduated from high school, and only 3 percent had at least a bachelor's degree. By 2003, 17 percent of the older population had at least a bachelor's degree, and 72 percent had graduated high school.

Net Migration by Region, 2002–2003 (thousands)

	Northeast	Midwest	South	West
65 and over	−31	15	16	0
65 to 75	−30	1	36	−6
75 and over	−1	14	−20	6

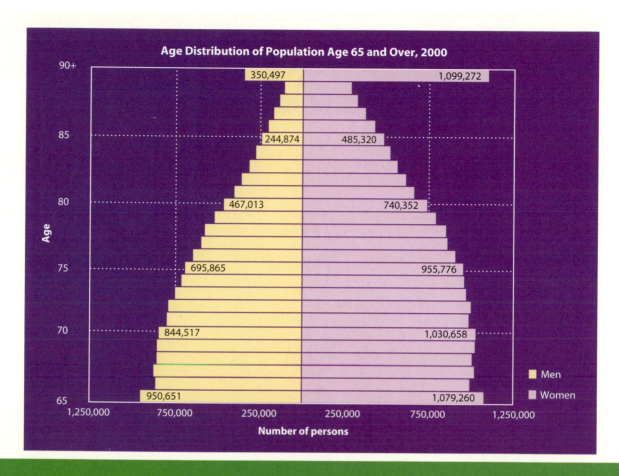

Age Distribution of Population Age 65 and Over, 2000

- 90+: Men 350,497 | Women 1,099,272
- 85: Men 244,874 | Women 485,320
- 80: Men 467,013 | Women 740,352
- 75: Men 695,865 | Women 955,776
- 70: Men 844,517 | Women 1,030,658
- 65: Men 950,651 | Women 1,079,260

Age / Number of persons

Men / Women

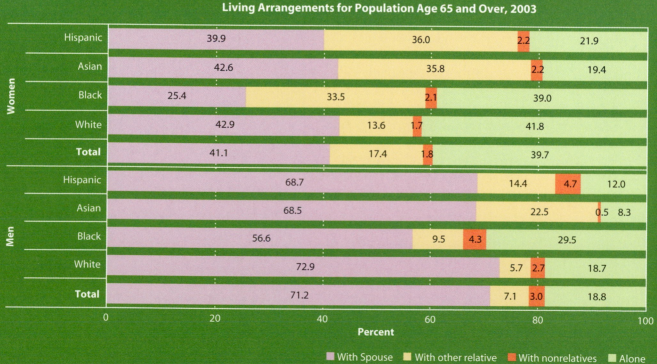

Living Arrangements for Population Age 65 and Over, 2003

Women
- Hispanic: 39.9 | 36.0 | 2.2 | 21.9
- Asian: 42.6 | 35.8 | 2.2 | 19.4
- Black: 25.4 | 33.5 | 2.1 | 39.0
- White: 42.9 | 13.6 | 1.7 | 41.8
- Total: 41.1 | 17.4 | 1.8 | 39.7

Men
- Hispanic: 68.7 | 14.4 | 4.7 | 12.0
- Asian: 68.5 | 22.5 | 0.5 | 8.3
- Black: 56.6 | 9.5 | 4.3 | 29.5
- White: 72.9 | 5.7 | 2.7 | 18.7
- Total: 71.2 | 7.1 | 3.0 | 18.8

Percent

With Spouse   With other relative   With nonrelatives   Alone

Life Expectancy and Mortality

The Center for Disease Control reported the deaths of 2,448,288 persons in 2003. The number of deaths was nearly equal for men and women. The life expectancy for a baby born in the United States in 1900 was only 47 years. By 2003, the life expectancy for newborns had increased to 74.8 years for men and 80.1 years for women.

Heart disease and cancer are the two leading causes of death for all races, but differences between top causes do exist. The chart to the right displays the top 10 causes of death for each race for comparison. Because only the top 10 are shown for each race, bars are not shown for all races and causes.

Although the causes of death varied by sex and race, variation was most dramatic between men of different races. For example, suicide rates were high for males of four out of the five most populous races, especially for whites and American Indian/Alaskan Natives. The only race without suicide in the top ten causes of death was blacks. Homicide also remains a leading cause of death for men of most races; it was listed as the cause of death for approximately one in every 25 black men who died in 2003. In 1980, one in every four deaths among American Indian or Alaskan Native men resulted from accident or unintentional injury. Although a smaller percentage died as a result of unintentional injury in 2003, the rate was still approximately three times higher than for most other races.

There are several notable differences in causes of death between men and women. For example, the tenth most common cause of death among men in 2003, Alzheimer's disease, ranked fifth among women. Alzheimer's disease resulted in the deaths of almost three times as many women as men.

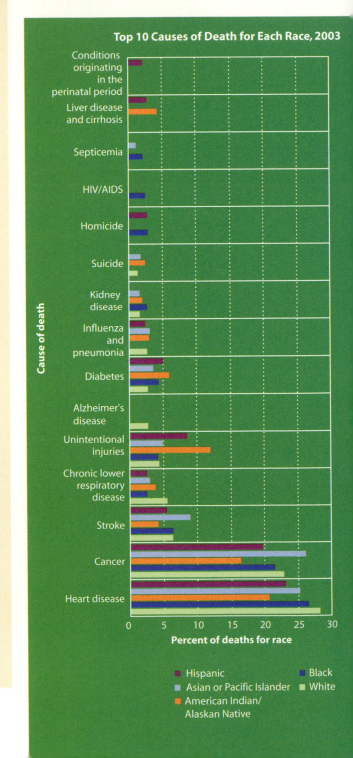

Top 10 Causes of Death for Each Race, 2003

Cause of death / Percent of deaths for race

Causes (top to bottom): Conditions originating in the perinatal period, Liver disease and cirrhosis, Septicemia, HIV/AIDS, Homicide, Suicide, Kidney disease, Influenza and pneumonia, Diabetes, Alzheimer's disease, Unintentional injuries, Chronic lower respiratory disease, Stroke, Cancer, Heart disease

Legend:
- Hispanic
- Asian or Pacific Islander
- American Indian/Alaskan Native
- Black
- White

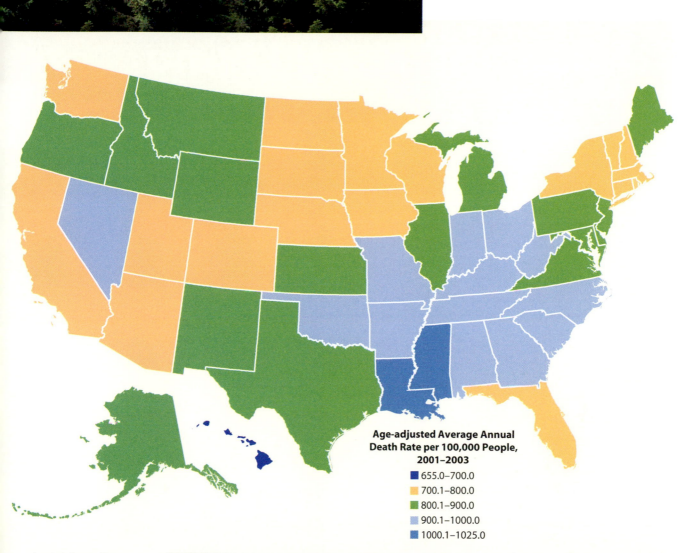

Age-adjusted Average Annual Death Rate per 100,000 People, 2001–2003

- 655.0–700.0
- 700.1–800.0
- 800.1–900.0
- 900.1–1000.0
- 1000.1–1025.0

In 1980, heart disease was the leading cause of death and responsible for almost 40 percent of the nation's deaths. By 2003 that figure had dropped to just under 28 percent. During the same period, however, deaths caused by cancer increased from 20.9 percent to 22.8 percent.

In 1980, only 1.3 percent of male deaths were a result of diabetes. By 2003, that rate had more than doubled to 2.9 percent.

Leading Causes of Death in the United States, 1980 and 2003

Cause	1980	Cause	2003
Heart disease	38.25%	Heart disease	27.98%
Cancer	20.93%	Cancer	22.75%
Stroke	8.55%	Stroke	6.44%
Unintentional injury	5.31%	Chronic lower respiratory disease	5.16%
Chronic obstructive pulmonary disease	2.82%	Unintentional injury	4.46%
Influenza and pneumonia	2.74%	Diabetes	3.03%
Diabetes	1.75%	Influenza and pneumonia	2.66%
Liver disease and cirrhosis	1.54%	Alzheimer's disease	2.59%
Atherosclerosis	1.48%	Kidney failure	1.73%
Suicide	1.35%	Septicemia	1.39%

Urban and Rural Living

Any county with more than 50 percent of its residents living in urban areas is considered mostly urban; 99 percent or more is considered completely urban. Similarly, counties with less than 50 percent of their residents living in urban areas are considered mostly rural, while counties with one percent or less living in urban areas are considered completely rural.

Fifteen percent of the U.S. population lives in rural or mostly rural counties, with 732 out of 3,141 counties having no urban population. In contrast, only 84 counties are completely urban, but these counties contain 26 percent of the population. Only 39 percent of counties are mostly or completely urban, but 85 percent of the nation's population is found in these densely populated areas.

As a result of the high population density, urban areas typically offer greater access to post-secondary education, recreational activities, and business opportunities. Unfortunately, along with the benefits, urban areas sometimes have higher rates of crime, poverty, and environmental pollutants (lead pipes and airborne pollutants, for example), as well as a decreased sense of community.

Urban and rural areas differ in many ways, including racial composition, age distribution, income levels, and the extent of poverty. Housing characteristics also differ. In 2000, 23 percent of rural housing units were unoccupied, whereas only six percent of urban housing units were vacant. Additionally, urban households are more than twice as likely to be rented (47 percent of urban households) than rural households (21 percent of rural households).

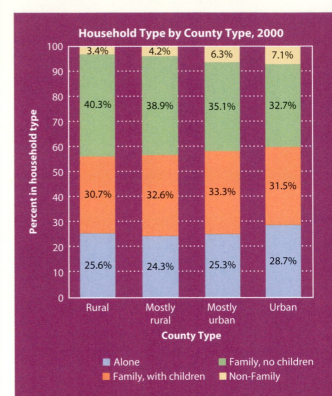

The highest percentages of persons living alone and in non-family households occur in urban counties, while rural areas have the highest percentage of families with no children under 18. As may be expected, the areas with the highest share of families with children are the mostly urban counties.

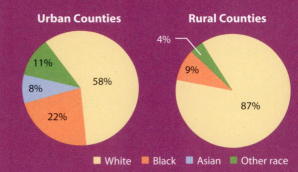

Urban counties are more racially diverse: 42 percent of city dwellers are non-white compared to only 13 percent in rural areas.

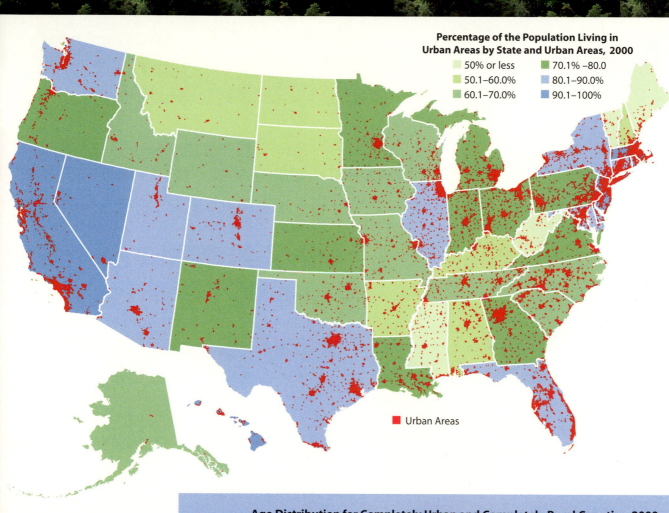

**Percentage of the Population Living in
Urban Areas by State and Urban Areas, 2000**

- 50% or less
- 50.1–60.0%
- 60.1–70.0%
- 70.1 –80.0
- 80.1–90.0%
- 90.1–100%

■ Urban Areas

Age Distribution for Completely Urban and Completely Rural Counties, 2000

Age group (vertical axis): 85+, 80-84, 75-79, 70-74, 65-69, 60-64, 55-59, 50-54, 45-49, 40-44, 35-39, 30-34, 25-29, 20-24, 15-19, 10-14, 5-9, 0-5

Percent (horizontal axis): 10 8 6 4 2 0 2 4 6 8 10

- Completely urban
- Completely rural

Urban residents tend to be younger than people in rural counties. Almost fifteen percent of the rural population is over 65, while only 12 percent of those living in urban areas have reached the same milestone. Children are represented differently in urban (higher 0 to 9) and rural counties (higher 10 to 17), but about one-fourth of residents are under age 18.

Marriage and Divorce

Traditional wedding vows include the phrase, "until death do us part." The altered phrase, "until divorce do us part," probably has not made its way into many marriage ceremonies, but divorce is a reality for many Americans. While divorce can be one of the most difficult experiences a person can go through, the option to get a divorce also offers a freedom from troubled marriages that people once did not have.

People are waiting longer to get married than ever before. The median age of first marriage for men in 2005 was 27, while the median age for women was younger, at 25.5 years. In 2005, 55.6 percent of people age 15 and older were married. Increased education levels are associated with lower divorce rates, as are later marriages, higher incomes, stronger religious affiliations, and full-time employment.

According to the Center for Disease Control and Prevention, "forty-three percent of first marriages end in separation or divorce within 15 years." Those marriages ending in divorce had lasted a median of eight years. In 2005, 10.2 percent of people age 15 and older were divorced.

The frequency of remarriage varies by cohort. About 15 percent of people born between 1935 and 1939 had been married two or more times by their 40th birthday. Of those born from 1945 to 1949, 22 percent had remarried by age 40. About 50 percent of people who remarry after their first marriage do so within three to four years of the divorce.

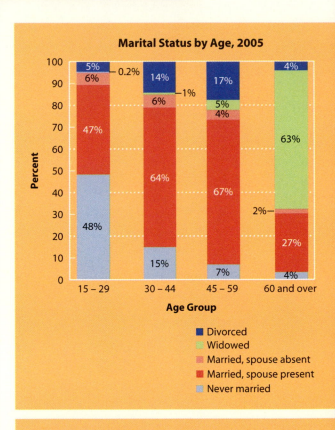

Marital Status by Age, 2005

Legend:
- Divorced
- Widowed
- Married, spouse absent
- Married, spouse present
- Never married

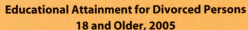

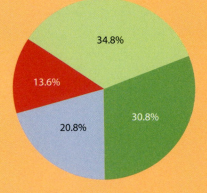

Educational Attainment for Divorced Persons 18 and Older, 2005

- 34.8%
- 30.8%
- 20.8%
- 13.6%

Educational attainment
- No high school diploma
- High school or equivalent
- Some college, less than 4-year degree
- Bachelor's or higher degree

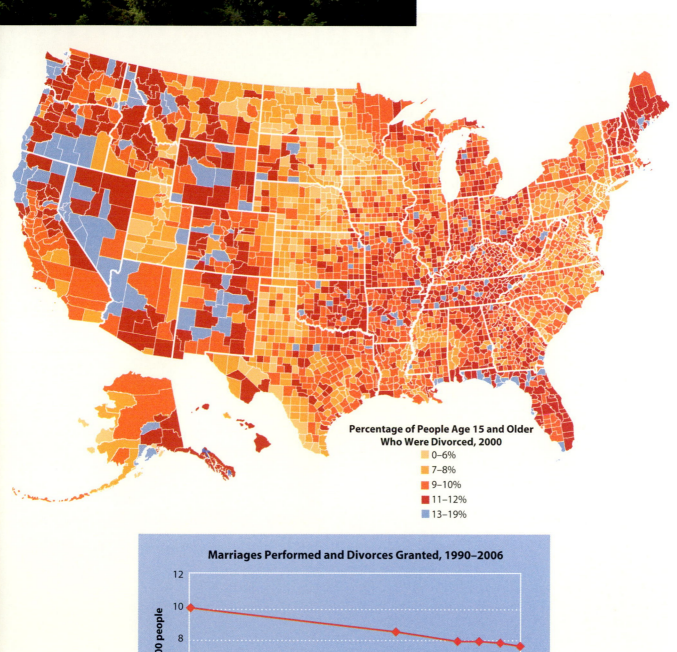

**Percentage of People Age 15 and Older
Who Were Divorced, 2000**

- 0–6%
- 7–8%
- 9–10%
- 11–12%
- 13–19%

Marriages Performed and Divorces Granted, 1990–2006

Number per 1,000 people

Year

Divorce rate — Marriage rate

Blood, Marriage, or Adoption
Family Structure

A household consists of one or more persons living in a housing unit. In order for a household to be considered a family according to the census, two or more people must be related by blood, marriage, or adoption, and one of them must be the householder. In 2005, there were nearly 75 million family households. Of these households, 47.2 percent had children under age 18.

The majority of children lived with both of their parents in 2004. Sixty-five percent of Hispanic children, 77 percent of white children, and 83 percent of Asian children lived with both parents. Among blacks, only 35 percent of children lived with both their mother and father. Over 50 percent lived with a mother only and over 9 percent lived with neither parent. Across all racial groups, it was much more common for children who lived with only one parent to live with their mothers rather than their fathers. Only 4.6 percent of all children lived with only their father.

In married-couple families, median family income is, as expected, higher, since many married-couple families benefit from the collective income of two parents. Married-couple families with children have a higher median family income than married couples without children. In contrast, households with only a male or female householder and no spouse present have lower family incomes when children are living in the household than when children are not.

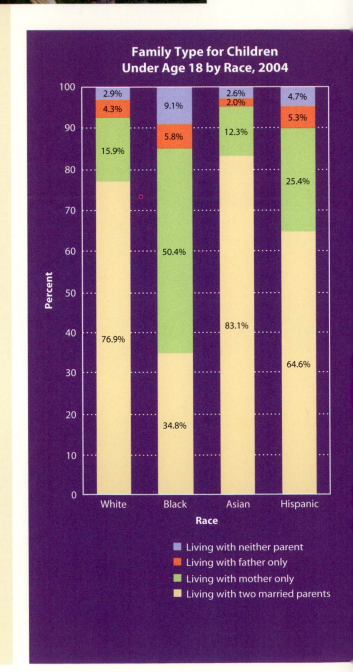

Family Type for Children Under Age 18 by Race, 2004

Percent / Race

White: 76.9%, 15.9%, 4.3%, 2.9%
Black: 34.8%, 50.4%, 5.8%, 9.1%
Asian: 83.1%, 12.3%, 2.0%, 2.6%
Hispanic: 64.6%, 25.4%, 5.3%, 4.7%

■ Living with neither parent
■ Living with father only
■ Living with mother only
■ Living with two married parents

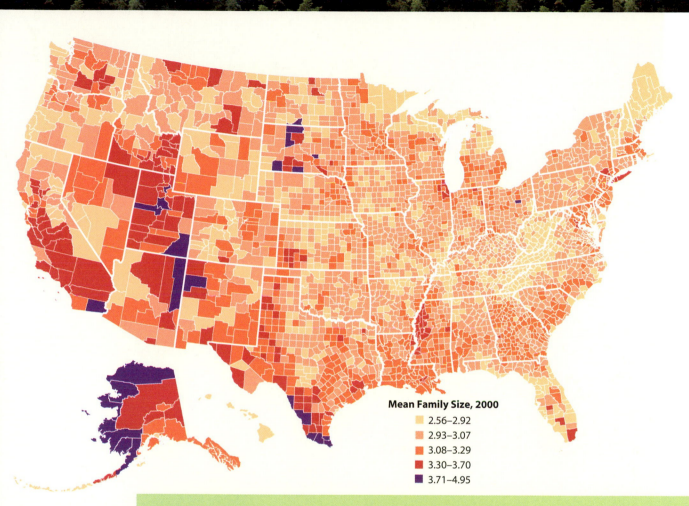

Mean Family Size, 2000

- 2.56–2.92
- 2.93–3.07
- 3.08–3.29
- 3.30–3.70
- 3.71–4.95

**Median Family Income in the Past 12 Months
by Family Type, 2005**

Median income (dollars)

Total — Married-couple family: With own children under 18 years; No own children under 18 years — Male householder, no wife present: With own children under 18 years; No own children under 18 years — Female householder, no husband present: With own children under 18 years; No own children under 18 years

Family type

Blood, Marriage, or Adoption: Family Structure

In 2003, there were an estimated 23.2 million married-couple families with children under age 15. In 5.5 million of these families, one parent was in the labor force and the other parent stayed home with the expressed purpose of caring for the home and children. As women have joined the work force, there has been a decline in the number of traditional 1950s-style stay-at-home mothers. However, of the estimated 5.5 million stay-at-home parents in 2003, over 98 percent were mothers. Sixty-five percent of stay-at-home parents had children under age six.

In 2005, there were 25 million married-couple families with their own children under age 18 living in their household. Parents (as defined by the Census Bureau) are not limited only to biological parents, but also include stepparents and those who have legally adopted their children. There were about 12.6 million family households with children under 18 and a parent householder, but no spouse present. This is only an approximation of single-parent households. For example, it does not account for parents who are living together without having ever married, or same-sex parents.

Furthermore, in many cases, though children may be living with just one parent, they are living with other adults. In 2003, when children lived with a mother, other adults were present in 41 percent of cases. When children lived with a father but no mother, other adults were present 60 percent of the time.

In 2005, 3.6 percent of children lived with their grandparents. Of grandparents living with their grandchildren, about 43 percent were the primary caretakers. Two-thirds of grandparents who were caretakers were between the ages of 30 and 59, while the remaining third was age 60 or above.

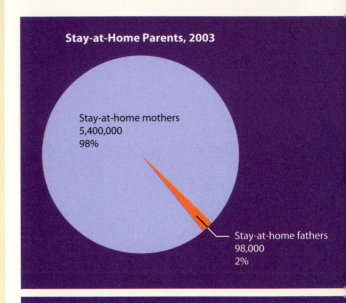

Stay-at-Home Parents, 2003

Stay-at-home mothers
5,400,000
98%

Stay-at-home fathers
98,000
2%

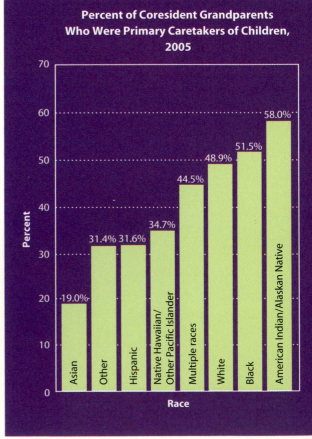

Percent of Coresident Grandparents Who Were Primary Caretakers of Children, 2005

Asian: 19.0%
Other: 31.4%
Hispanic: 31.6%
Native Hawaiian/Other Pacific Islander: 34.7%
Multiple races: 44.5%
White: 48.9%
Black: 51.5%
American Indian/Alaskan Native: 58.0%

Percent

Race

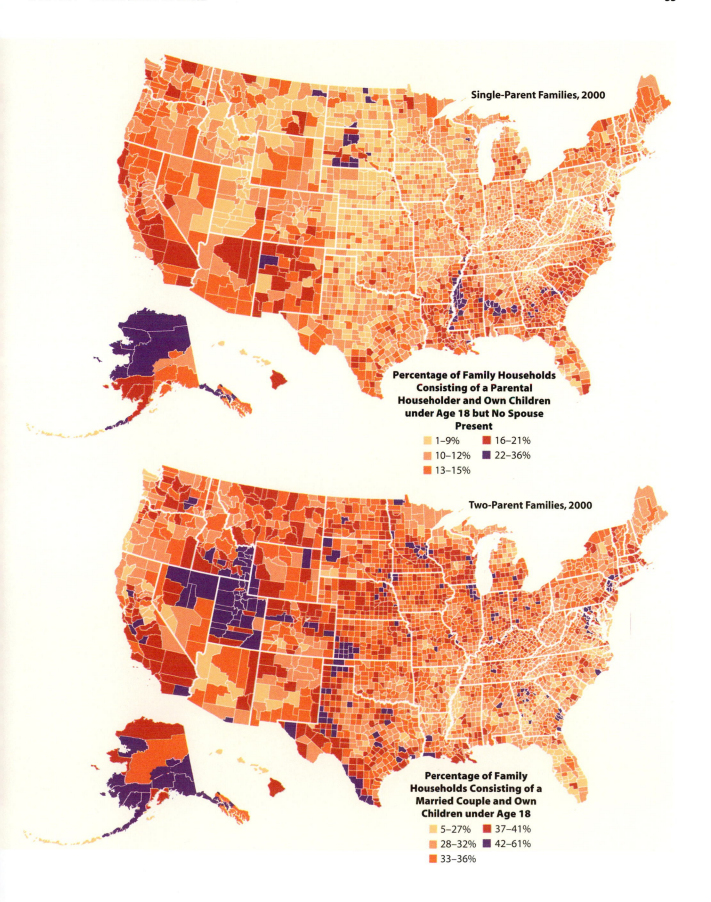

Single-Parent Families, 2000

Percentage of Family Households Consisting of a Parental Householder and Own Children under Age 18 but No Spouse Present

1–9%	16–21%
10–12%	22–36%
13–15%	

Two-Parent Families, 2000

Percentage of Family Households Consisting of a Married Couple and Own Children under Age 18

5–27%	37–41%
28–32%	42–61%
33–36%	

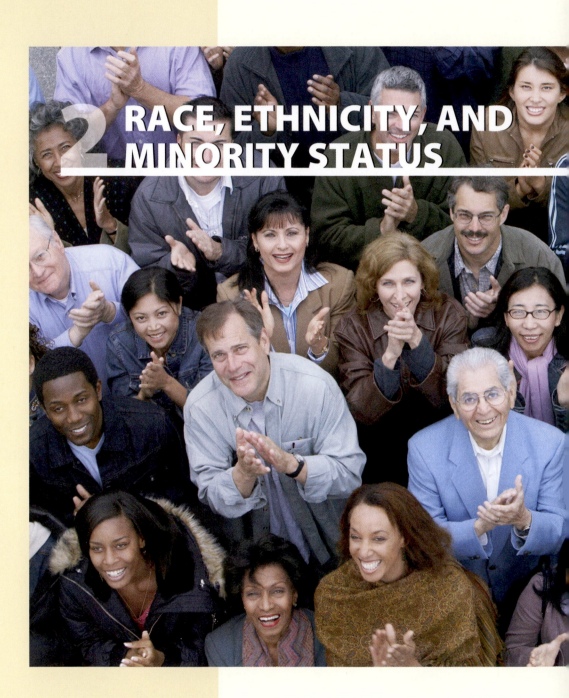

2 RACE, ETHNICITY, AND MINORITY STATUS

- **Racial Groups and Inequalities**

- **White Ancestry**

- **Black Americans**

- **Hispanic Americans**

- **Asians and Pacific Islanders**

- **American Indians and Alaskan Natives**

- **Our Segregated Cities**

- **Gay, Lesbian, and Bisexual Americans**

Racial Groups and Inequalities

While the United States is the home to people of all races, racial differences and inequalities exist. The standard classifications of race include seven groups: white, black, Hispanics, American Indian and Alaskan Native, Asian, Hawaiian and Pacific Islander (sometimes included with Asian), and some other race. Although some studies consider an Hispanic background to be an ethnicity rather than a race, it is generally included as a distinct group where races are concerned. The classification of two or more races is also taken into account in the census.

In 2005, over 98 percent of the population reported being only one race. Almost 15 percent of people identified as Hispanic. Whites accounted for about 67 percent of the population, but by 2050, whites are projected to account for only 50 percent of the population. Hispanics are expected to double from only 12 to 24 percent of the population, increasing from only 35 to 102 million people. Asians are expected to triple from almost 11 million to 33 million people.

In 2004, income was only one of the major social inequalities between races. Thirty-nine percent of whites and 31 percent of Asians were in families with annual incomes of less than $40,000. For both blacks and American Indians, 59 percent lived in families with incomes less than $40,000.

The multiracial population, those reporting two or more races, accounted for only 1.6 percent of the population in 2000. The census allows people to choose up to six races, but 93 percent of those who identified as multiracial selected only two races.

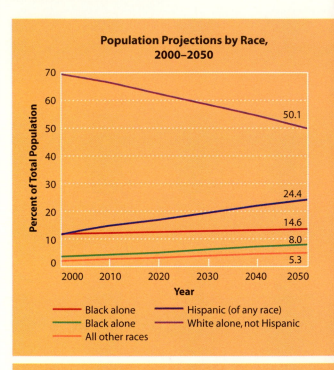

Population Projections by Race, 2000–2050

Percent of Total Population

Year	
2050	50.1
2050	24.4
2050	14.6
2050	8.0
2050	5.3

— Black alone   — Hispanic (of any race)
— Black alone   — White alone, not Hispanic
— All other races

Number of Persons Who Reported Two Races, 2000

	Black or African American	American Indian / Alaskan Native	Asian	Pacific Islander	Some other race
White	784,764	1,082,683	868,395	112,964	2,206,251
Black		182,494	106,782	29,876	417,249
American Indian / Alaskan Native			52,429	7,328	93,842
Asian				138,802	249,108
Pacific Islander					35,108

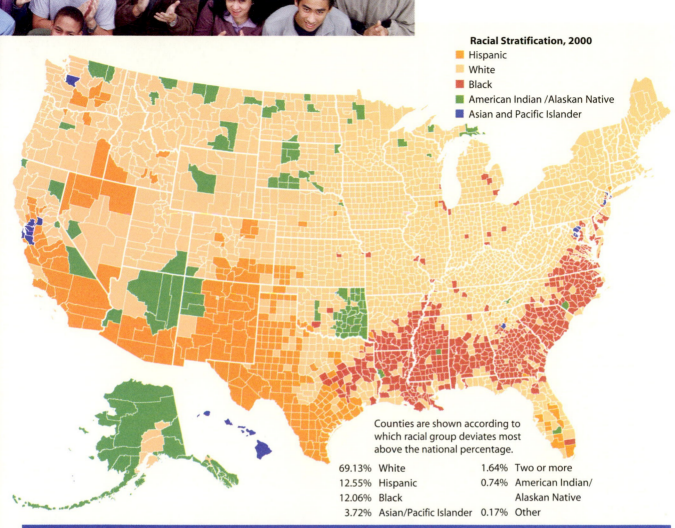

Racial Stratification, 2000
- Hispanic
- White
- Black
- American Indian /Alaskan Native
- Asian and Pacific Islander

Counties are shown according to which racial group deviates most above the national percentage.

69.13% White	1.64% Two or more
12.55% Hispanic	0.74% American Indian/
12.06% Black	Alaskan Native
3.72% Asian/Pacific Islander	0.17% Other

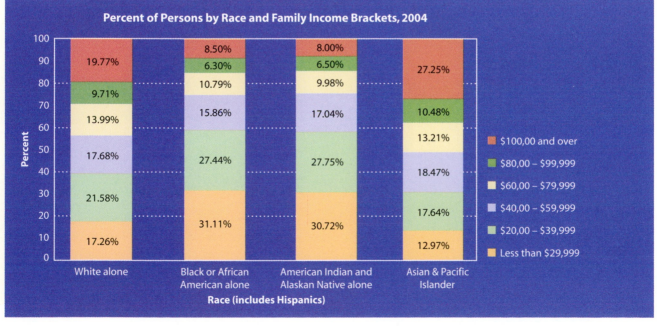

Percent of Persons by Race and Family Income Brackets, 2004

Percent

Income Bracket	White alone	Black or African American alone	American Indian and Alaskan Native alone	Asian & Pacific Islander
$100,00 and over	19.77%	8.50%	8.00%	27.25%
$80,00 – $99,999	9.71%	6.30%	6.50%	10.48%
$60,00 – $79,999	13.99%	10.79%	9.98%	13.21%
$40,00 – $59,999	17.68%	15.86%	17.04%	18.47%
$20,00 – $39,999	21.58%	27.44%	27.75%	17.64%
Less than $29,999	17.26%	31.11%	30.72%	12.97%

Race (includes Hispanics)

White Ancestry

I n 2004, 67.3 percent of the population identified as white. Although this group has historically been the overwhelming majority of the population for two centuries, it is projected to account for only 50.1 percent of the population by 2050.

According to the Census Bureau, "white" refers to people having origins in Europe, the Middle East, or North Africa. It includes people who indicated their race as "white" or wrote in entries such as Irish, German, Italian, Lebanese, Near Easterner, Arab, or Polish. Although the census allows people to identify as many as six races, it limits responses for ancestry to only two.

Although the United States was colonized by the Spanish, Dutch, and English, the top two white ancestries as of 2000 were German and Irish.

People with common ancestries often formed communities, with remnants still evident today: Italians in New Jersey and near New York City; French in Louisiana and adjacent to Canada's Quebec province; people of Irish ancestry in parts of New York and Massachusetts; English communities in Vermont, New Hampshire, and Maine; Dutch communities in Western Michigan; Finnish communities in Northern Michigan; and Norwegian communities in North Dakota and parts of Minnesota.

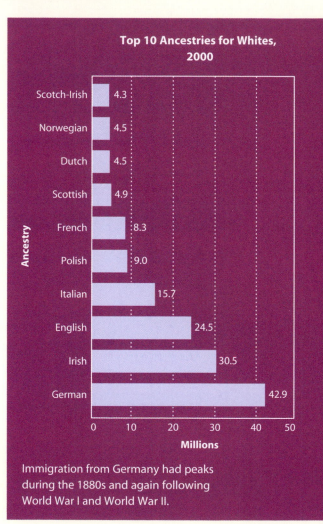

Top 10 Ancestries for Whites, 2000

Ancestry	Millions
Scotch-Irish	4.3
Norwegian	4.5
Dutch	4.5
Scottish	4.9
French	8.3
Polish	9.0
Italian	15.7
English	24.5
Irish	30.5
German	42.9

Immigration from Germany had peaks during the 1880s and again following World War I and World War II.

The immigration chart to the right includes those countries from which at least 1 million people emigrated since 1821. Although more people have emigrated from Italy since 1871 than anywhere else, it ranks fourth in terms of people claiming it as an ancestry.

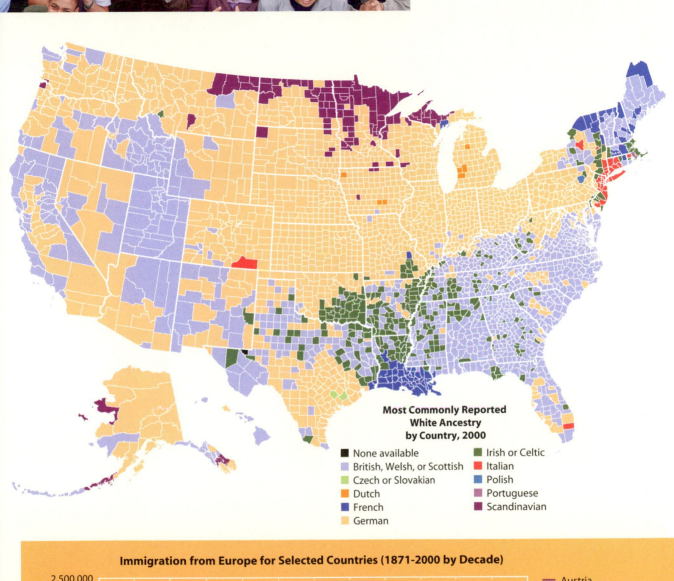

**Most Commonly Reported
White Ancestry
by Country, 2000**

- ■ None available
- ■ British, Welsh, or Scottish
- ■ Czech or Slovakian
- ■ Dutch
- ■ French
- ■ German
- ■ Irish or Celtic
- ■ Italian
- ■ Polish
- ■ Portuguese
- ■ Scandinavian

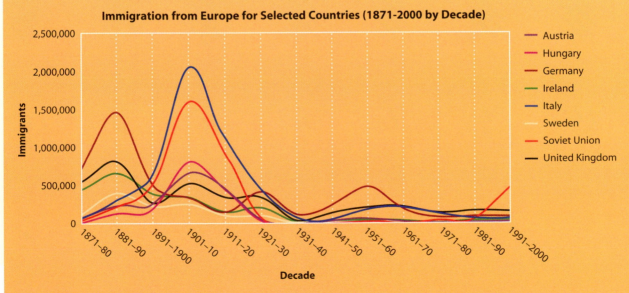

Immigration from Europe for Selected Countries (1871-2000 by Decade)

- — Austria
- — Hungary
- — Germany
- — Ireland
- — Italy
- — Sweden
- — Soviet Union
- — United Kingdom

Immigrants

2,500,000
2,000,000
1,500,000
1,000,000
500,000
0

1871–80   1881–90   1891–1900   1901–10   1911–20   1921–30   1931–40   1941–50   1951–60   1961–70   1971–80   1981–90   1991–2000

Decade

Black Americans

I n 2000, there were 36.2 million blacks in the United States, accounting for 12.9 percent of the population. Of these, 1.9 million reported being two or more races.

Geographically, 55.3 percent of blacks lived in the South. While only 79 percent of the total population lived in urban areas, 90 percent of the black population resided in these population centers.

In the total population, educational attainment levels were generally higher among men than women. Among blacks, however, women had higher educational attainment levels. About 15 percent of black women had received a bachelor's degree, while only 13 percent of black men had received an equivalent degree. Similarly, 29.7 percent of black women had achieved an associate's degree or had some college experience. Only 26.5 percent of men had achieved this level of education.

In the total population, labor force participation rates differed between men and women by over 13 percent: 70.7 percent of men worked compared to 57.5 percent of women. Among blacks, labor force participation rates were nearly equal between men and women: 60.9 percent of men worked compared to 59.6 percent of women.

Poverty rates were much higher for blacks than for the general population: one in four blacks lived in poverty. In the total population, only one in eight people lived in poverty.

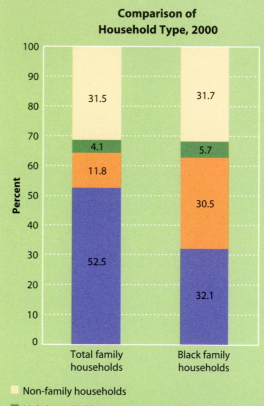

Comparison of Household Type, 2000

Non-family households
Male householder, no spouse present
Female householder, no spouse present
Married couple

Over one-half of all households were run by married couples but, among blacks, married couple households accounted for only one-third of households. The share of households headed by women, however, was almost three times higher among blacks. The median household income for black, female-headed households was only $20,631.

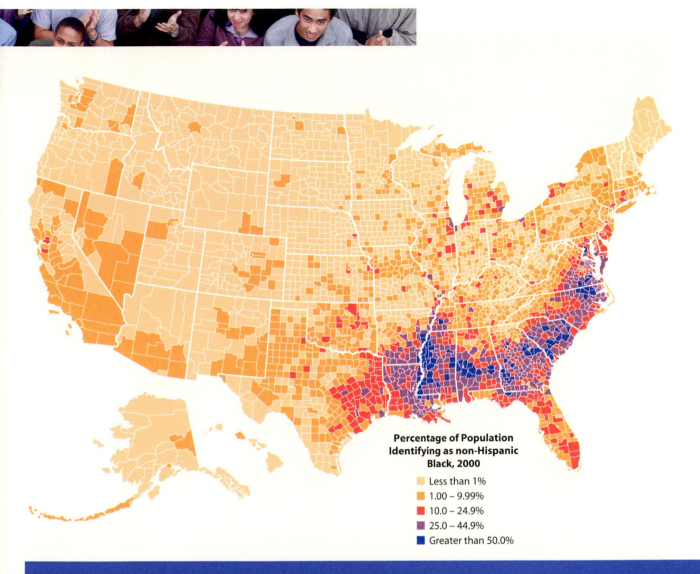

**Percentage of Population
Identifying as non-Hispanic
Black, 2000**

- Less than 1%
- 1.00 – 9.99%
- 10.0 – 24.9%
- 25.0 – 44.9%
- Greater than 50.0%

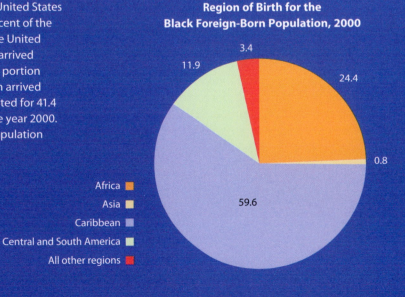

In 2000, 94 percent of blacks in the United States were native born. Twenty-seven percent of the foreign-born population came to the United States prior to 1980, and 32 percent arrived between 1980 and 1990. The largest portion of the black foreign-born population arrived between 1990 and 2000 and accounted for 41.4 percent of foreign-born blacks in the year 2000. Sixty percent of the foreign-born population came from the Caribbean.

**Region of Birth for the
Black Foreign-Born Population, 2000**

3.4
11.9
24.4
0.8
59.6

- Africa
- Asia
- Caribbean
- Central and South America
- All other regions

Hispanic Americans

As of 2003, Hispanics became the largest minority group in the United States, with a population exceeding 38.8 million. With a growth rate that is more than three times that of the total population (9.8 percent since 2000 compared with 2.5 percent for the total population), in coming years Hispanics are projected to make up almost 25 percent of the population.

The Hispanic population is concentrated in the South and the West and Hispanic individuals are more likely to be found in urban areas than the rest of the U.S. population, with nearly half of Hispanics residing in central cities. The Hispanic population is also one of the youngest demographic groups in the United States; their median age is 25.9, while the nation's median age is eight years older.

More than two in five Hispanics are foreign born, a rate much higher than the rest of the U.S. population, and those born in Latin America account for 52.2 percent of the entire U.S. foreign-born population. According to Jeff Passel of the Pew Hispanic Center, more than one in five Hispanics is in the United States without authorization.

Twenty-one percent of all Hispanics fall below the poverty line (national average: 12 percent), and while 88.7 percent of non-Hispanic whites have completed high school, the rate for Hispanics is only 57 percent. In general, foreign-born Hispanics tend to show the greatest deviations from the total population, mainly because of the difficulties adjusting to language and cultural differences. Later generations tend to be more similar to national averages in terms of education and income.

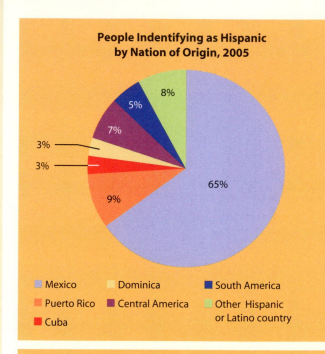

People Indentifying as Hispanic by Nation of Origin, 2005

- Mexico — 65%
- Puerto Rico — 9%
- Cuba — 3%
- Dominica — 3%
- Central America — 7%
- South America — 5%
- Other Hispanic or Latino country — 8%

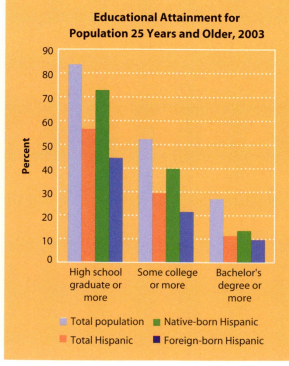

Educational Attainment for Population 25 Years and Older, 2003

- Total population
- Total Hispanic
- Native-born Hispanic
- Foreign-born Hispanic

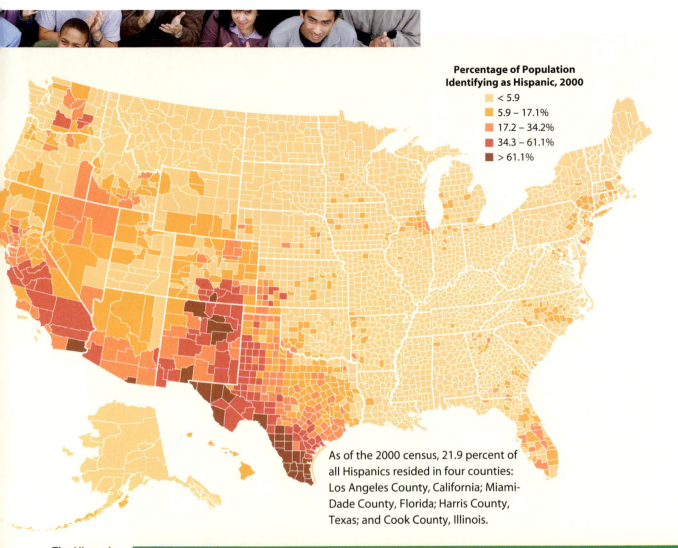

Percentage of Population Identifying as Hispanic, 2000

- < 5.9
- 5.9 – 17.1%
- 17.2 – 34.2%
- 34.3 – 61.1%
- > 61.1%

As of the 2000 census, 21.9 percent of all Hispanics resided in four counties: Los Angeles County, California; Miami-Dade County, Florida; Harris County, Texas; and Cook County, Illinois.

The Hispanic population is expected to grow by more than 1.7 million a year, 100,000 every three weeks, or 5,000 people a day.

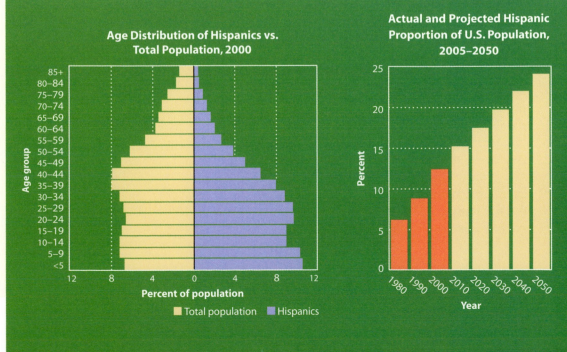

Age Distribution of Hispanics vs. Total Population, 2000

Age group: 85+, 80–84, 75–79, 70–74, 65–69, 60–64, 55–59, 50–54, 45–49, 40–44, 35–39, 30–34, 25–29, 20–24, 15–19, 10–14, 5–9, <5

Percent of population

■ Total population   ■ Hispanics

Actual and Projected Hispanic Proportion of U.S. Population, 2005–2050

Percent

Year: 1980, 1990, 2000, 2010, 2020, 2030, 2040, 2050

Asians and Pacific Islanders

In 2000, there were approximately 10.7 million people identifying as Asian living in the United States. According to projections released in 2004, that figure is expected to more than triple by 2050, increasing to over 33.4 million. That corresponds to an increase from 3.8 percent to 8.0 percent of the population over a span of 50 years.

Many Asians live in ethnic clusters, often in or around metropolitan areas. Over 50 percent of the total Asian population lives in only 20 counties. Of the 10 counties with largest Asian populations, 6 are in California. Data for 2004 indicated that 47.9 percent of the Asian population lived in the Western region of the country.

According to figures for 2004, the levels of education for Asians differed from the rest of the population. Whereas only 27.7 percent of the general population over the age of 25 had received a bachelor's degree or more, 49.4 percent of Asians had achieved that level of education. Similarly, although only 9.6 percent of the general population had acquired a degree beyond a bachelor's, 19.6 percent of Asians had received an advanced degree. On the other hand, while only 3.3 percent of non-Hispanic whites (and 6.3 percent of the general population) had less than a 9th grade education, 8.2 percent of Asians had never attended high school.

Asian families tend to be larger than the average U.S. family. In 2004, 33.2 percent of all families, and 42.5 percent of Asian families, had four or more people. Additionally, Asian families were nearly twice as likely as the total population to have seven or more people.

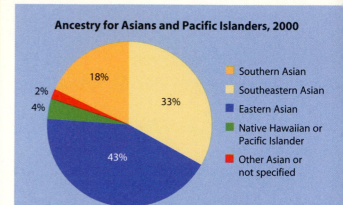

Ancestry for Asians and Pacific Islanders, 2000

- Southern Asian
- Southeastern Asian
- Eastern Asian
- Native Hawaiian or Pacific Islander
- Other Asian or not specified

Although the 12 million Asians in the United States reported ancestry from over 20 different countries in 2004, China (2.83 million, not including Taiwan), India (2.25 million), Philippines (2.15 million), Vietnam (1.27 million), and Korea (1.25 million) were most commonly reported.

Top 10 Counties Contributing to Total Asian Population, 2000

County	Percent of total U.S. Asian population
Los Angeles County, California	10.96%
Honolulu County, Hawaii	4.50%
Santa Clara County, California	4.12%
Orange County, California	3.74%
Queens County, New York	3.72%
Alameda County, California	2.87%
Cook County, Illinois	2.48%
San Diego County, California	2.46%
San Francisco County, California	2.31%
King County, Washington	1.86%

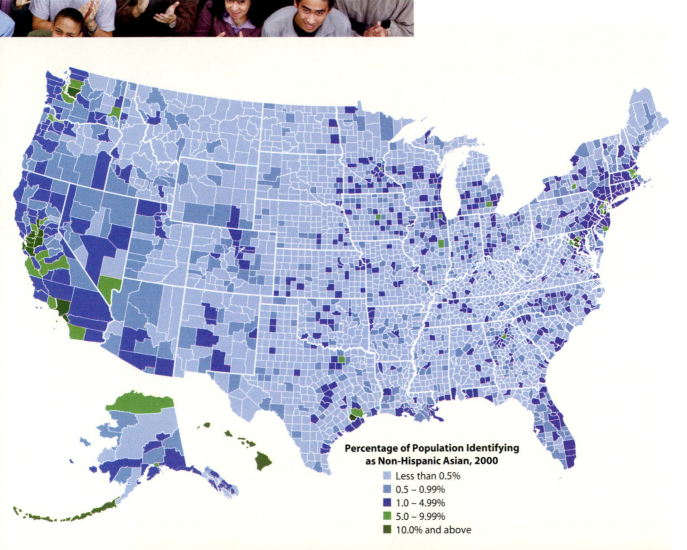

Percentage of Population Identifying as Non-Hispanic Asian, 2000

- Less than 0.5%
- 0.5 – 0.99%
- 1.0 – 4.99%
- 5.0 – 9.99%
- 10.0% and above

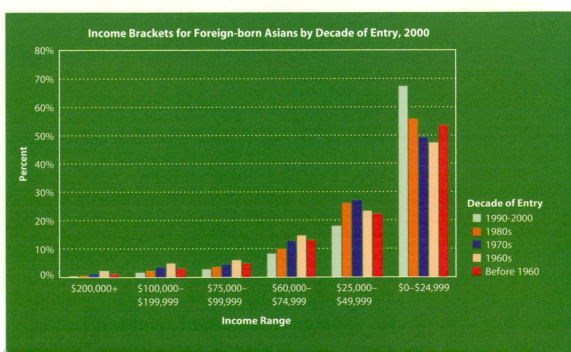

Income Brackets for Foreign-born Asians by Decade of Entry, 2000

Percent

Income Range

Decade of Entry
- 1990-2000
- 1980s
- 1970s
- 1960s
- Before 1960

American Indians and Alaskan Natives

The Census Bureau uses the term "American Indian and Alaskan Native" to refer to people whose ancestry ties back to the original peoples of North and South America (including Central America), and who maintain tribal affiliation or community attachment. It includes people who reported as "American Indian and Alaskan Native" or wrote in their principal or enrolled tribe.

In 2005, about 4.5 million individuals identified as American Indian or Alaskan Native (AIAN). About 1.6 million AIANs identified as two or more races. As a percentage of the total population, AIANs comprised 1.5 percent, with 0.97 percent claiming AIAN as their only race. Furthermore, AIANs live in close proximity to other AIANs, many in the protected areas specified in the map. Almost half (43 percent) of all American Indians live in the West, and over half live in just ten states: California, Oklahoma, Arizona, Texas, New Mexico, New York, Washington, North Carolina, Michigan, and Alaska. As of 2000, 25 percent of the total AIAN population lived in only two states, California and Oklahoma, with 627,562 and 391,949 AIANs, respectively.

Six AIAN tribal groupings (the Chippewa tribal group, for example, includes 27 separate tribes) had over 100,000 people each as of 2000 and accounted for 40 percent of all AIANs: Cherokee, Navajo, Latin American Indian, Choctaw, Sioux, and Chippewa. A total of 729,533 people reported to be Cherokee, either alone or in combination with another race, making it the most common AIAN tribal grouping.

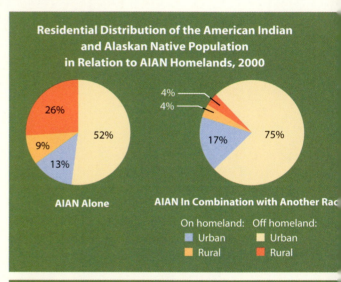

Residential Distribution of the American Indian and Alaskan Native Population in Relation to AIAN Homelands, 2000

AIAN Alone: 52%, 26%, 9%, 13%

AIAN In Combination with Another Race: 75%, 17%, 4%, 4%

On homeland:
- Urban (blue)
- Rural (orange)

Off homeland:
- Urban (tan)
- Rural (red)

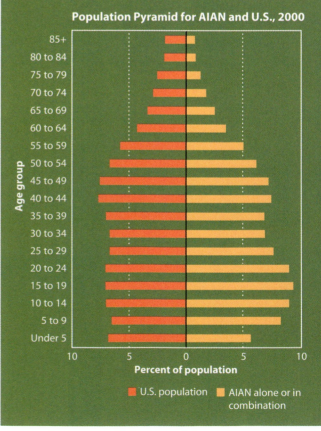

Population Pyramid for AIAN and U.S., 2000

Age group: 85+, 80 to 84, 75 to 79, 70 to 74, 65 to 69, 60 to 64, 55 to 59, 50 to 54, 45 to 49, 40 to 44, 35 to 39, 30 to 34, 25 to 29, 20 to 24, 15 to 19, 10 to 14, 5 to 9, Under 5

Percent of population

- U.S. population
- AIAN alone or in combination

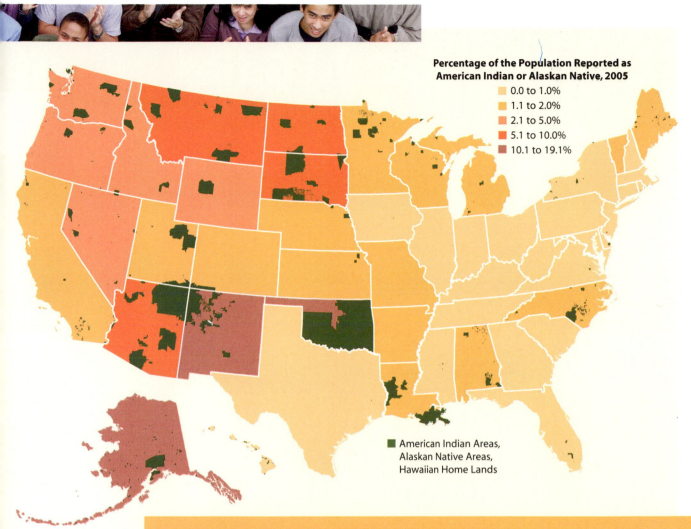

Percentage of the Population Reported as American Indian or Alaskan Native, 2005

- 0.0 to 1.0%
- 1.1 to 2.0%
- 2.1 to 5.0%
- 5.1 to 10.0%
- 10.1 to 19.1%

■ American Indian Areas, Alaskan Native Areas, Hawaiian Home Lands

Counties and Equivalent Areas with Highest Percentages of AIAN Population, 2000

Rank	County	Total Population	AIAN Alone or Combined	Percentage of Population Identified as AIAN
1	Shannon County, South Dakota	12,466	11,850	95.06%
2	Wade Hampton Census Area, Alaska	7,028	6,673	94.95%
3	Menominee County, Wisconsin	4,562	4,010	87.90%
4	Todd County, South Dakota	9,050	7,861	86.86%
5	Northwest Arctic Borough, Alaska	7,208	6,181	85.75%
6	Bethel Census Area, Alaska	16,006	13,680	85.47%
7	Sioux County, North Dakota	4,044	3,450	85.31%
8	Buffalo County, South Dakota	2,032	1,692	83.27%
9	Lake and Peninsula Borough, Alaska	1,823	1,453	79.70%
10	Nome Census Area, Alaska	9,196	7,274	79.10%
11	Apache County, Arizona	69,423	53,998	77.78%
12	McKinley County, New Mexico	74,798	57,126	76.37%
13	Dillingham Census Area, Alaska	4,922	3,753	76.25%
14	Dewey County, South Dakota	5,972	4,503	75.40%
15	Rolette County, North Dakota	13,674	10,185	74.48%

Our Segregated Cities

Although the civil rights movement of the mid-20th century intended to end institutionalized segregation with Supreme Court decisions like Brown v. Board of Education of Topeka in 1954, segregation still occurs within communities. Many of today's cities have neighborhoods with widely varied racial compositions resulting in residential segregation.

While the extent of segregation and its effects may differ for each city, the social implications concern subjects such as diversity in schools, local funding for education, accessibility to municipal resources, level of safety, and range of occupational opportunities. The mistreatment of minorities and immigrants throughout much of the nation's history prompted the mistreated to form their own communities. These resulting neighborhoods, which often have larger minority populations, may lack many benefits found in nearby neighborhoods. As these communities remain segregated, so too are the options available to the residents. This residential segregation, therefore, perpetuates a socioeconomic divide.

In 2000, for the third consecutive decade, the metropolitan area with the greatest segregation was Detroit, Michigan. Of the 325 metropolitan areas ranked for 2000, Redding, California was the least segregated.

Cities with greater and more diverse populations, such as Chicago or Los Angeles, often are more segregated than those cities with limited minority populations, such as Eugene, Oregon or Boulder, Colorado.

The maps show several examples of racial and ethnic distribution across metropolitan areas. Darker colors indicate that the unit is substantially composed of a single race. Lighter colors indicate that the area contains substantial populations beyond that of the most prevalent race/ethnicity.

SAN FRANCISCO

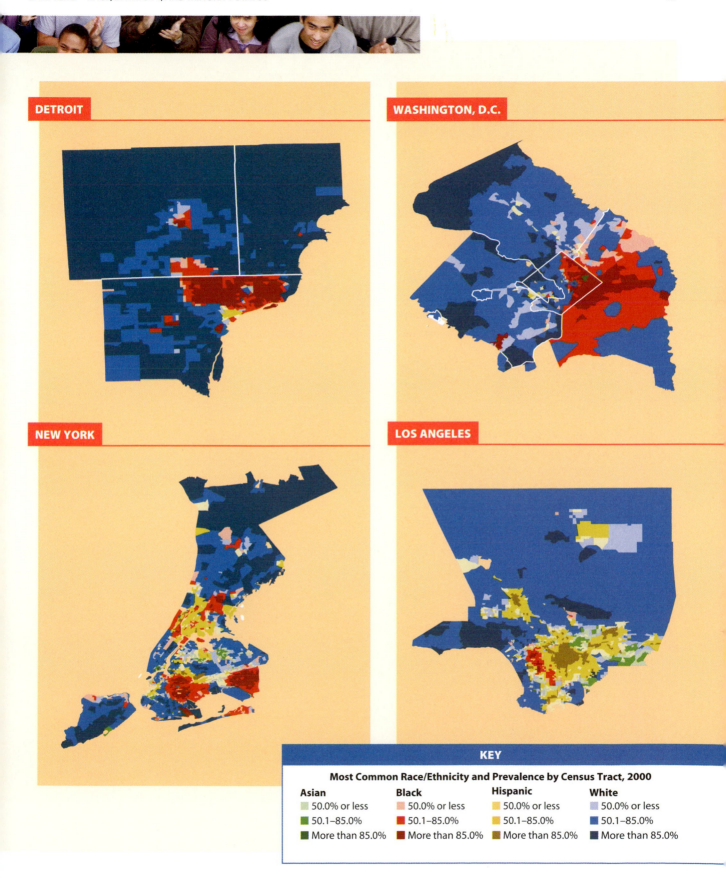

DETROIT

WASHINGTON, D.C.

NEW YORK

LOS ANGELES

KEY

Most Common Race/Ethnicity and Prevalence by Census Tract, 2000

Asian	Black	Hispanic	White
50.0% or less	50.0% or less	50.0% or less	50.0% or less
50.1–85.0%	50.1–85.0%	50.1–85.0%	50.1–85.0%
More than 85.0%	More than 85.0%	More than 85.0%	More than 85.0%

Gay, Lesbian, and Bisexual America

The Defense of Marriage Act (DOMA) passed by Congress in 1996 recognizes only opposite-sex marriages at the federal level. It defines marriage as "a legal union between one man and one woman." For both federal benefits and tax purposes, same-sex couples are not eligible as married couples. States have taken initiative to enact their own laws. Some states have fortified the federal statute by implementing constitutional bans against same-sex civil marriages. Other states have granted more equal treatment for homosexual couples. As of early 2007, only Massachusetts recognized same-sex and opposite-sex marriages as equivalent.

In 2000, there were an estimated 594,391 same-sex households in the United States. However, the *Journal of Pediatrics* reports that because the census cannot ask specifically about gay and lesbian couples, this number could undercount the number of same-sex couples, possibly missing up to 19 percent.

Every two years, the Massachusetts Department of Education surveys students in 9th through 12th grades. In 2003, nearly 4,000 students from randomly selected schools participated in the voluntary and anonymous survey. Of these high school students, 3.5 percent identified as gay, lesbian, or bisexual, and an additional 2.5 percent had engaged in sexual contact with someone of the same sex. The survey found that homosexual students were more likely to report suicide attempts or violent confrontations.

TOP 10
Percentage of Same-Sex Households Out of All Households, 2000

2.7%	San Francisco, CA	1.7%	Atlanta, GA
2.1%	Fort Lauderdale, FL	1.6%	Minneapolis, MN
1.9%	Seattle, WA	1.5%	Washington, DC
1.8%	Oakland, CA	1.4%	Long Beach, CA
1.8%	Berkeley, CA	1.3%	Portland, OR

Places with a population of 100,000 or more

Same-sex couples are more likely than opposite-sex couples to live in the central area of metropolitan cities. Of all coupled households, 25.3 percent live in city centers. Of same-sex coupled households, 41.6 percent live in city centers.

Percentage of Couples Raising Children by Sexual Orientation of Couple, 2000

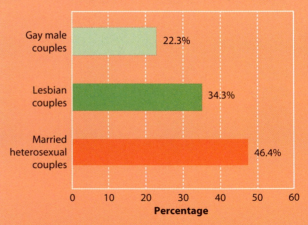

Gay male couples — 22.3%
Lesbian couples — 34.3%
Married heterosexual couples — 46.4%

Percentage

In many cases, the children being raised by gay and lesbian couples are from relationships prior to the current same-sex partnership.

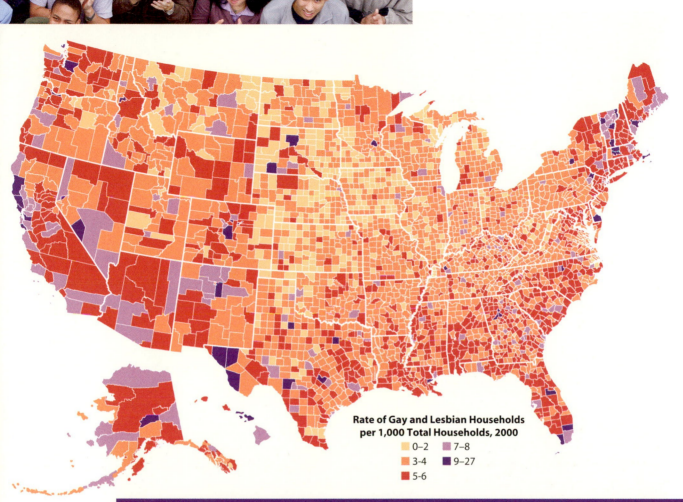

**Rate of Gay and Lesbian Households
per 1,000 Total Households, 2000**

0–2		7–8	
3-4		9–27	
5-6			

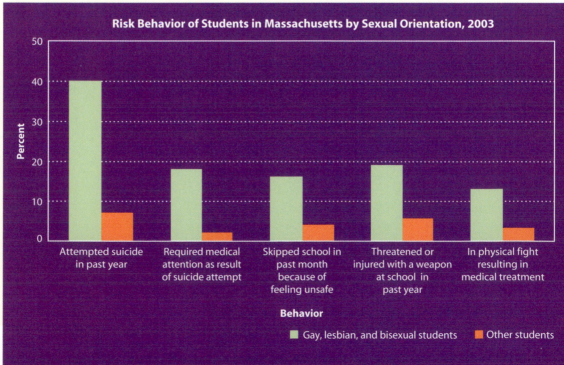

Risk Behavior of Students in Massachusetts by Sexual Orientation, 2003

Percent

Behavior

- Attempted suicide in past year
- Required medical attention as result of suicide attempt
- Skipped school in past month because of feeling unsafe
- Threatened or injured with a weapon at school in past year
- In physical fight resulting in medical treatment

- Gay, lesbian, and bisexual students
- Other students

3 WEALTH, INCOME, AND OPPORTUNITY

- **Chasing the American Dream**

- **Over Our Heads: Consumer Debt**

- **The Persistence of Poverty**

- **Educational Attainment and Life Chances**

- **Unfinished Business: High School and College Dropouts**

- **Alternatives to Public Education**

Chasing the American Dream

The United States is almost exclusively a land of immigrants. Since immigrants first started settling the areas of Virginia and Massachusetts during the early 17th century, the land we now know as the United States was seen as a land of opportunity and offered freedom from persecution. This promise still exists today, both to the new immigrants as well as to the progeny of those who came to these shores in the past four centuries. The concept of the "American Dream" encourages each individual to improve his or her own quality of life.

Although many individuals still come to the United States to escape persecution, for economic opportunities, for higher education, ownership of both homes and businesses draw many immigrants as well. From 1997 to 2002, the number of businesses owned by minorities increased much more quickly than the overall rate. In those five years, the number of businesses owned by women increased by 20 percent, but businesses owned by Blacks, Asians, Hispanics, and Native Hawaiians grew much more quickly, at 45, 24, 31, and 67 percent, respectively. Businesses owned by American Indians or Alaskan Natives accounted for 8 percent of all firms in Alaska and 5 percent of firms in both Oklahoma and New Mexico.

Census data reveal that residents who immigrated before the 1980s are more financially successful than the non-immigrants. While 61.8 percent of non-immigrants of working age earned less than $25,000 in 2000, only 57.2, 57.5, and 60.1 percent of immigrants who entered the country in the 1950s, 1960s, and 1970s, respectively, were in that same income bracket.

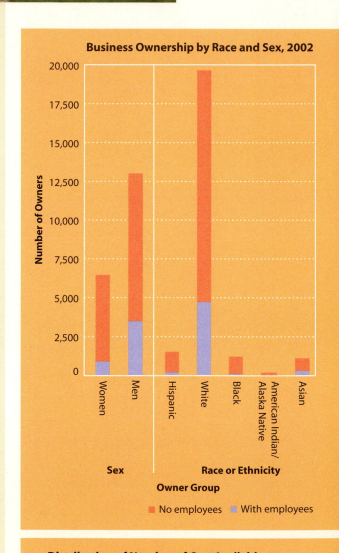

Business Ownership by Race and Sex, 2002

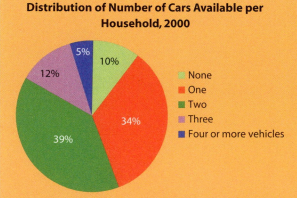

Distribution of Number of Cars Available per Household, 2000

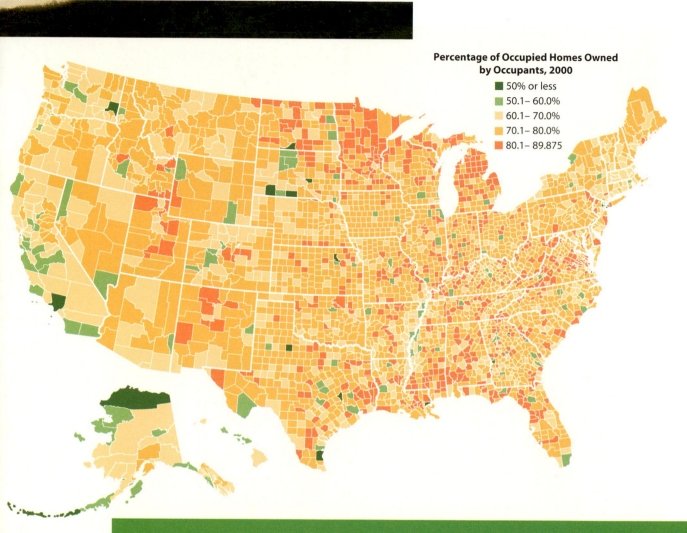

Percentage of Occupied Homes Owned by Occupants, 2000
- 50% or less
- 50.1– 60.0%
- 60.1– 70.0%
- 70.1– 80.0%
- 80.1– 89.875

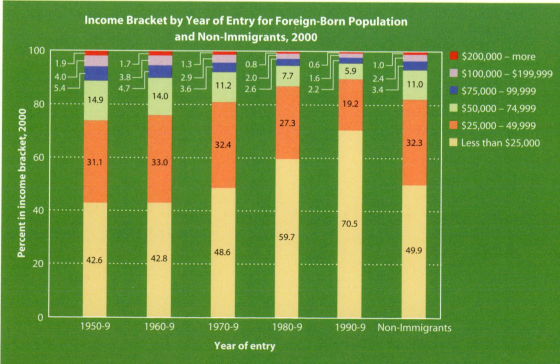

Income Bracket by Year of Entry for Foreign-Born Population and Non-Immigrants, 2000

Percent in income bracket, 2000 (vertical axis)

Year of entry (horizontal axis)

Legend:
- $200,000 – more
- $100,000 – $199,999
- $75,000 – 99,999
- $50,000 – 74,999
- $25,000 – 49,999
- Less than $25,000

Year of entry	1950-9	1960-9	1970-9	1980-9	1990-9	Non-Immigrants
$200,000 – more	1.9	1.7	1.3	0.8	0.6	1.0
$100,000 – $199,999	4.0	3.8	2.9	2.0	1.6	2.4
$75,000 – 99,999	5.4	4.7	3.6	2.6	2.2	3.4
$50,000 – 74,999	14.9	14.0	11.2	7.7	5.9	11.0
$25,000 – 49,999	31.1	33.0	32.4	27.3	19.2	32.3
Less than $25,000	42.6	42.8	48.6	59.7	70.5	49.9

Over Our Heads: Consumer Debt

Some Americans dream of winning the lottery. Others dream of striking it rich on some newfangled invention. Still others consider hard work and honesty the only proper way to achieve economic security. Methods may differ from one individual to the next, but everywhere hopes for financial freedom linger. Unfortunately, by early 2006, Americans had accumulated almost 2.2 trillion dollars in consumer debt!

In 2001, 76.4 percent of families reported being in debt. The most common types of debt were mortgages, installment loans, and credit card balances. In 2000, 70 percent of owner-occupied housing was mortgaged. In 2005, households spent 13.8 percent of their disposable income paying debtors.

While credit cards help to avoid the initial upfront costs of large purchases, inability to pay off credit card balances can be a quick way to dig deeper into debt. In 2001, almost 73 percent of families had at least one general purpose credit card, such as MasterCard, Visa, Optima, and Discover cards.

A general guideline for budgeting is that 30 percent of personal income should be spent on housing. In 2004, forty-five percent of all rent-paying households spent more than 30 percent of household income on rent. Ninety percent of those overspending on rent earn less than $35,000 per year.

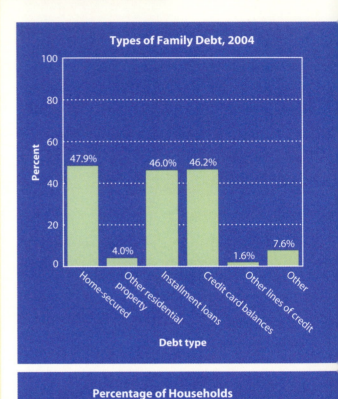

Types of Family Debt, 2004

Home-secured: 47.9%
Other residential property: 4.0%
Installment loans: 46.0%
Credit card balances: 46.2%
Other lines of credit: 1.6%
Other: 7.6%

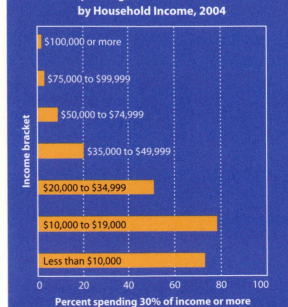

Percentage of Households Overspending on Rent in the Last Year by Household Income, 2004

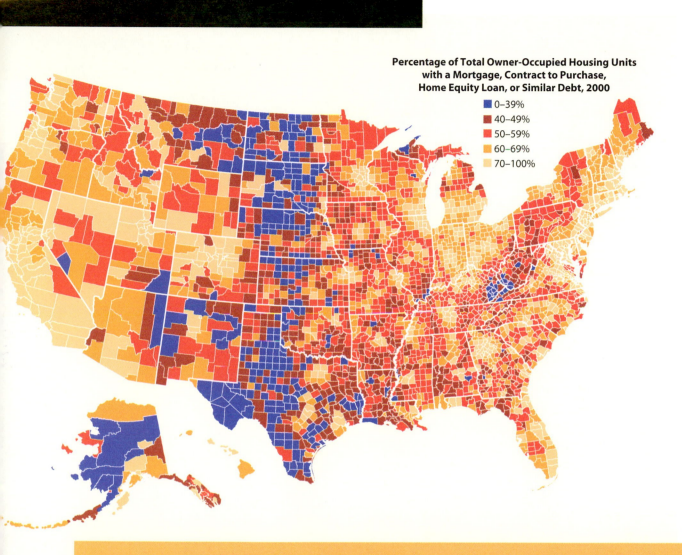

**Percentage of Total Owner-Occupied Housing Units
with a Mortgage, Contract to Purchase,
Home Equity Loan, or Similar Debt, 2000**

■ 0–39%
■ 40–49%
■ 50–59%
■ 60–69%
■ 70–100%

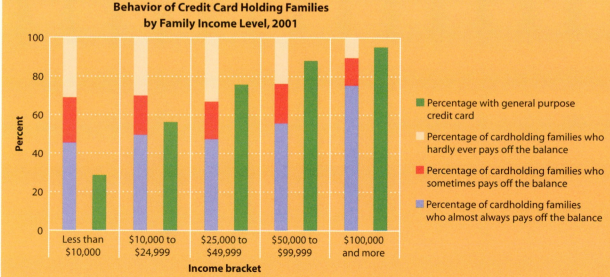

**Behavior of Credit Card Holding Families
by Family Income Level, 2001**

■ Percentage with general purpose
credit card

□ Percentage of cardholding families who
hardly ever pays off the balance

■ Percentage of cardholding families who
sometimes pays off the balance

■ Percentage of cardholding families
who almost always pays off the balance

Income bracket: Less than $10,000 | $10,000 to $24,999 | $25,000 to $49,999 | $50,000 to $99,999 | $100,000 and more

The Persistence of Poverty

Despite the many advances made in modern societies, poverty remained a problem for about 37 million Americans in 2005. Although the poverty rate had declined to just over 13 percent in 2005 (about half of the poverty rate 45 years before), over 25 percent of blacks and American Indians still lived below the poverty level.

Poverty status is also linked with educational attainment. While only 3.5 percent of individuals with a bachelor's degree or higher were living beneath the poverty level in 2005, 23.6 percent of those who had not finished high school were reported to be under the poverty line.

Although poverty may be difficult to quantify in general, the Census Bureau determines thresholds annually based on the age and number of household occupants. In 2005, for example, the threshold for a household with one individual under the age of 65 was a family income of $10,160. For a household with two adults and three children under age 18 related to the householder, the threshold was $23,307. The calculated thresholds are based primarily on costs of family food consumption, and adjusted annually based on the consumer price index.

Implications of poverty extend well beyond financial limitations of obtaining food. As a result of a reduced income, families living below the poverty line often have difficulty paying bills, lack adequate health insurance and health care, suffer from reduced access to educational opportunities, and many other problems.

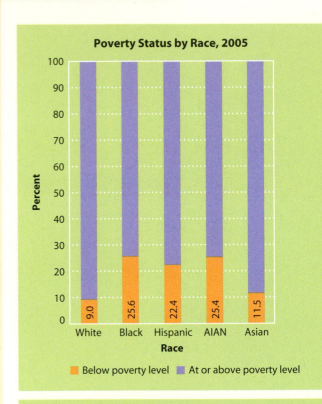

Poverty Status by Race, 2005

White 9.0, Black 25.6, Hispanic 22.4, AIAN 25.4, Asian 11.5

Race

Percent

■ Below poverty level   ■ At or above poverty level

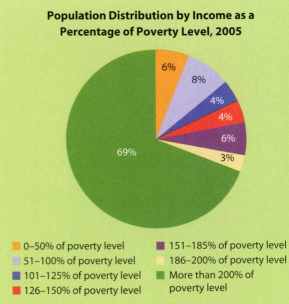

Population Distribution by Income as a Percentage of Poverty Level, 2005

6%, 8%, 4%, 4%, 6%, 3%, 69%

■ 0–50% of poverty level
■ 51–100% of poverty level
■ 101–125% of poverty level
■ 126–150% of poverty level
■ 151–185% of poverty level
■ 186–200% of poverty level
■ More than 200% of poverty level

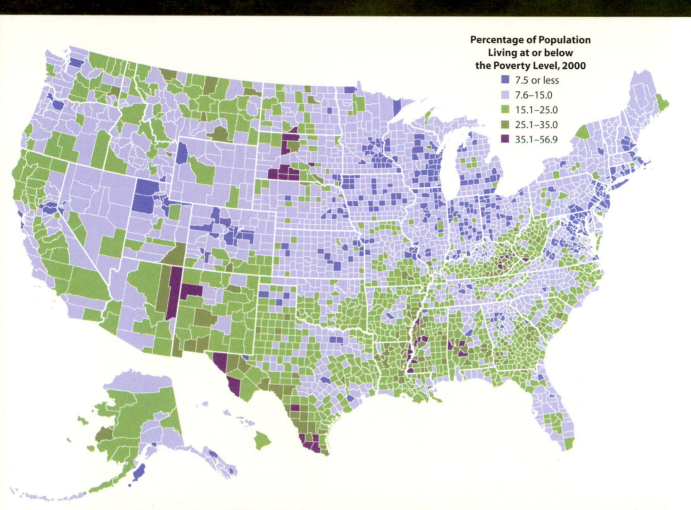

**Percentage of Population
Living at or below
the Poverty Level, 2000**

- 7.5 or less
- 7.6–15.0
- 15.1–25.0
- 25.1–35.0
- 35.1–56.9

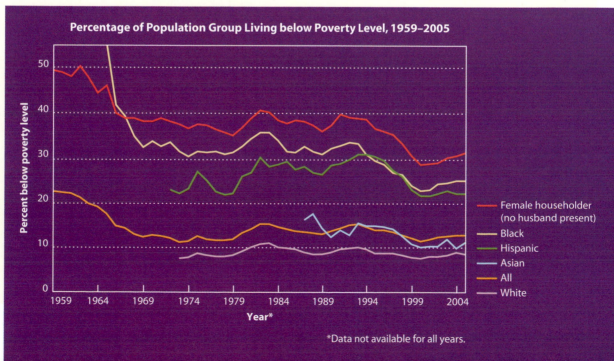

Percentage of Population Group Living below Poverty Level, 1959–2005

Percent below poverty level

Year*

- Female householder
  (no husband present)
- Black
- Hispanic
- Asian
- All
- White

*Data not available for all years.

The Persistence of Poverty

Children are the largest and fastest growing group of low-income people in the country. They account for 36 percent of low-income persons in the United States. In 2000, 38 percent of all children lived in low-income families, and 17 percent of all children lived below the poverty level.

Depending on family composition and income, individuals are assigned a poverty threshold by the government. "Poor" status is assigned to individuals who fall below their given poverty threshold. "Near poor" status is assigned to those whose family income falls between 100 to 200 percent of their given threshold. The "low-income" category encompasses both poor and near-poor individuals.

People often associate the poor status with lack of a desire or ability to work. It is important to note, however, that of the low-income children in America in 2003, 56 percent lived in families whose parents worked full time. Only 16 percent lived in families with no employed parent.

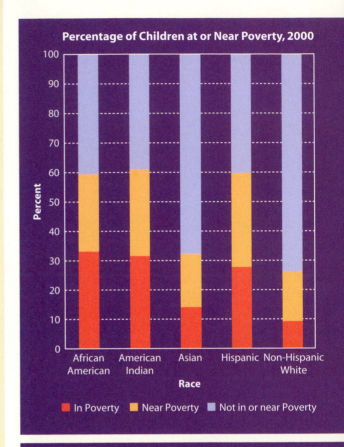

Percentage of Children at or Near Poverty, 2000

Legend: ■ In Poverty ■ Near Poverty ■ Not in or near Poverty

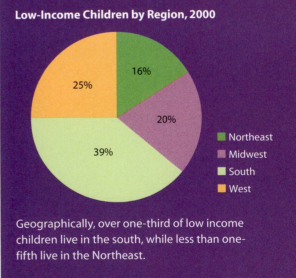

Low-Income Children by Region, 2000

Northeast 16%, Midwest 20%, South 39%, West 25%

Geographically, over one-third of low income children live in the south, while less than one-fifth live in the Northeast.

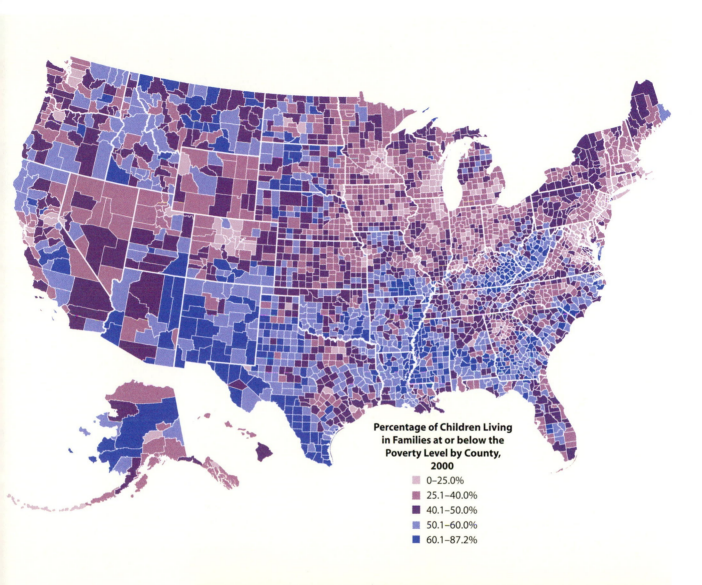

**Percentage of Children Living
in Families at or below the
Poverty Level by County,
2000**

- 0–25.0%
- 25.1–40.0%
- 40.1–50.0%
- 50.1–60.0%
- 60.1–87.2%

Many low-income families rely on the government to provide health care for their children, but approximately one-fifth of low-income children go without health insurance.

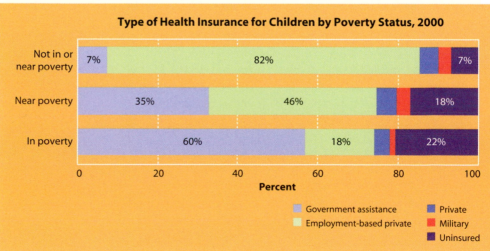

Type of Health Insurance for Children by Poverty Status, 2000

Not in or near poverty: 7% | 82% | 7%

Near poverty: 35% | 46% | 18%

In poverty: 60% | 18% | 22%

Percent

- Government assistance
- Employment-based private
- Private
- Military
- Uninsured

Educational Attainment and Life Chances

E qual access to quality education has been championed as an American right for all individuals. The famous Supreme Court case, Brown v. The Board of Education, established the legal obligation to provide fair education for everyone. While the debate continues over how to best fulfill this obligation, educational attainment levels are higher than at any point in America's history.

In 2003, 27 percent of persons age 25 and older had a bachelor's degree. The percentage of Americans age 25 and older with a high school diploma increased from 13.5 percent in 1910 to 85 percent in 2003. While this number continues to grow, educational attainment varies by race. In 2004, 90 percent of whites had a high school diploma; the same was true for only 81.1 percent of blacks and 58.4 percent of Hispanics.

In 2004, two of three people in poverty had not attended college; of those who had not finished high school, 22.8 percent reported incomes below the poverty level, compared to 10.6 percent of high school graduates and 3.1 percent of people with graduate-level degrees.

Los Alamos County, New Mexico, the county with the highest percentage of individuals having graduate or professional degrees, is home to the Los Alamos National Laboratory, which was established as a research facility for the Manhattan Project. Thirty-six percent of the population in this county had an advanced degree in 2000, compared with a national rate of 8.9 percent in 2003.

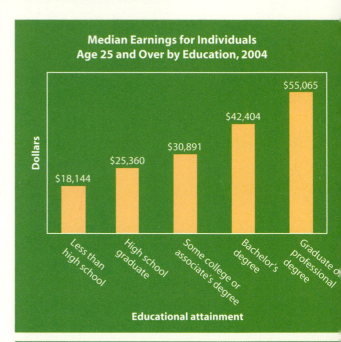

Median Earnings for Individuals Age 25 and Over by Education, 2004

- Less than high school: $18,144
- High school graduate: $25,360
- Some college or associate's degree: $30,891
- Bachelor's degree: $42,404
- Graduate or professional degree: $55,065

Dollars (y-axis)
Educational attainment (x-axis)

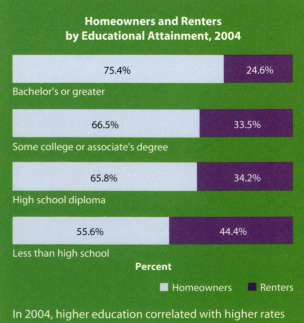

Homeowners and Renters by Educational Attainment, 2004

- Bachelor's or greater: 75.4% / 24.6%
- Some college or associate's degree: 66.5% / 33.5%
- High school diploma: 65.8% / 34.2%
- Less than high school: 55.6% / 44.4%

Percent

■ Homeowners   ■ Renters

In 2004, higher education correlated with higher rates of homeownership. Overall, one-third of the population lived in a rental residence.

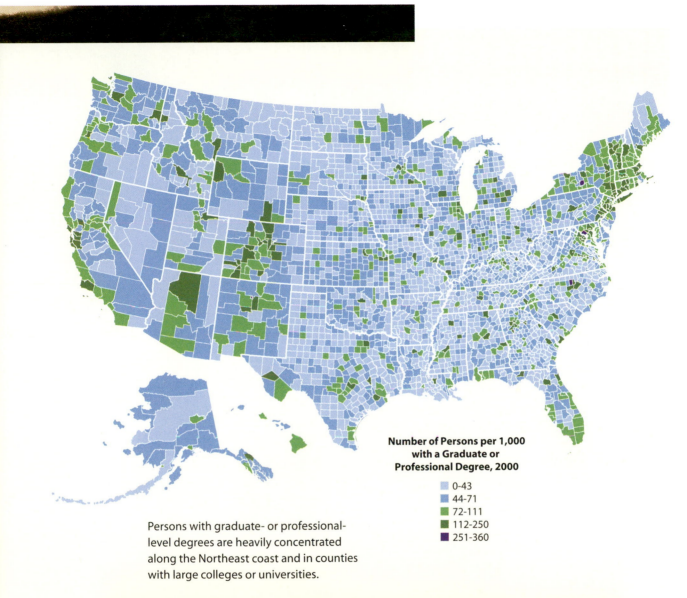

**Number of Persons per 1,000
with a Graduate or
Professional Degree, 2000**

- 0-43
- 44-71
- 72-111
- 112-250
- 251-360

Persons with graduate- or professional-
level degrees are heavily concentrated
along the Northeast coast and in counties
with large colleges or universities.

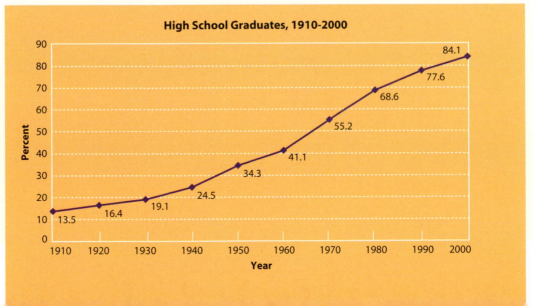

High School Graduates, 1910-2000

13.5, 16.4, 19.1, 24.5, 34.3, 41.1, 55.2, 68.6, 77.6, 84.1

Unfinished Business:
High School and College Dropouts

A high school diploma is often necessary to open doors to new employment opportunities and high-paying jobs. As a result, those individuals who drop out prior to finishing high school can face many challenges obtaining jobs and attaining incomes above the poverty level. Difficulty acquiring a desirable occupation has led many to remove themselves from the work force, relying on assistance from family, friends, or the government. Fortunately, some dropouts return to school to obtain a diploma or General Equivalence Degree (GED), thereby expanding their options.

In 2004, 30 million individuals age 25 or over had never completed high school or received a GED. Of men age 25 or over, 16.4 percent had never completed high school. Of women age 25 or over, 15.7 percent had dropped out prior to receiving a diploma or equivalent.

Receipt of a high school diploma is typically considered a major milestone in an individual's academic life, but today, more than ever, a college education is highly valued in the workforce. Some students enroll in college, but never complete a degree, and are often considered college dropouts. As of 2000, 33 million Americans age 25 or over had started college but had not obtained a degree and no longer attended school. Although all of these individuals may not be considered dropouts, they represent a large portion of the 80 million Americans who had attended college.

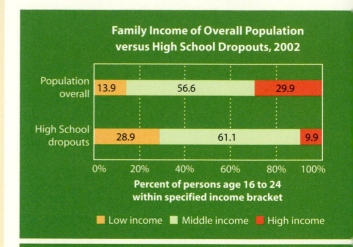

Family Income of Overall Population versus High School Dropouts, 2002

Population overall: 13.9 | 56.6 | 29.9

High School dropouts: 28.9 | 61.1 | 9.9

Percent of persons age 16 to 24 within specified income bracket

■ Low income ■ Middle income ■ High income

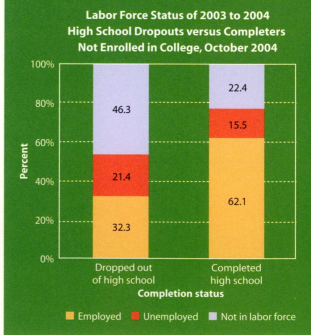

Labor Force Status of 2003 to 2004 High School Dropouts versus Completers Not Enrolled in College, October 2004

Dropped out of high school: Employed 32.3 | Unemployed 21.4 | Not in labor force 46.3

Completed high school: Employed 62.1 | Unemployed 15.5 | Not in labor force 22.4

Completion status

■ Employed ■ Unemployed ■ Not in labor force

As adults, dropouts face financial hardships. In 2000, 22.7 percent of high school dropouts age 25 and above reported incomes below the poverty level, compared to only 7 percent of high school graduates. Students from low-income homes made up a disproportionately high percentage of high school dropouts in 2002.

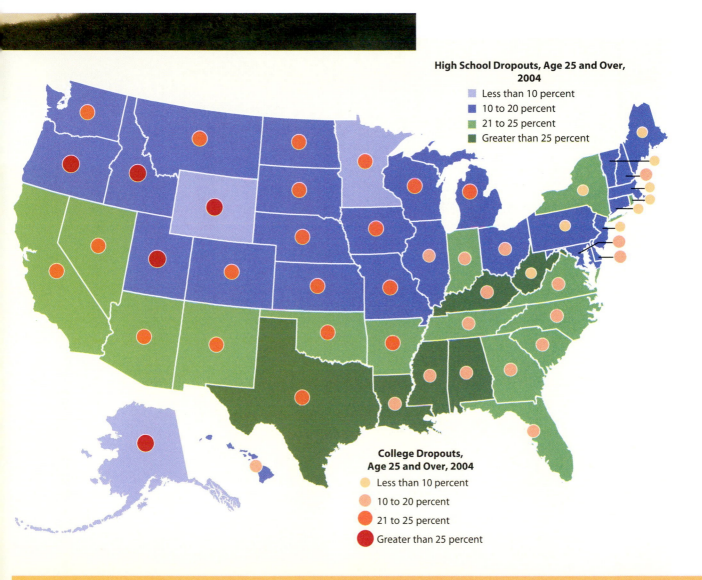

High School Dropouts, Age 25 and Over, 2004
- Less than 10 percent
- 10 to 20 percent
- 21 to 25 percent
- Greater than 25 percent

College Dropouts, Age 25 and Over, 2004
- Less than 10 percent
- 10 to 20 percent
- 21 to 25 percent
- Greater than 25 percent

In 2002, 10.5 percent of Americans age 16 to 24 were high school dropouts. Though this was only a slight reduction from 10 years earlier when the dropout rate was 11 percent, it was a large decrease from 1960 when more than 27 percent of the population had not completed high school. Since the early 1970s, dropout rates have decreased for all races, but still remained highest for Hispanics at 25.7 percent in 2002. While only 45 percent of Hispanic youths were foreign-born, immigrants accounted for 72 percent of Hispanic dropouts.

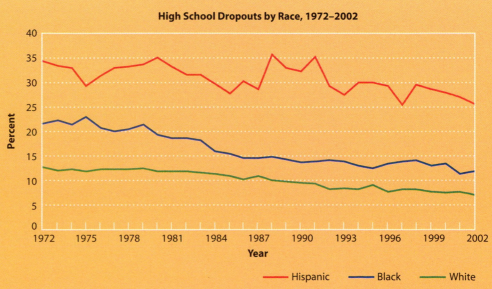

High School Dropouts by Race, 1972–2002

Alternatives to Public Education

In 1852, Massachusetts passed the first compulsory education law. By 1918, elementary-level education was compulsory throughout the nation. Protection for alternative education was strengthened in 1925, when the Supreme Court ruled that education need not be provided solely by public institutions.

An estimated 1,096,000 students were homeschooled in 2003. Homeschooled students tend to live in larger families and tend to be from rural areas. Though only 43.7 percent of all students lived in families with 3 or more children, 62.0 percent of homeschooled children were from families with three or more children. In 2003, 20.8 percent of all students lived in the rural areas, but 27.6 percent of homeschooled children were from rural areas. Parents of homeschooled kids were more likely to have a college or graduate level education.

Nationally, about 10 percent of students were enrolled in private schools in the 2001–2002 school year. Higher income families send more children to private schools. Twenty-three percent of children from families making over $75,000 per year were enrolled in private elementary schools in 2002, whereas only 5 percent of children from families earning under $25,000 annually were in the same schools.

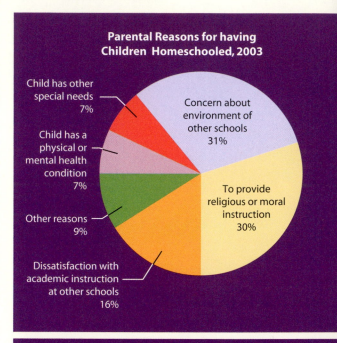

Parental Reasons for having Children Homeschooled, 2003

- Child has other special needs 7%
- Child has a physical or mental health condition 7%
- Other reasons 9%
- Dissatisfaction with academic instruction at other schools 16%
- Concern about environment of other schools 31%
- To provide religious or moral instruction 30%

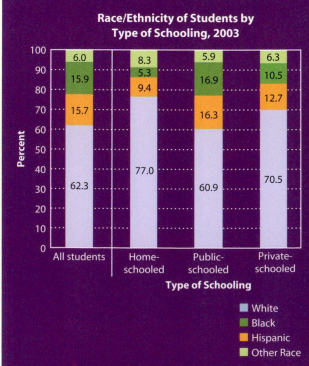

Race/Ethnicity of Students by Type of Schooling, 2003

Type of Schooling	White	Hispanic	Black	Other Race
All students	62.3	15.7	15.9	6.0
Home-schooled	77.0	9.4	5.3	8.3
Public-schooled	60.9	16.3	16.9	5.9
Private-schooled	70.5	12.7	10.5	6.3

Percent

Type of Schooling

Legend:
- White
- Black
- Hispanic
- Other Race

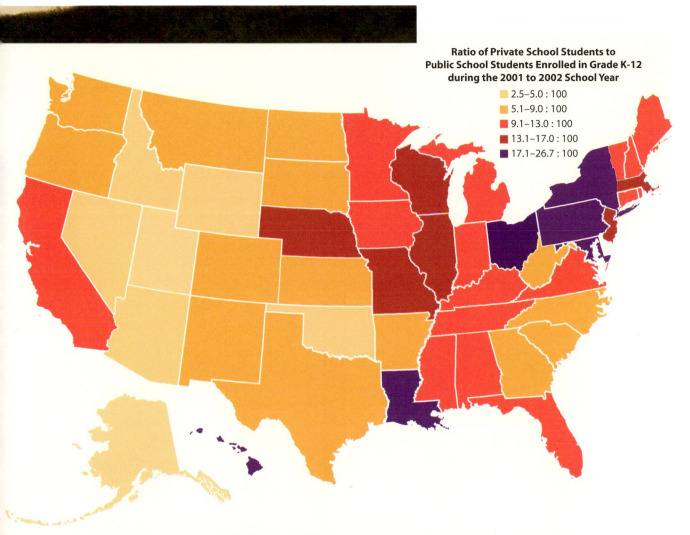

Ratio of Private School Students to Public School Students Enrolled in Grade K-12 during the 2001 to 2002 School Year

- 2.5–5.0 : 100
- 5.1–9.0 : 100
- 9.1–13.0 : 100
- 13.1–17.0 : 100
- 17.1–26.7 : 100

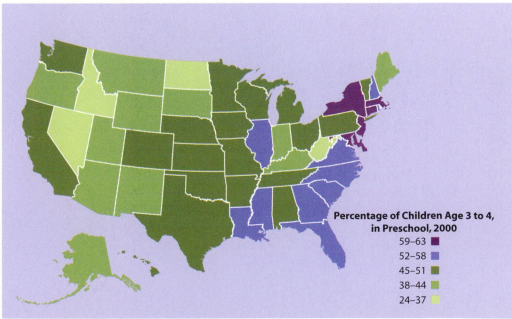

Getting a Head Start: Preschool Enrollment

Nationally, 49.3 percent of children age 3 and 4 were enrolled in preschool in 2000. Enrollment was highest in New Jersey, at 63.2 percent, and lowest in North Dakota, at 34.4 percent.

Preschool enrollment does not appear to correspond with wealth. Enrollment is high in the "rich" Northeast, but also in the "poor" Mississippi delta; average to low enrollments are found in both the relatively poor Great Plains states and wealthy California.

Percentage of Children Age 3 to 4, in Preschool, 2000

- 59–63
- 52–58
- 45–51
- 38–44
- 24–37

4 THE ECONOMY AND WORKPLACE

Earning Our Keep: The American Workforce

The United States economy is defined by the products produced and services offered by the nation's workforce. In a diverse job market, people can choose from an extensive list of occupations, both conventional and inventive. In 2002, the health and social services sector employed more individuals than any other sector, with over 15 million employees nationwide. Manufacturing and retail trade also had high employment levels. At the county level, manufacturing was more common than any other industry in 1,715 counties.

International trade between the United States and other nations of the world is also crucial in the U.S. economy. In 2005, exports of goods and services from the United States to other countries reached almost $1.3 trillion. The cost of total imports was even higher at almost $2 trillion. The balance in exports has been consistently negative since 1971. However, in 1971, the trade deficit was only $1.3 billion; it has been on the rise since then. In 2005, the deficit reached $716.7 billion, over 550 times higher.

Median earnings for individual employees differed among industries in 2004. Median earnings in the management of companies and enterprises sector were highest, while median earnings were lowest in the accommodations and food services sector. The wholesale trade industry sector had the highest value of sales, but when ranked by median earnings for its employees, wholesale trade fell near the middle.

Median Annual Earnings by Industry Sector for Full-time Year-round Employees, Age 16 and Over, 2005

Industry sector	Median annual earnings
Accommodation and food services	$21,915
Administrative and support and waste management services	$29,728
Agriculture, forestry, fishing, hunting	$25,829
Arts, entertainment, and recreation	$31,537
Construction	$35,854
Educational services	$40,156
Finance and insurance	$45,341
Health care and social assistance	$34,815
Information	$49,248
Management of companies and enterprises	$59,926
Manufacturing	$40,482
Mining	$50,482
Other services, except public administration	$30,029
Professional, scientific, and technical services	$57,620
Public administration	$45,928
Real estate and rental and leasing	$38,363
Retail trade	$30,421
Transportation and warehousing	$42,065
Utilities	$54,630
Wholesale trade	$40,514

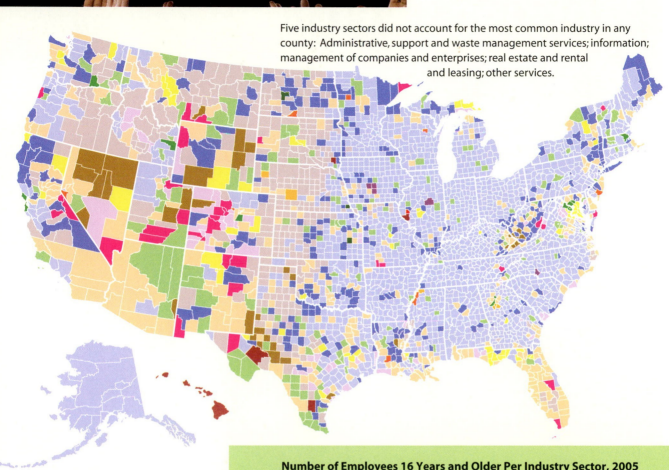

Five industry sectors did not account for the most common industry in any county: Administrative, support and waste management services; information; management of companies and enterprises; real estate and rental and leasing; other services.

Most common industry according to number of people working in each industry, 2000

- Accomodation and food services
- Agriculture, forestry, fishing and hunting
- Arts, entertainment, and recreation
- Construction
- Educational services
- Finance and insurance
- Healthcare and social assistance
- Manufacturing
- Mining
- Professional, scientific, and technical services
- Public administration
- Retail trade
- Transportation and warehousing
- Utilities
- Wholesale trade
- Two equally common industries

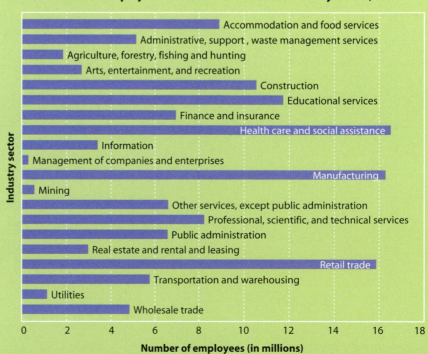

Number of Employees 16 Years and Older Per Industry Sector, 2005

Industry sector

- Accommodation and food services
- Administrative, support , waste management services
- Agriculture, forestry, fishing and hunting
- Arts, entertainment, and recreation
- Construction
- Educational services
- Finance and insurance
- Health care and social assistance
- Information
- Management of companies and enterprises
- Manufacturing
- Mining
- Other services, except public administration
- Professional, scientific, and technical services
- Public administration
- Real estate and rental and leasing
- Retail trade
- Transportation and warehousing
- Utilities
- Wholesale trade

0   2   4   6   8   10   12   14   16   18

Number of employees (in millions)

Working Overtime: Labor Conditions

Work is a major cause of stress for many Americans. The CDC reports that "high levels of emotional exhaustion at the end of the workday are the norm for 25 percent to 30 percent of the workforce." Days away from work due to anxiety, stress, and neurotic disorders tend to differ among occupations and may be tied to the level of stress induced by such positions.

The percentage of workers receiving benefits varies widely by specific benefit, job type, and union membership. Generally, higher-paid and higher-status workers, union members, full-time employees, and goods-producing (as opposed to service-producing) workers receive more benefits.

Overall, on-the-job fatalities decreased by about 1.2 percent from 1992 to 2002; nonfatal injuries decreased by 55.5 percent, according to the Bureau of Labor Statistics. In 2003, men accounted for 92 percent of all workplace-related fatalities even though only 54 percent of people in the workforce were men. Victims were women in 56 percent of all job-related highway incidents and 73 percent of on-the-job homicides. Men were more likely to be victims of accidents such as falls or contact with objects and equipment.

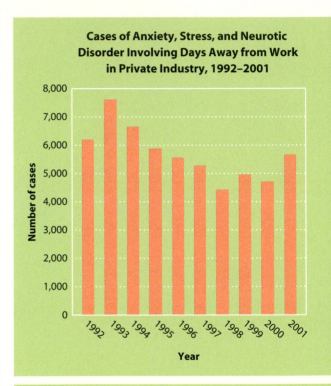

Cases of Anxiety, Stress, and Neurotic Disorder Involving Days Away from Work in Private Industry, 1992–2001

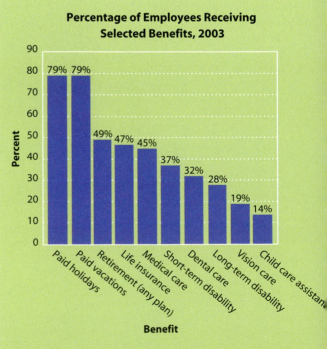

Percentage of Employees Receiving Selected Benefits, 2003

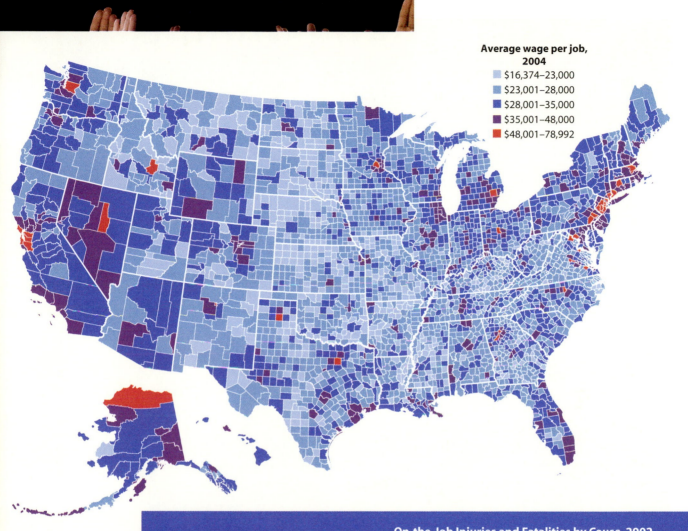

Average wage per job, 2004

- $16,374–23,000
- $23,001–28,000
- $28,001–35,000
- $35,001–48,000
- $48,001–78,992

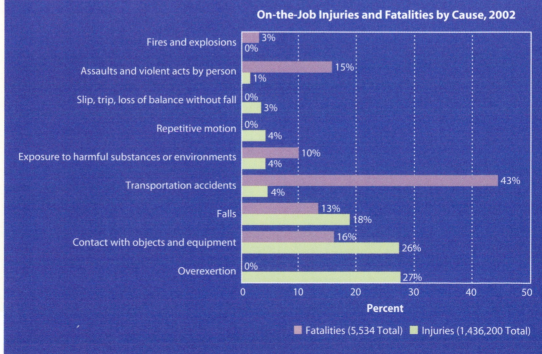

On-the-Job Injuries and Fatalities by Cause, 2002

Cause	Fatalities	Injuries
Fires and explosions	3%	0%
Assaults and violent acts by person	15%	1%
Slip, trip, loss of balance without fall	0%	3%
Repetitive motion	0%	4%
Exposure to harmful substances or environments	10%	4%
Transportation accidents	43%	4%
Falls	13%	18%
Contact with objects and equipment	16%	26%
Overexertion	0%	27%

Percent

■ Fatalities (5,534 Total)   ■ Injuries (1,436,200 Total)

The State of the Unions: Organized Labor

Union membership has declined steadily since the 1950s. However, membership increased slightly after a 1962 executive order that legalized public sector unions. There are many reasons for the overall decline, including the disappearance of traditionally unionized industries, the growth of industries that are more difficult to organize, insufficient organizing, and union-limiting legislation.

Many states have passed "right-to-work" laws prohibiting mandatory union membership, and union membership tends to be lowest in these states. Union membership is highest in the Great Lakes region, New England, and on the West Coast.

In 2005, union members had a median weekly salary that was 29 percent higher than non-members. Union members are also more likely to receive benefits such as health care. Many of the states with high rates of unionization also have a minimum wage above the federal level.

Union membership differs between demographic groups. In 2005, 13.5 percent of men were union members compared to 11.3 percent of women. Membership was highest among blacks (15.1 percent) and lowest among Hispanics (10.4 percent). While 13.7 percent of full-time workers have union memberships, only 6.5 percent of part-time workers are union members.

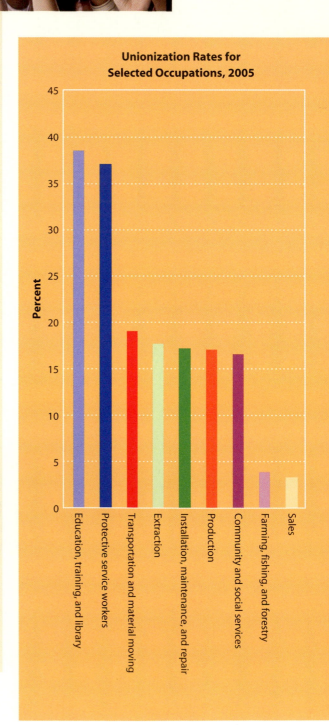

Unionization Rates for Selected Occupations, 2005

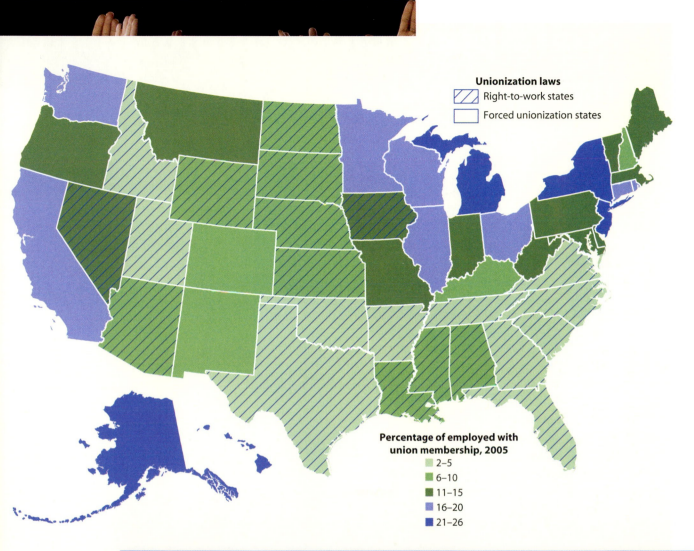

Unionization laws

- ⧄ Right-to-work states
- ▢ Forced unionization states

Percentage of employed with union membership, 2005

- 2–5
- 6–10
- 11–15
- 16–20
- 21–26

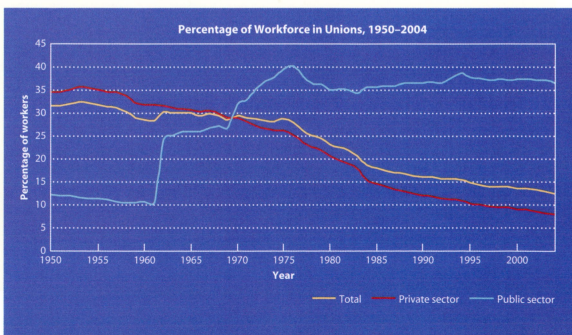

Percentage of Workforce in Unions, 1950–2004

— Total   — Private sector   — Public sector

Equal Opportunity Employment: Diversity in the Workforce

Today's bustling workforce reflects the diversity of the nation. Equal-opportunity laws aim to protect all individuals from unfair discrimination and exist to ensure that people are fairly hired, retained, and promoted. Two of the most important laws include the Equal Pay Act of 1963 and Title VII of the Civil Rights Act of 1964. The Equal Pay Act prohibits sex-based wage discrimination, while Title VII prohibits employment discrimination based on race, color, religion, sex, or national origin. The Age Discrimination in Employment Act of 1967 and the Americans with Disabilities Act of 1990 provide additional employment protections not covered by the earlier laws.

Minorities account for about 30 percent of the population in the United States. Within different career groups, minorities make up varying percentages of workers. Minorities account for a higher percentage of teachers and nurses than lawyers, but minorities are increasing as a percentage of lawyers at legal firms.

A 2005 national Gallup poll conducted in conjunction with the Equal Employment Opportunity Commission (EEOC) shows that despite equal employment laws, perceptions of employment discrimination remain among workers: 15 percent of workers reported to pollsters that they felt they had been subject to unfair treatment and on-the-job discrimination. Feelings of discrimination were highest among Asians: 31 percent of Asians surveyed felt they had experienced incidents of discrimination. The second highest rate was among blacks: 26 percent expressed feelings of workplace discrimination.

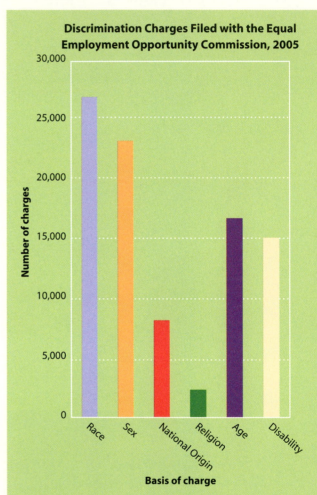

Discrimination Charges Filed with the Equal Employment Opportunity Commission, 2005

The Equal Employment Opportunity Commission (EEOC) enforces federal equal-opportunity laws.

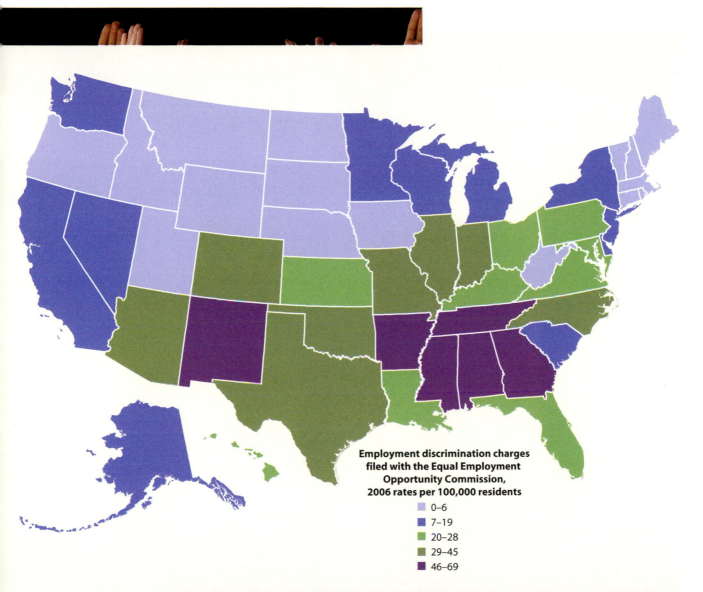

Employment discrimination charges filed with the Equal Employment Opportunity Commission, 2006 rates per 100,000 residents

- 0–6
- 7–19
- 20–28
- 29–45
- 46–69

In 1975, only about 3 percent of lawyers at large legal firms were minorities, but in 2002, minorities accounted for nearly 13 percent of lawyers at large firms: 5.3 percent were Asian, 4.4 percent were blacks, and 2.9 percent were Hispanic.

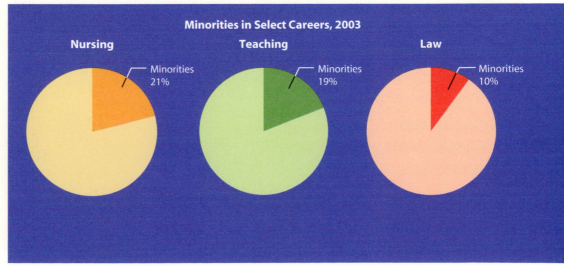

Minorities in Select Careers, 2003

Nursing
Minorities 21%

Teaching
Minorities 19%

Law
Minorities 10%

The Workplace Gender Gap

Though the labor force is now nearly equally divided between women and men, there are still many occupations that are dominated by one sex. Though management and professional occupations seem almost equally divided, there is much division within the occupations that make up this category. Eighty-five percent of farmers and 86 percent of architects are men. Of healthcare practitioners, 73 percent are women.

Predominately female occupations tend to pay less than predominately male occupations. Though the law states that men and women must receive equal compensation for the same position, average salaries for women continue to be lower since more women work in lower level jobs.

Less than one-third (30 percent) of men make less than $20,000 per year while nearly half of women (46 percent) fall into this lower income bracket (includes part-time workers). Fifty-seven percent of people earning less than $20,000 are women. Higher income levels are dominated by men; of those earning $75,000 or more per year, 77 percent are men.

Median earnings increase directly with educational attainment. However, the difference in the income of men and women also increases. Among people at the same educational level, men make more on average than women. While the difference in median annual earnings between men and women without high school degrees is only about $7,000, the difference between men and women with advanced degrees is over $20,000.

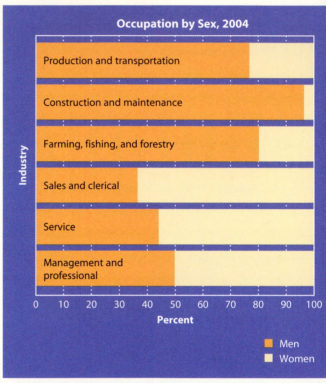

Occupation by Sex, 2004

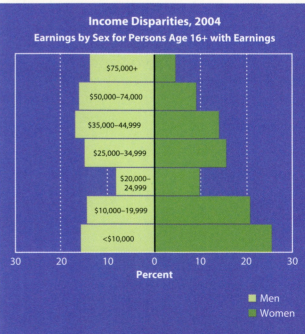

Income Disparities, 2004
Earnings by Sex for Persons Age 16+ with Earnings

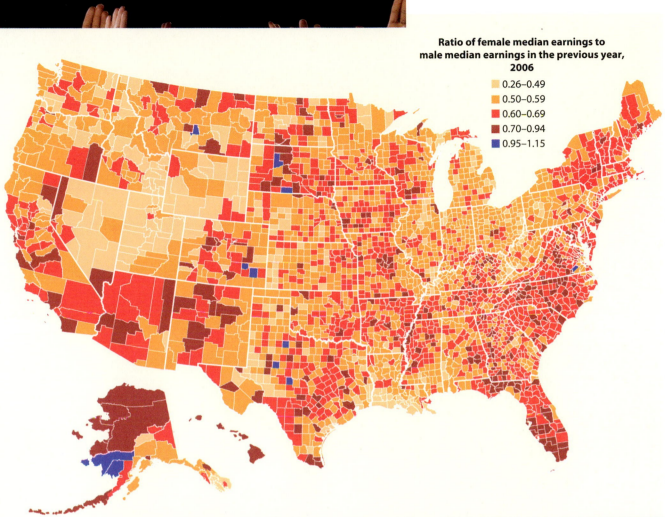

Ratio of female median earnings to male median earnings in the previous year, 2006

- 0.26–0.49
- 0.50–0.59
- 0.60–0.69
- 0.70–0.94
- 0.95–1.15

The gap in labor force participation has narrowed since the 1850s when nearly 100 percent of people in the labor force were men. During World War II, women joined the workforce while their husbands went to war. The rethinking of traditional gender roles during the 1950s and 1960s led to a greater percentage of women workers. In 2000, 53.5 percent of people in the workforce were men and 46.5 percent of people in the workforce were women.

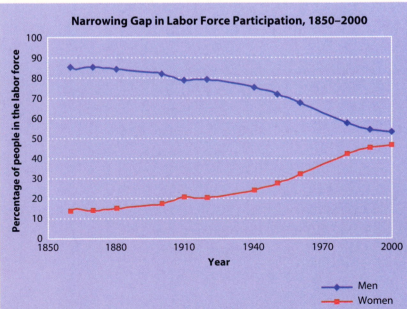

Narrowing Gap in Labor Force Participation, 1850–2000

5 HEALTH AND WELLNESS

Health Insurance: The Haves and Have-Nots

Health care can be expensive, and unexpected hospital bills are one of the leading causes of personal bankruptcy filings. In 2005, 15.6 percent of the population reported never having health care coverage for the previous year.

Health insurance can be provided by either the government or private organizations. In 2004, almost 80 million individuals (about 27 percent of the population) were covered through government insurance programs. In addition to Medicare and Medicaid, the government also provides insurance to military personnel.

The majority of Americans, however, receive coverage from private insurance carriers. Although rates dropped slightly from 1998, about 60 percent of the population received private health care coverage through an employer in 2004, and an additional 9.3 percent purchased private insurance plans on their own.

Those families with the lowest incomes are also least likely to have health care coverage. In fact, of individuals belonging to families with annual incomes below $25,000 in 2004, almost 27 percent had no health care coverage. Similarly, almost 30 percent of individuals age 25 and over without a high school diploma reported being uninsured during the same period. In contrast, less than nine percent of those individuals having a bachelor's degree or more reported being uninsured, and only seven percent of individuals belonging to families having incomes over $75,000 lacked insurance in 2004.

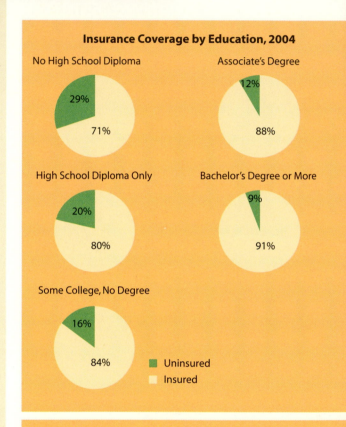

Insurance Coverage by Education, 2004

No High School Diploma
29% Uninsured / 71% Insured

Associate's Degree
12% Uninsured / 88% Insured

High School Diploma Only
20% Uninsured / 80% Insured

Bachelor's Degree or More
9% Uninsured / 91% Insured

Some College, No Degree
16% Uninsured / 84% Insured

■ Uninsured
□ Insured

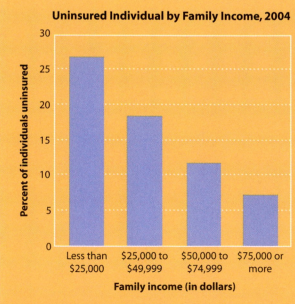

Uninsured Individual by Family Income, 2004

Percent of individuals uninsured (y-axis: 0 to 30)

Family income (in dollars): Less than $25,000; $25,000 to $49,999; $50,000 to $74,999; $75,000 or more

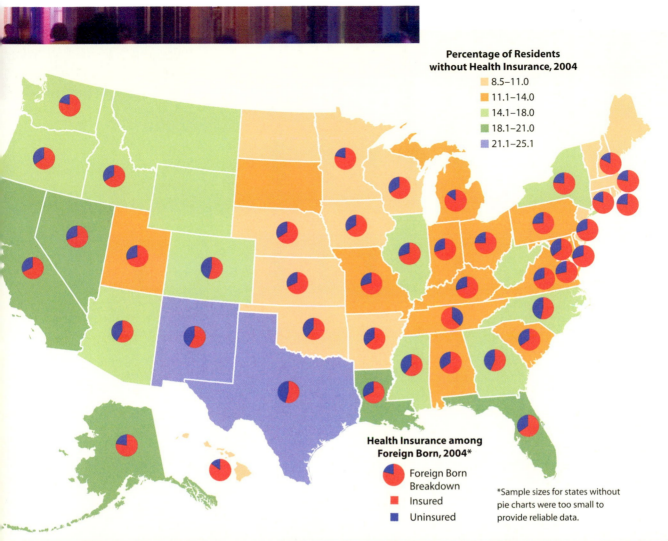

Percentage of Residents without Health Insurance, 2004

- 8.5–11.0
- 11.1–14.0
- 14.1–18.0
- 18.1–21.0
- 21.1–25.1

Health Insurance among Foreign Born, 2004*

- Foreign Born Breakdown
- Insured
- Uninsured

*Sample sizes for states without pie charts were too small to provide reliable data.

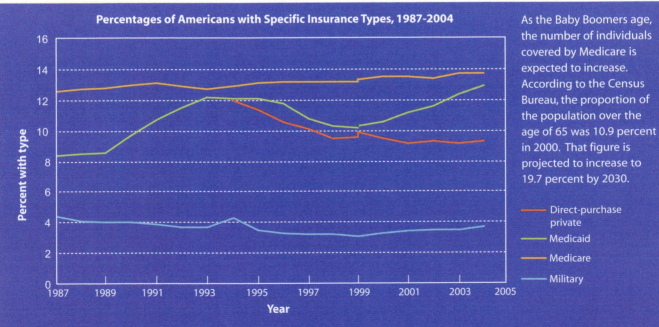

Percentages of Americans with Specific Insurance Types, 1987-2004

Percent with type vs *Year*

As the Baby Boomers age, the number of individuals covered by Medicare is expected to increase. According to the Census Bureau, the proportion of the population over the age of 65 was 10.9 percent in 2000. That figure is projected to increase to 19.7 percent by 2030.

- Direct-purchase private
- Medicaid
- Medicare
- Military

Living on the Edge: Behavioral Risk Factors

In 2000, the top three causes of death due to behavioral risks in the U.S. were a result of tobacco use (18.1 percent of all deaths), poor diet, and physical inactivity (16.6 percent), and alcohol consumption (3.5 percent).

For many years, the social use of tobacco products was considered "cool" and was depicted casually in entertainment and advertising media. Increased awareness of the health risks associated with this activity has led to a decline in its prevalence, but smoking is still relatively common today. Between 1995 and 1999, there was an average of 442,398 smoking-related deaths per year.

California reported the most people per capita who considered smoking to be a risk to health and had the second a lowest percentage of smokers in 2002. At the other extreme was Kentucky, with the most smokers of any state, and the lowest percentage of people who deemed smoking to be risky.

Nearly two-thirds of American adults weigh more than is deemed healthy, with 30.9 percent classified as obese. From 1974 to 2000, the number of overweight and obese people increased from 47.7 to 64.5 percent, and the prevalence of obesity doubled from 14.6 to 30.6 percent. Over the same period, children and adolescents 6 to 19 years old showed an increase in obesity from 5 to 15 percent.

In 2000, an estimated $75 billion was spent on overweight- and obesity-related health care. Carrying extra pounds correlates with a host of health problems, including diabetes, high blood pressure, asthma, arthritis, and heart disease.

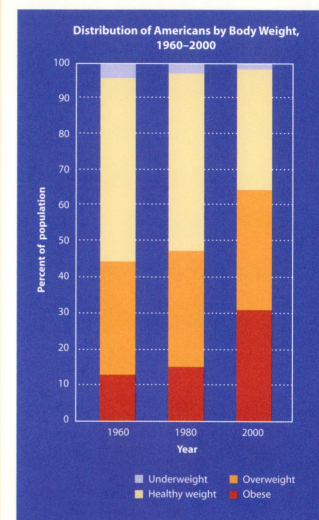

Distribution of Americans by Body Weight, 1960–2000

Overweight is defined as having a body mass index (BMI) of 25 or greater. Obese refers to a BMI of 30 or greater. BMI is based on a person's height and weight. A person who stands 5' 8" would be overweight at 164 pounds, and obese at 197 pounds.

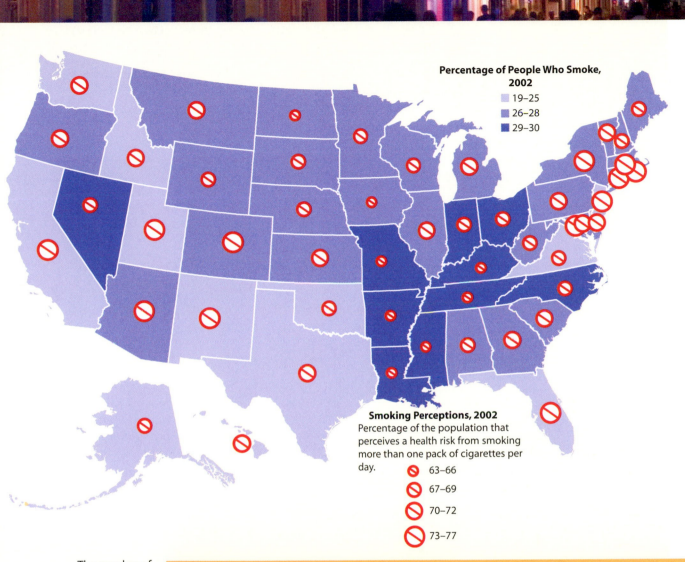

Percentage of People Who Smoke, 2002

- 19–25
- 26–28
- 29–30

Smoking Perceptions, 2002

Percentage of the population that perceives a health risk from smoking more than one pack of cigarettes per day.

- 63–66
- 67–69
- 70–72
- 73–77

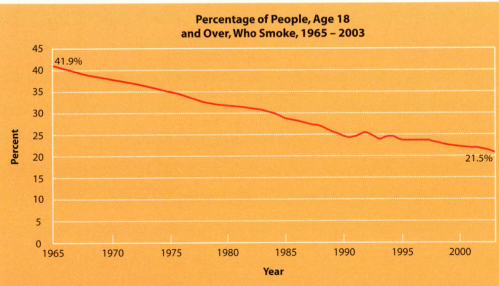

The number of smokers dropped from 41.9 percent of the population in 1965 to only 21.5 percent of the population in 2003.

Percentage of People, Age 18 and Over, Who Smoke, 1965 – 2003

41.9%

21.5%

Percent

Year

Living on the Edge: Behavioral Risk Factors

Alcohol consumption is widespread in today's culture. Almost 41,000 Americans died in 2001 from acute alcohol-related causes, including motor vehicle crashes. The number of men who died from acute alcohol-related causes was three times higher than the number of women who died from the same causes. Almost 35,000 people died due to chronic alcohol-related problems such as liver disease.

In 2003, two out of five men who were current drinkers reported moderate to heavy levels of alcohol consumption. Only one in every five women who were current drinkers reported moderate to heavy levels of alcohol consumption. The difference between men and women is much more pronounced for moderate drinkers than for heavy drinkers.

Awareness about drunk driving has increased, but an estimated 10 to 22 percent of car accidents involved people under the influence of drugs and alcohol. In 2004, there were 1,433,382 reported arrests for driving under the influence. Unfortunately, a very small percentage of those driving illegally are ever arrested and charged with driving under the influence (DUI).

Drunk driving remains a concern, but there have been other encouraging trends related to driving behavior. Seatbelt usage has increased from just 59 percent in 1994 to 79 percent in 2003. Between 2002 and 2003, 17 percent of seatbelt non-users chose to start buckling up regularly. Seatbelts are about 50 percent effective in preventing fatalities in collisions that would otherwise result in death. Driving laws and penalties may have contributed to this rise in seatbelt usage and may partially explain why the number of wearers differs by state.

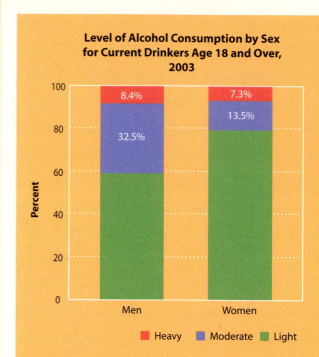

Level of Alcohol Consumption by Sex for Current Drinkers Age 18 and Over, 2003

Heavy drinking is defined as having more than 14 drinks a week for men and more than 7 drinks a week for women. Moderate drinking is defined as having between 4 and 14 drinks per week for men and between 3 and 6 drinks per week for women.

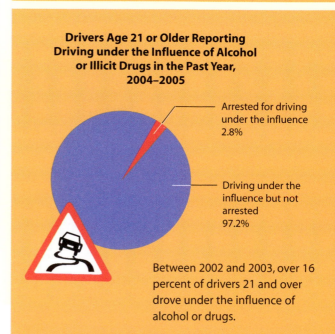

Drivers Age 21 or Older Reporting Driving under the Influence of Alcohol or Illicit Drugs in the Past Year, 2004–2005

Arrested for driving under the influence 2.8%

Driving under the influence but not arrested 97.2%

Between 2002 and 2003, over 16 percent of drivers 21 and over drove under the influence of alcohol or drugs.

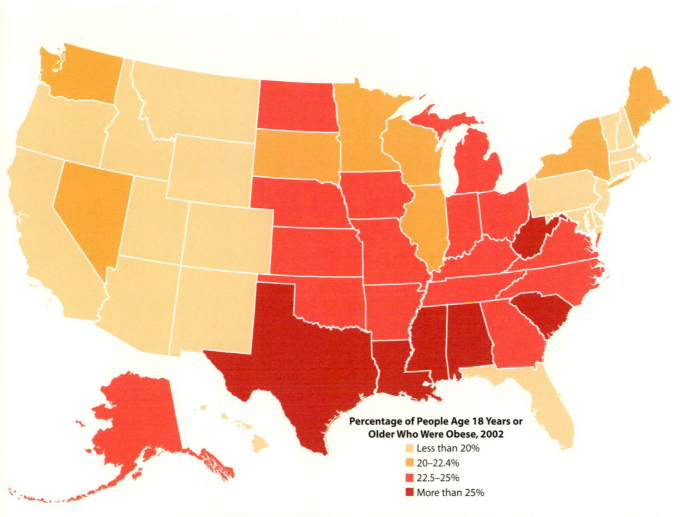

Percentage of People Age 18 Years or Older Who Were Obese, 2002

- Less than 20%
- 20–22.4%
- 22.5–25%
- More than 25%

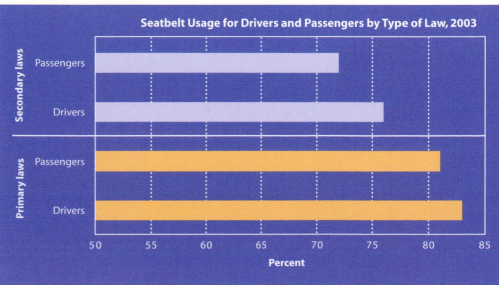

Seatbelt Usage for Drivers and Passengers by Type of Law, 2003

Secondary laws
- Passengers
- Drivers

Primary laws
- Passengers
- Drivers

Percent

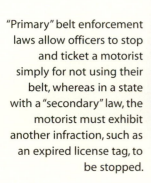

"Primary" belt enforcement laws allow officers to stop and ticket a motorist simply for not using their belt, whereas in a state with a "secondary" law, the motorist must exhibit another infraction, such as an expired license tag, to be stopped.

The Threat of Pandemic Disease

Since the late 1990s, Americans have been warned about threats of several diseases including smallpox, anthrax, severe acute respiratory syndrome (SARS), mad cow disease, West Nile virus, and pandemic flu. Although media outlets may have sensationalized the extent of such threats, the concern it generated likely encouraged increased vigilance on the part of both government agencies and the general public. For example, when bovine spongiform encephalopathy (BSE, also known as mad cow disease) was identified and linked with the human disease variant Creutzfeldt-Jakob disease (vCJD), the government not only increased regulations for the import and export of beef but also increased research and testing for both BSE and vCJD.

Terrorism in the first few years of the 21st century resulted in increased fear of threats such as anthrax and smallpox. *Bacillus anthracis,* the bacterium which causes anthrax, was sent through the mail with limited results in 2001 and 2002, but no cases of smallpox had been seen by early 2007.

While the threats posed by some diseases such as SARS may have been exaggerated, experts have warned of the potential for a flu outbreak with consequences similar to the H1N1 strain, which caused the 1918 pandemic and killed at least 50 million people worldwide. The H5N1 virus, commonly known as avian flu, has renewed concern. Although the H5N1 virus had caused fewer than a thousand human deaths by the beginning of 2007, a mutation allowing human-to-human transmission would likely cause infection rates to explode.

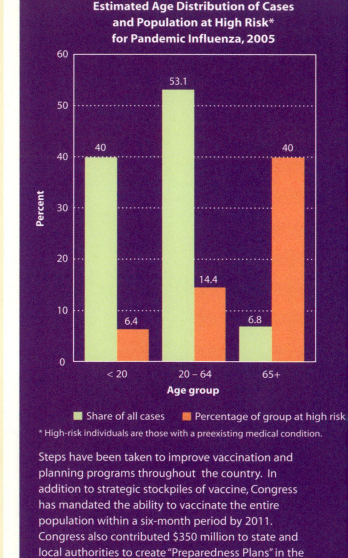

Estimated Age Distribution of Cases and Population at High Risk* for Pandemic Influenza, 2005

Percent (y-axis)

Age group (x-axis): < 20, 20 – 64, 65+

- < 20: Share of all cases 40; Percentage of group at high risk 6.4
- 20 – 64: Share of all cases 53.1; Percentage of group at high risk 14.4
- 65+: Share of all cases 6.8; Percentage of group at high risk 40

■ Share of all cases   ■ Percentage of group at high risk
* High-risk individuals are those with a preexisting medical condition.

Steps have been taken to improve vaccination and planning programs throughout the country. In addition to strategic stockpiles of vaccine, Congress has mandated the ability to vaccinate the entire population within a six-month period by 2011. Congress also contributed $350 million to state and local authorities to create "Preparedness Plans" in the event of a pandemic flu.

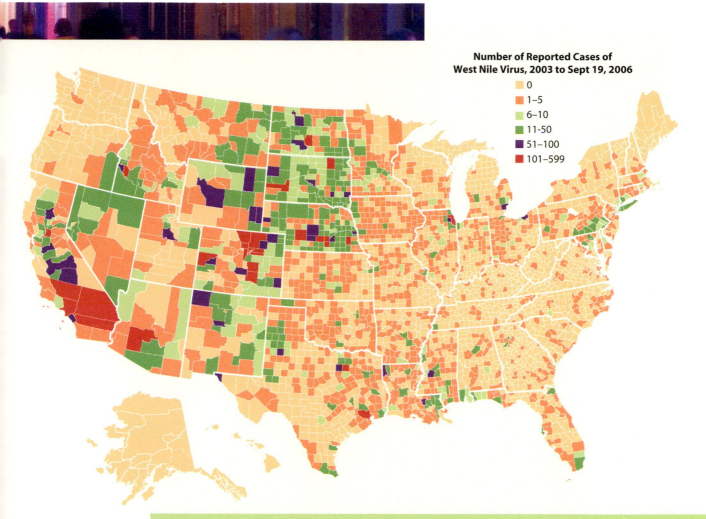

**Number of Reported Cases of
West Nile Virus, 2003 to Sept 19, 2006**

- 0
- 1–5
- 6–10
- 11-50
- 51–100
- 101–599

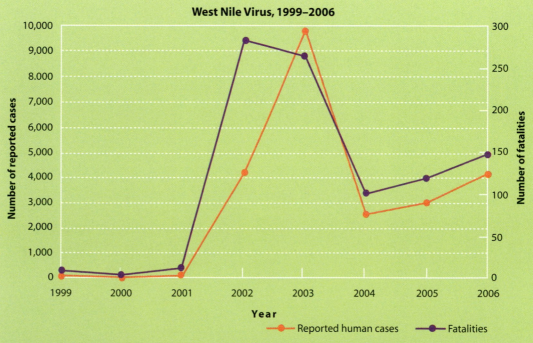

West Nile Virus, 1999–2006

States only report confirmed and probable cases of West Nile virus to the Centers for Disease Control and Prevention. As a consequence, many cases may go either undiagnosed or unreported.

— Reported human cases   — Fatalities

A Matter of Life and Death: Cancer

Cancer, the second leading cause of death in the United States, is actually more than 100 different diseases. The National Cancer Institute estimated there were 1.40 million new cancer cases and 545,000 cancer deaths in 2006. At the beginning of 2003, approximately 10.5 million people had a history of cancer. Although cancer affects all races and ethnicities, whites are most likely to develop the disease. In contrast, black women and Asian and Pacific Islander men and women are least likely to develop cancer.

The National Cancer Institute predicts that 45.3 percent of men and 37.9 percent of women will be diagnosed with a type of cancer at some point. Only a few decades ago, men would have had about a 40 percent chance of surviving for five years after diagnosis, and women did not fare much better. More recently, health care and education has improved the five-year survival rate to nearly 70 percent for both men and women.

According to the National Cancer Institute, over 40 percent of babies born in 2006 will be diagnosed with cancer at some point during their lives. Additionally, the National Cancer Institute estimated that 8.7 million years of life were lost due to cancer in 2003 alone.

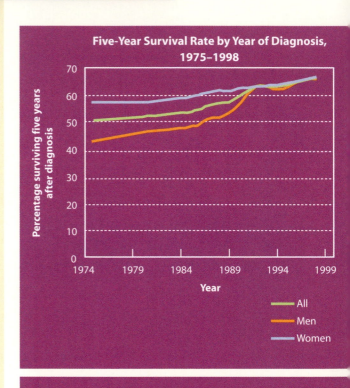

Five-Year Survival Rate by Year of Diagnosis, 1975–1998

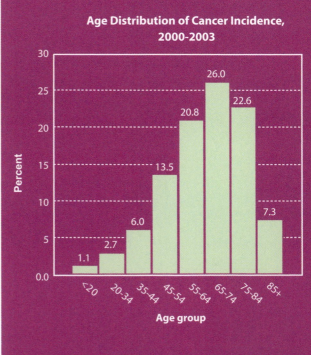

Age Distribution of Cancer Incidence, 2000-2003

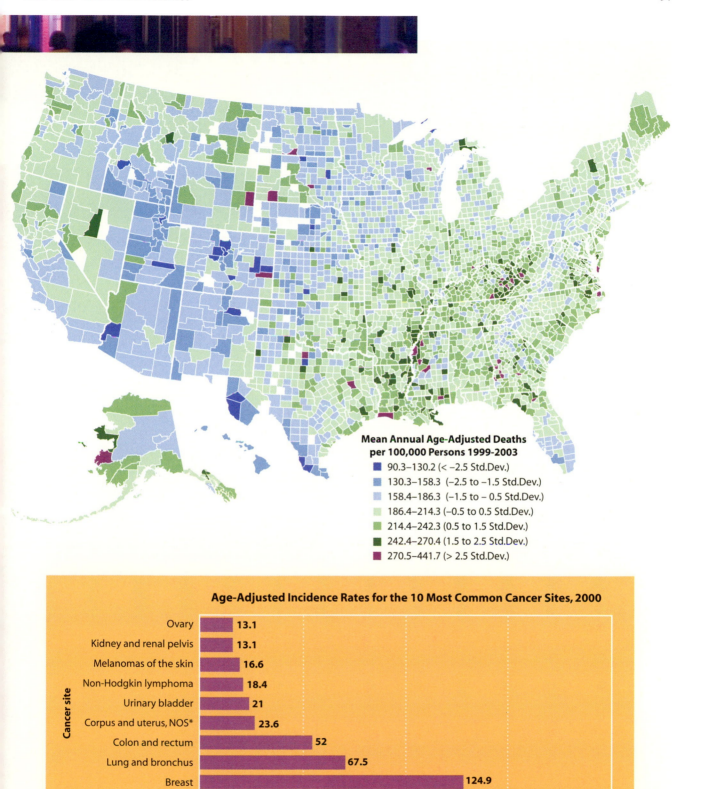

**Mean Annual Age-Adjusted Deaths
per 100,000 Persons 1999-2003**

- 90.3–130.2 (< –2.5 Std.Dev.)
- 130.3–158.3 (–2.5 to –1.5 Std.Dev.)
- 158.4–186.3 (–1.5 to – 0.5 Std.Dev.)
- 186.4–214.3 (–0.5 to 0.5 Std.Dev.)
- 214.4–242.3 (0.5 to 1.5 Std.Dev.)
- 242.4–270.4 (1.5 to 2.5 Std.Dev.)
- 270.5–441.7 (> 2.5 Std.Dev.)

Age-Adjusted Incidence Rates for the 10 Most Common Cancer Sites, 2000

Cancer site

Ovary	13.1
Kidney and renal pelvis	13.1
Melanomas of the skin	16.6
Non-Hodgkin lymphoma	18.4
Urinary bladder	21
Corpus and uterus, NOS*	23.6
Colon and rectum	52
Lung and bronchus	67.5
Breast	124.9
Prostate	161.2

0   50   100   150   200

Annual diagnoses per 100,00 persons

* NOS: Not Otherwise Specified

Sexually Transmitted Diseases

Sexually transmitted diseases (STDs) have long plagued Americans. During both World Wars I and II, American armed forces personnel received materials educating them on how to avoid STDs and their potential health risks.

Next to abstinence, condoms are the best defense against spreading STDs. Condom usage has increased at different rates for whites, blacks, and Hispanics. White women reported the least dramatic increase in condom use, from 13.1 percent in 1982, to 21.7 percent in 2002. Black and Hispanic women, however, experienced increases from 6.3 percent and 6.9 percent, respectively, in 1982, to 29.6 percent and 24.1 percent, respectively, in 2002.

Chlamydia trachomatis infections (commonly known as chlamydia) are the most commonly reported infectious disease in the United States. In 2004, the Centers for Disease Control and Prevention (CDC) received reports of 319.6 chlamydia cases per 100,000 persons, more than 2.5 times the rate of reported cases of gonorrhea (113.5 cases per 100,000 persons). While the chlamydia rates were 3.3 times higher for women, gonorrhea rates were about 2 times higher for men. Some good news: the rates for reported gonorrhea cases in 2004 were the lowest ever.

Human papillomavirus (HPV), which causes genital warts, and genital herpes are thought to be the most prevalent STDs. In fact, at any given time, 20 million Americans may have transmittable genital HPV infections. Other reports from 1997 estimated that 45 million Americans were infected with genital herpes virus.

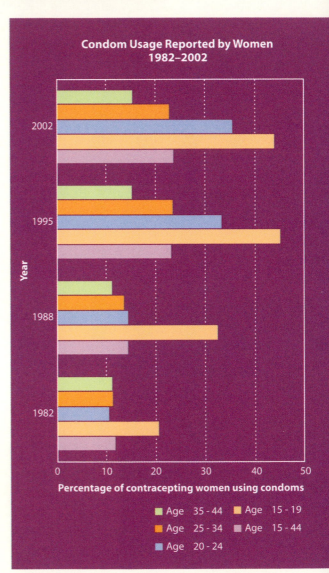

Condom Usage Reported by Women 1982–2002

Year / Percentage of contracepting women using condoms

Legend:
- Age 35 - 44
- Age 25 - 34
- Age 20 - 24
- Age 15 - 19
- Age 15 - 44

The percentage of women who use condoms as contraception has increased substantially. Women age 15 to 24 have increased usage the most. For women age 15 to 19, condom usage increased from 20.8 percent in 1982 to 44.6 percent in 2002. Women age 20 to 24 increased usage from 10.7 percent to 36.0 percent during the same period.

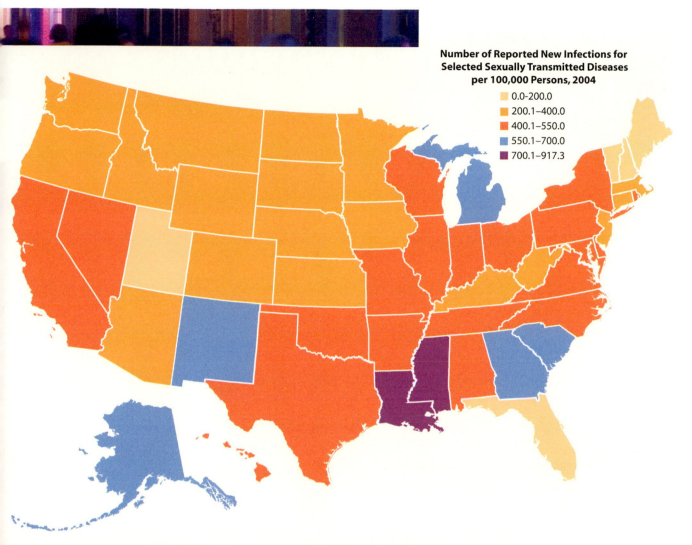

Number of Reported New Infections for Selected Sexually Transmitted Diseases per 100,000 Persons, 2004

- 0.0-200.0
- 200.1–400.0
- 400.1–550.0
- 550.1–700.0
- 700.1–917.3

Although health care providers are not required to report every genital warts or genital herpes diagnosis to the CDC, estimates are compiled. Because there is currently no cure for either virus, those who contract these viruses will always have them.

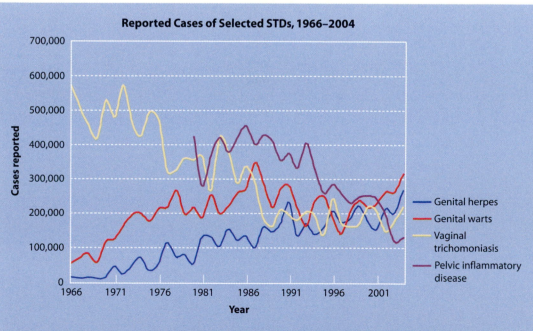

Reported Cases of Selected STDs, 1966–2004

Cases reported

700,000
600,000
500,000
400,000
300,000
200,000
100,000
0

1966   1971   1976   1981   1986   1991   1996   2001

Year

— Genital herpes
— Genital warts
— Vaginal trichomoniasis
— Pelvic inflammatory disease

Battling the Epidemic: AIDS in America

Since 1981 almost 1.5 million Americans have been infected with HIV and over 500,000 have died due to AIDS.

The District of Columbia has the highest prevalence of AIDS (144.7 persons per 10,000), while the next highest rate is in New York, with a rate of 33.1. States with large urban areas such as Illinois, California, and Texas tend to have higher prevalence rates, as do states in the Southeast. Federal funding to the states for the prevention and treatment of AIDS is generally proportional to infection rates, although there is disproportionately high funding in the densely populated Northeast.

Those in poverty are at a higher risk for AIDS and may lack the insurance necessary to obtain costly medications; 41 percent of all men and 64 percent of all women with AIDS had annual incomes below $10,000 in 2002.

The rate of new HIV infections for children under age 13 has fallen the most dramatically, mainly due to stricter blood monitoring and the prevention of HIV transmission from mother to child. In 1992 there were 925 cases diagnosed, while in 2000 there were only 92. Despite a decline in infection rates among children, people under age 25 still account for over half of all new HIV infections.

Men have been more impacted by HIV/AIDS than women, but the female share has risen from seven percent in 1986 to 26 percent in 2001. Among teenagers age 13 to 19, women accounted for 57 percent of all new HIV infections.

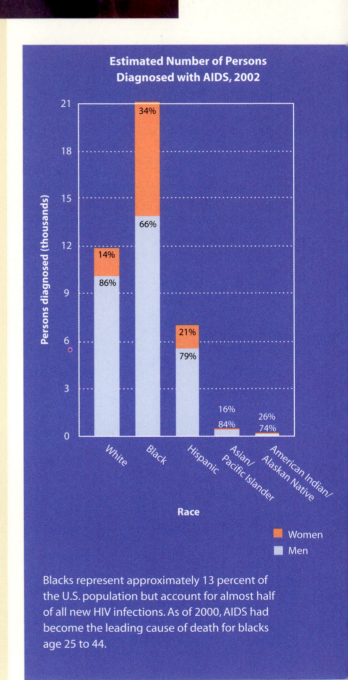

Estimated Number of Persons Diagnosed with AIDS, 2002

Persons diagnosed (thousands)

White — Men 86%, Women 14%
Black — Men 66%, Women 34%
Hispanic — Men 79%, Women 21%
Asian/Pacific Islander — Men 84%, Women 16%
American Indian/Alaskan Native — Men 74%, Women 26%

Race

■ Women
■ Men

Blacks represent approximately 13 percent of the U.S. population but account for almost half of all new HIV infections. As of 2000, AIDS had become the leading cause of death for blacks age 25 to 44.

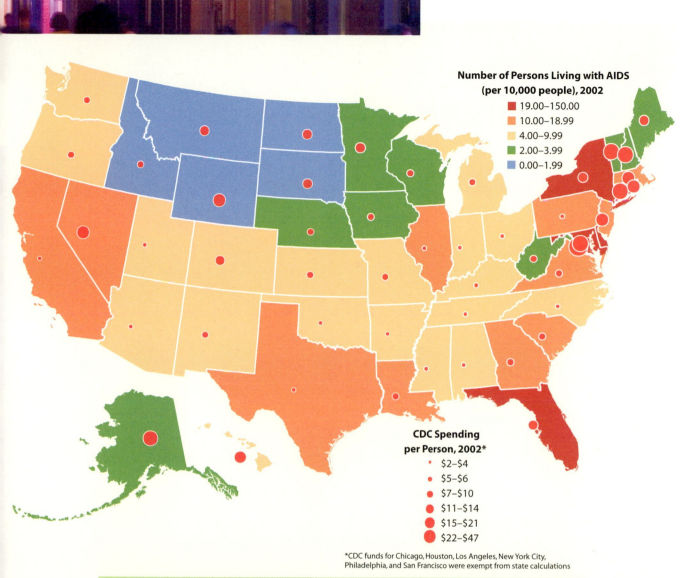

**Number of Persons Living with AIDS
(per 10,000 people), 2002**

- 19.00–150.00
- 10.00–18.99
- 4.00–9.99
- 2.00–3.99
- 0.00–1.99

**CDC Spending
per Person, 2002***

- $2–$4
- $5–$6
- $7–$10
- $11–$14
- $15–$21
- $22–$47

*CDC funds for Chicago, Houston, Los Angeles, New York City,
Philadelphia, and San Francisco were exempt from state calculations

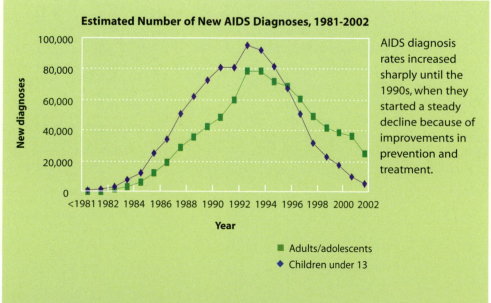

Estimated Number of New AIDS Diagnoses, 1981-2002

New diagnoses (y-axis): 0, 20,000, 40,000, 60,000, 80,000, 100,000

Year (x-axis): <1981 1982 1984 1986 1988 1990 1992 1994 1996 1998 2000 2002

AIDS diagnosis rates increased sharply until the 1990s, when they started a steady decline because of improvements in prevention and treatment.

- ■ Adults/adolescents
- ◆ Children under 13

Americans with Disabilities

According to the Census Bureau, 51.2 million Americans have some level of disability. Since the passage of the Americans with Disabilities Act (ADA) in 1990, persons with disabilities have been guaranteed equal employment opportunities as well as access to transportation, public accommodations, commercial facilities, government services, and telecommunications.

The term disability often conjures stereotypical images of wheelchairs or assistance animals, but some conditions may be less visible. Chronic heart disease and arthritis are the two most frequent causes of disability. In 2006, approximately 1.8 million individuals age 15 and over were blind, and 1 million were deaf. At least 2.0 million individuals had difficulty having their speech understood; 600,000 were without speech. Of those individuals age 15 and over, 2.6 million used a wheelchair and another 9.1 million used an aid such as a cane or walker. Additionally, 14.3 million people reported a mental disability.

Because of the ADA, there are more employment opportunities for persons having a disability. Despite this legal protection, persons having a disability are still less likely to be employed, earn less on average, and are more likely to live in poverty than individuals without a disability. In 2005 the poverty rate for those without a disability was 8 percent; for those with a non-severe disability, 11 percent; for those with a severe disability, 26 percent.

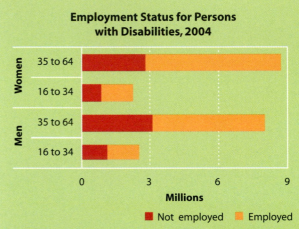

Employment Status for Persons with Disabilities, 2004

■ Not employed ■ Employed

Of individuals age 21 to 64, 82 percent with a non-severe disability and 43 percent with a severe disability reported working during the previous year, compared with 88 percent of those without a disability. The median earnings for those with a severe disability was $12,800 in 2005; those without a disability had median earnings of $25,000.

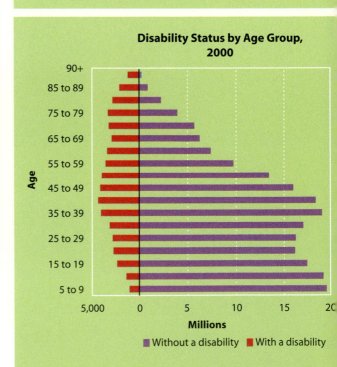

Disability Status by Age Group, 2000

■ Without a disability ■ With a disability

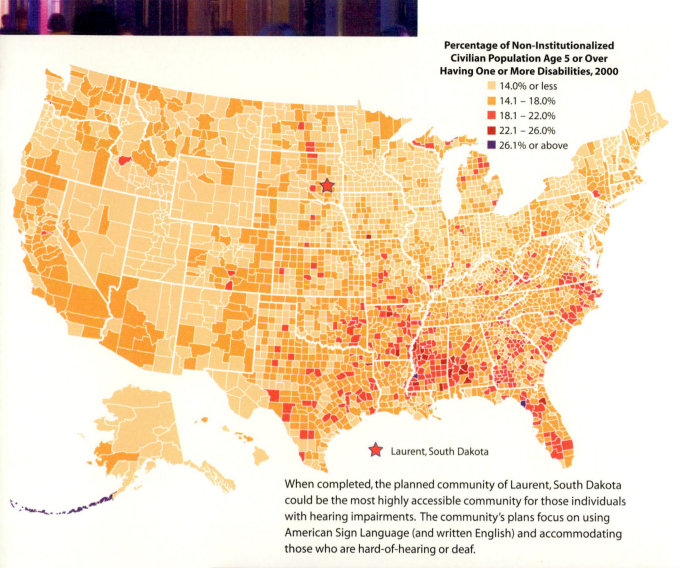

Percentage of Non-Institutionalized Civilian Population Age 5 or Over Having One or More Disabilities, 2000

- 14.0% or less
- 14.1 – 18.0%
- 18.1 – 22.0%
- 22.1 – 26.0%
- 26.1% or above

⭐ Laurent, South Dakota

When completed, the planned community of Laurent, South Dakota could be the most highly accessible community for those individuals with hearing impairments. The community's plans focus on using American Sign Language (and written English) and accommodating those who are hard-of-hearing or deaf.

The concept of "disability" is a broad social construction describing a functional limitation typically corresponding to a physical, sensory, or mental condition. Furthermore, an individual's impairment may not be a disability. Many persons with hearing impairments assert that they have no disability. Additionally, the same impairment might be a disability to an individual in one environment, but benign to another person elsewhere.

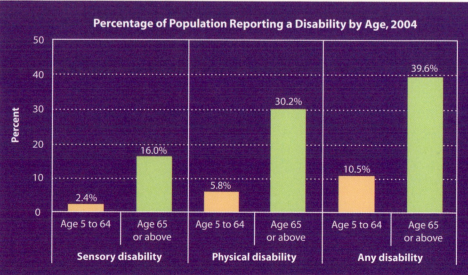

Percentage of Population Reporting a Disability by Age, 2004

Percent

	Sensory disability	Physical disability	Any disability
Age 5 to 64	2.4%	5.8%	10.5%
Age 65 or above	16.0%	30.2%	39.6%

Mental Health and Disability

Since the mid-20th century, perspectives regarding mental health have evolved dramatically. For example, as recently as the 1950s, mental health disorders in children were limited to "maladjustment" and "disturbance." In decades since, research has identified numerous developmental and other psychiatric disorders that affect children and adults. In fact, recent studies have estimated that 50 percent of the population has had a mental health condition at one time or another, with 26.2 percent of Americans 18 and over having had a mental health condition in any given year. Approximately six percent have a serious mental impairment. By 2003, antidepressants had become the most often prescribed class of medication for women and the second most common for the population overall.

Substance abuse and suicide are strongly related to mental illness. As much as 90 percent of the approximately 30,000 people who commit suicide each year have a diagnosable mental disorder. Recent studies, however, have shown reductions in suicidal thoughts among high school students, from 29 percent of students in 1991, down to 16.9 percent in 2003. Unfortunately, the percentage of students who attempted suicide increased during the same period.

The costs related to mental health and disability are exceptionally high. The direct costs of mental health services for 1996 were in excess of $99.3 billion. Indirect costs were estimated to be almost $80 million for the same year.

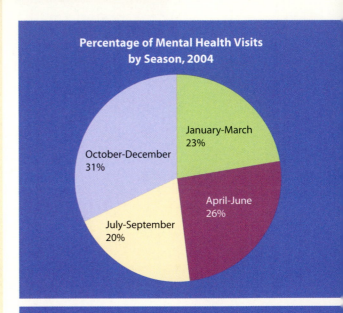

Percentage of Mental Health Visits by Season, 2004

- January-March 23%
- April-June 26%
- July-September 20%
- October-December 31%

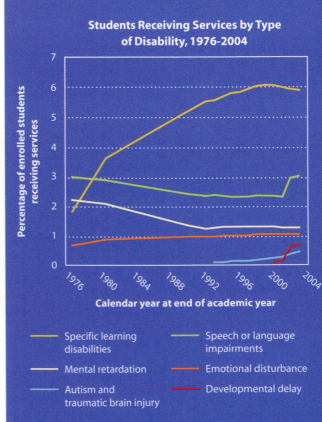

Students Receiving Services by Type of Disability, 1976-2004

Percentage of enrolled students receiving services

Calendar year at end of academic year

- Specific learning disabilities
- Mental retardation
- Autism and traumatic brain injury
- Speech or language impairments
- Emotional disturbance
- Developmental delay

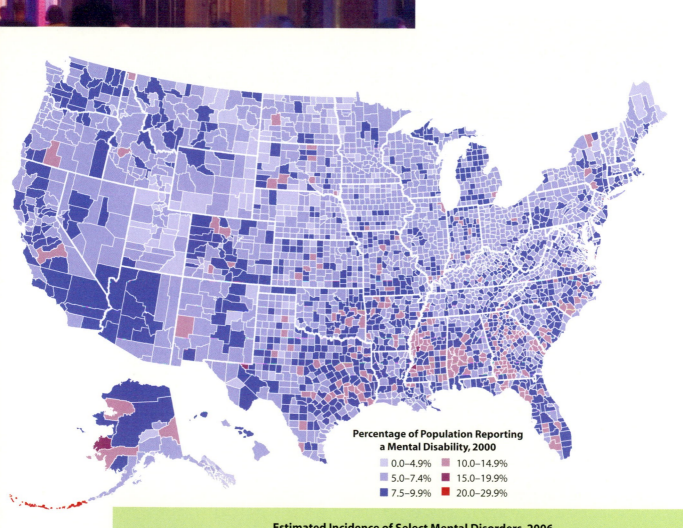

**Percentage of Population Reporting
a Mental Disability, 2000**

- 0.0–4.9%
- 5.0–7.4%
- 7.5–9.9%
- 10.0–14.9%
- 15.0–19.9%
- 20.0–29.9%

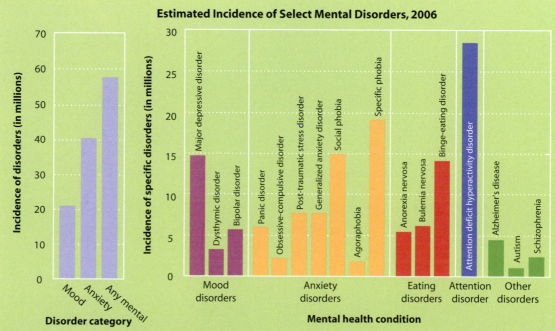

Estimated Incidence of Select Mental Disorders, 2006

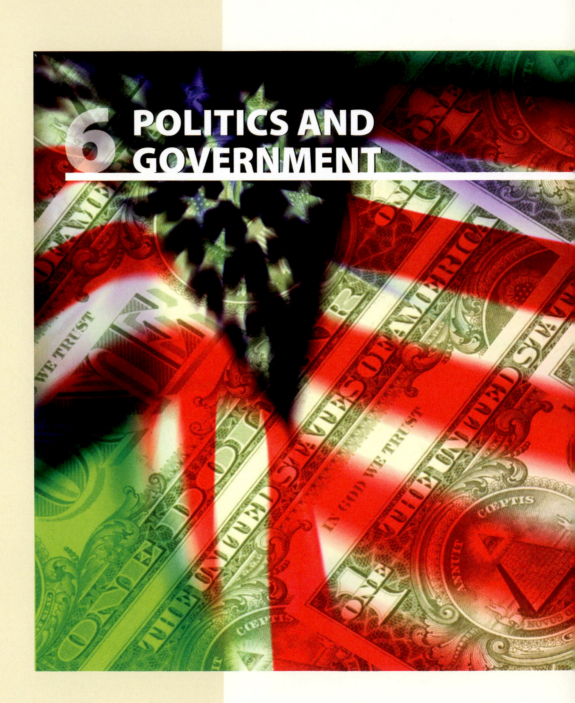

6 POLITICS AND GOVERNMENT

The Federal Purse: Government Spending

Whether you like to spend money or you are someone who keeps to a tight budget, there is one big wallet that you do not have direct control over. Government spending, from the federal level down to state and local governments, affects each and every person and community in the United States. Fortunately, U.S. citizens have the right to help oversee the financial decisions by voting for officials with desirable fiscal viewpoints.

In order to fund its many expenses, the government collects taxes. The federal government depends largely on income taxes—taxes on individual and business earnings. At the state level, funds are raised through both income taxes and taxes on consumption. Local governments, on the other hand, earn their revenue through property taxes. In addition to paying a mortgage on a home, for example, the homeowner is also often subject to property taxation. Additional sources of funding include payments for toll roads or entrance fees at parks.

One way of measuring federal spending is to consider the spending as a portion of the gross domestic product (GDP). In 1925, federal spending equaled only 3 percent of the GDP. During World War II, federal spending reached 42 percent of the GDP. In 2000, the fiscal budget was only 18 percent of the GDP, but later this century, spending could rival the heightened spending of World War II. The gross debt in fiscal year 2003 totaled $6.8 trillion.

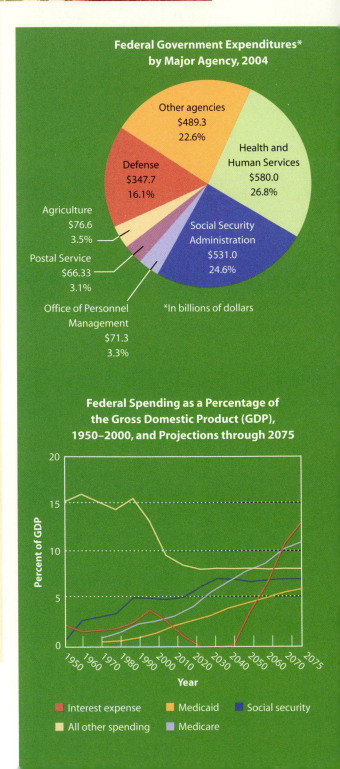

Federal Government Expenditures*
by Major Agency, 2004

Other agencies $489.3 22.6%

Health and Human Services $580.0 26.8%

Defense $347.7 16.1%

Agriculture $76.6 3.5%

Postal Service $66.33 3.1%

Office of Personnel Management $71.3 3.3%

Social Security Administration $531.0 24.6%

*In billions of dollars

Federal Spending as a Percentage of the Gross Domestic Product (GDP), 1950–2000, and Projections through 2075

Percent of GDP

20

15

10

5

0

1950 1960 1970 1980 1990 2000 2010 2020 2030 2040 2050 2060 2070 2075

Year

■ Interest expense   ■ Medicaid   ■ Social security
■ All other spending   ■ Medicare

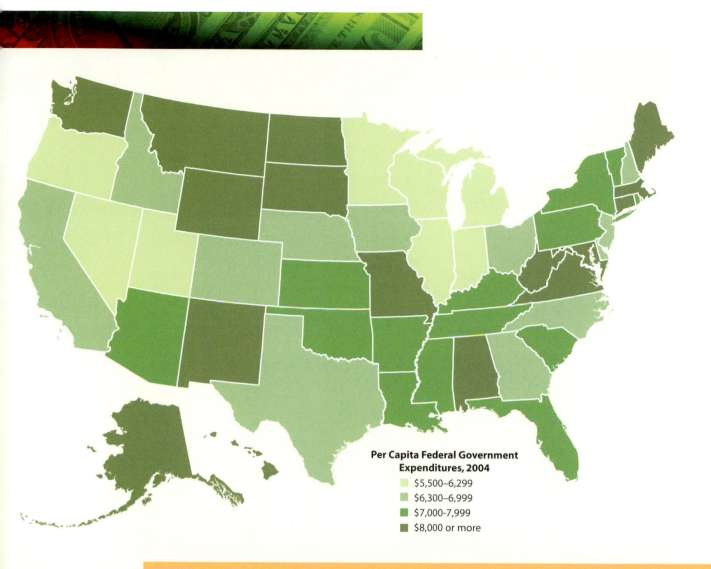

Per Capita Federal Government
Expenditures, 2004

- $5,500–6,299
- $6,300–6,999
- $7,000-7,999
- $8,000 or more

States retain
jurisdiction over the
educational sphere,
but the federal
government does
provide some
monetary support.
Per pupil amounts for
current spending on
public elementary and
secondary school
systems (including
federal, state, and local
resources) were
highest in the east.

Highest Annual Expenditures per Student	
New Jersey	$12,981
New York	$12,930
District of Coumbia	$12,801
Vermont	$11,128
Connecticut	$10,788

Lowest Annual Expenditures per Student	
Mississippi	$6,237
Oklahoma	$6,176
Arizona	$6,036
Idaho	$6,028
Utah	$5,008

Dollars Spent on Public Primary and Secondary Education by Government Level, 2004

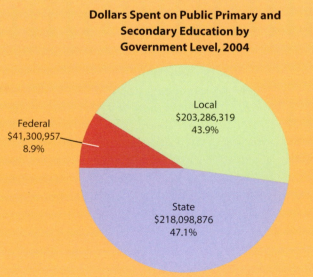

Federal
$41,300,957
8.9%

Local
$203,286,319
43.9%

State
$218,098,876
47.1%

Exercising Your Right: Voter Participation

The right to vote in the United States once belonged to only a small fraction of the population. Historically, discriminatory policies were used to deny people the right to vote.

After the Civil War, blacks were technically granted the right to vote by the 15th amendment, but intimidation policies and strategic limitation methods were often used to prevent blacks from effectively exercising their right to vote. A full century later during the civil rights movement, the Voting Rights Act of 1965 passed, making it illegal to use poll taxes and literacy tests to limit voter participation.

In the late 1800s and early 1900s, the women's suffrage movement worked hard to gain voting rights for women in the country. In 1919, a bill passed in Congress granting women the right to vote. By the 1920 election, every state had ratified the bill and women throughout the country were able to voice their opinion on general election ballots for the first time.

Despite the efforts of suffragists, many people still fail to vote. Voter participation is lower in off-year general election years not involving a presidential election, but voter turnout even in presidential election years hovers around only 60 to 70 percent. In 2004, only 64 percent of voting-aged citizens voted in the general election. In Hawaii, only 51 percent of voting-aged citizens exercised their right to vote. On the other hand, in Minnesota, almost 80 percent of potential voters voted in the election.

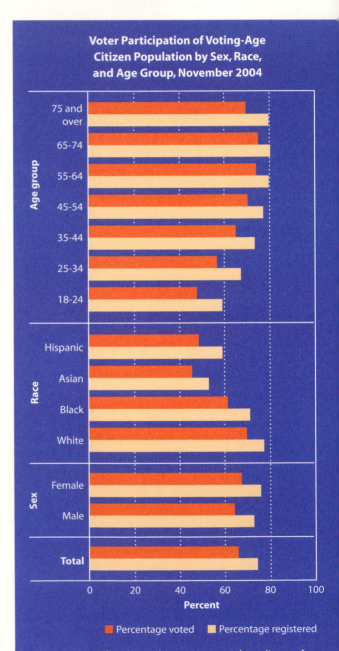

Voter Participation of Voting-Age Citizen Population by Sex, Race, and Age Group, November 2004

■ Percentage voted   ■ Percentage registered

The number of registered voters is a good predictor of voter turnout: 89 percent of registered voters did vote in the 2004 general election. Unfortunately, only 72 percent of potential voters were registered in 2004. About 55 million citizens were not registered.

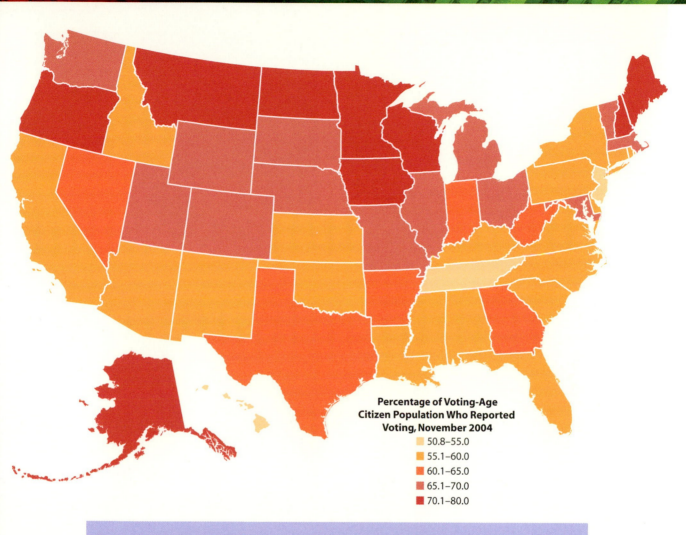

**Percentage of Voting-Age
Citizen Population Who Reported
Voting, November 2004**

- 50.8–55.0
- 55.1–60.0
- 60.1–65.0
- 65.1–70.0
- 70.1–80.0

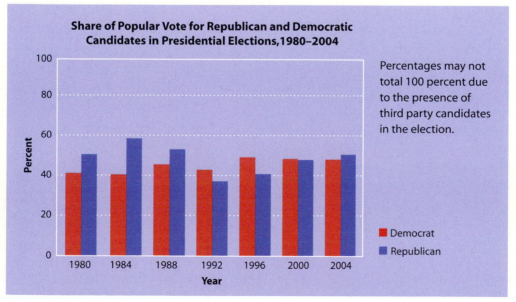

**Share of Popular Vote for Republican and Democratic
Candidates in Presidential Elections, 1980–2004**

Percentages may not total 100 percent due to the presence of third party candidates in the election.

Democrat
Republican

Exercising Your Right: Voter Participation

Of those who do cast their vote, 80 percent do so on election day. The other 20 percent vote prior to election day. Though options differ from state to state, all states offer alternative voting options, such as mail-in absentee ballots or in-person early voting. Some states have managed to minimize the rush to the polls. In Oregon, for example, 92.8 percent of the votes were cast prior to election day.

Even with early voting options, being out of town, forgetting to vote, and being too busy remain some of the most commonly reported reasons for not voting. Transportation problems, bad weather conditions, and inconvenient polling locations also continue to be reasons cited for not voting. Forty-six percent of people 65 and older reported illness or disability as a reason for not voting. In the age group 18 to 24 years old, where voting rates are the lowest of all age groups, almost one-third of non-voters reported that they were not interested, did not like the candidates or campaign issues, or refused to vote.

The idea that a single vote does not make a difference has been challenged in recent years. The race between George Bush and Al Gore was decided by just five electoral votes. In fact, while Bush won the election, Al Gore actually won the popular vote. Though not quite as controversial as the 2000 election, the 2004 Bush–Kerry presidential race was quite close as well. Five states—Wisconsin, Iowa, New Mexico, New Hampshire, and New York—were decided by a margin of less than two percent. Bush had a stronghold by more than 20 percent of the vote throughout the Great Plains states. Bush won with 286 electoral votes to Kerry's 251. One member of the Electoral College chose to vote for John Edwards, who was running as Kerry's vice president.

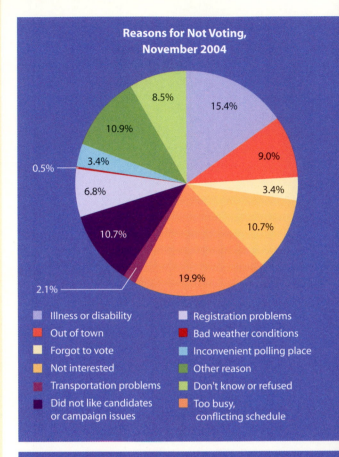

Reasons for Not Voting, November 2004

15.4%
9.0%
3.4%
10.7%
19.9%
2.1%
10.7%
6.8%
3.4%
0.5%
10.9%
8.5%

- Illness or disability
- Registration problems
- Out of town
- Bad weather conditions
- Forgot to vote
- Inconvenient polling place
- Not interested
- Other reason
- Transportation problems
- Don't know or refused
- Did not like candidates or campaign issues
- Too busy, conflicting schedule

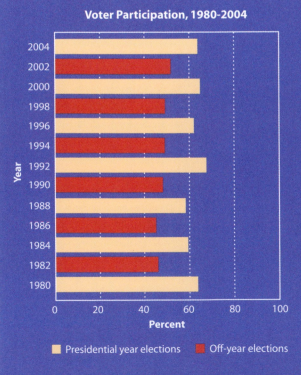

Voter Participation, 1980-2004

Year (axis): 2004, 2002, 2000, 1998, 1996, 1994, 1992, 1990, 1988, 1986, 1984, 1982, 1980

Percent (axis): 0, 20, 40, 60, 80, 100

- Presidential year elections
- Off-year elections

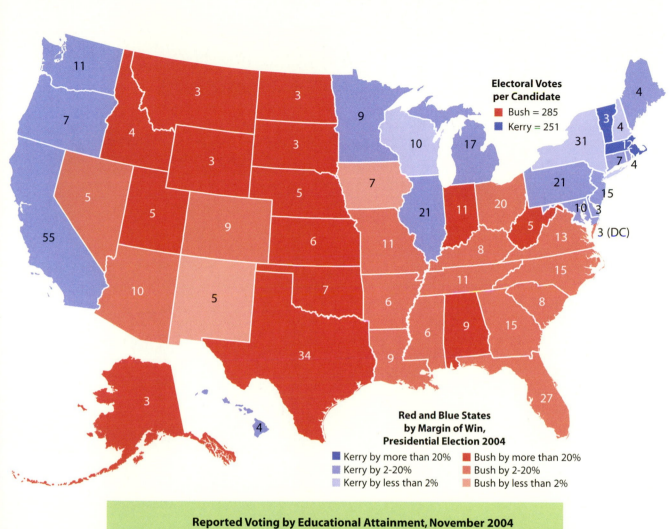

Electoral Votes
per Candidate
Bush = 285
Kerry = 251

Red and Blue States
by Margin of Win,
Presidential Election 2004

Kerry by more than 20%   Bush by more than 20%
Kerry by 2-20%   Bush by 2-20%
Kerry by less than 2%   Bush by less than 2%

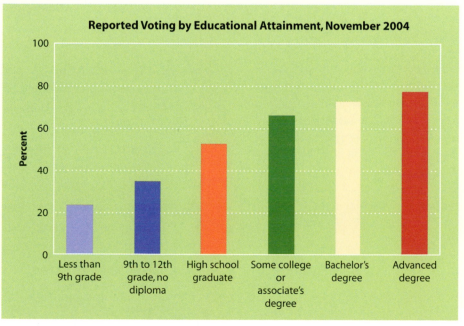

Reported Voting by Educational Attainment, November 2004

Diversity in Government

In a representative form of government such as that in the United States, the people rely on their representatives to act on their behalf. Despite being an extraordinarily diverse nation, politicians have often been white men, even in areas with large minority populations.

Women do not have proportional representation in the legislature. In 1917, Jeanette Rankin became the first woman to serve in Congress, representing Montana. Five years later, in 1922, the first female senator, Rebecca Felton, was sworn in. Felton's term, however, was largely ceremonial; she was appointed by the governor in October 1922, and was sworn in that November, serving as a senator for a single day. The first woman elected to the Senate was Hattie Wyatt Caraway in 1932. The governor of Arkansas appointed her to the position earlier to fill the vacancy resulting from her husband's death. Including Felton and Caraway, a total of 35 women have served in the Senate, 16 of whom were serving in early 2007.

In 1870, during Reconstruction, the first black senator, Hiram Revels, was elected to represent Mississippi. Later that year, Joseph Rainey became the first black member of the House of Representatives when he was sworn in to represent South Carolina. In 1875, Blanche Bruce was elected by the Mississippi legislature to represent them in the Senate, becoming the first and only former slave to ever serve as a senator. Bruce made further history by becoming the first black senator to preside over the Senate in 1879.

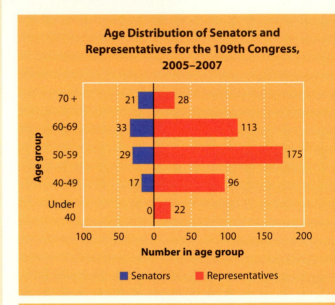

Age Distribution of Senators and Representatives for the 109th Congress, 2005–2007

Age group	Senators	Representatives
70 +	21	28
60-69	33	113
50-59	29	175
40-49	17	96
Under 40	0	22

Number in age group

■ Senators   ■ Representatives

Diversity in the Senate	
Black	Hiram R. Revels (R-Mississippi). 1870-71
	Blanche K. Bruce (R-Mississippi) 1875-81
	Edward W. Brooke (R-Massachusetts), 1967-79
	Carol Moseley-Braun (D-IIllinois), 1993-99
	Barack Obama (D-Illinois), 2005-
Asian	Hiram L. Fong (R-Hawaii), 1959-77
	Daniel K. Inouye (D-Hawaii), 1963-
	Samuel I. Hayakawa (R-California), 1977-1983
	Spark M. Matsunaga (D-Hawaii), 1977-90
	Daniel K. Akaka (D-Hawaii), 1990-
Hispanic	Octavano Larrazolo (R-New Mexico), 1928-29
	Dennis Chavez (D-New Mexico), 1935-62
	Joseph M. Montoya (D-New Mexico), 1964-77
	Ken L. Salazar (R-Colorado), 2005-
	Melquiades R. Martinez (R-Florida), 2005-
	Robert Menendez (D-New Jersey), 2006-
American Indian	Charles Curtis (R-Kansas), 1907-13; 1915-29
	Robert Owen (D-Oklahoma), 1907-1925
	Ben Nighthorse Campbell (R-Colorado), 1993-2005

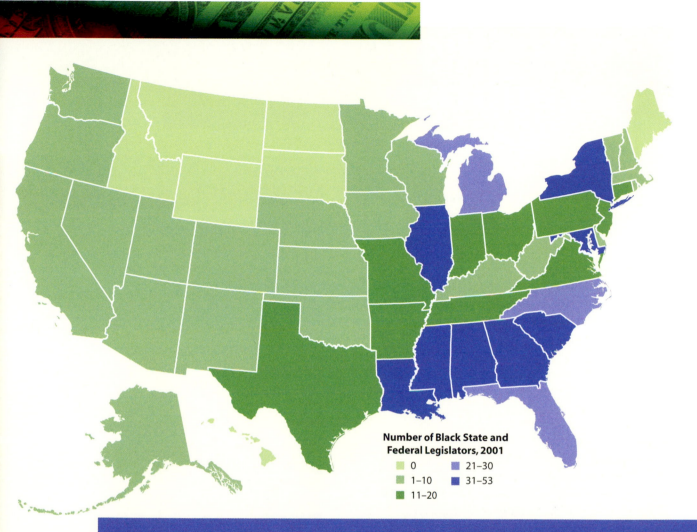

Number of Black State and Federal Legislators, 2001

- 0
- 1–10
- 11–20
- 21–30
- 31–53

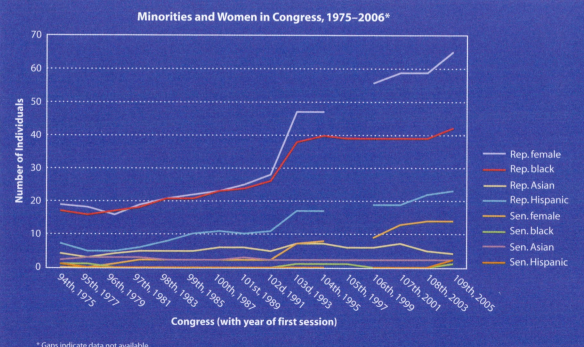

Minorities and Women in Congress, 1975–2006*

- Rep. female
- Rep. black
- Rep. Asian
- Rep. Hispanic
- Sen. female
- Sen. black
- Sen. Asian
- Sen. Hispanic

Number of Individuals

Congress (with year of first session)

* Gaps indicate data not available.

Defending the Nation: The Military

The nation depends on its military force for security and protection. The men and women of the military ensure the peace and safety for all U.S. citizens. In the past, the nation relied heavily on conscription, or the draft, but today, military participation depends on volunteers.

Since the tragedies of September 11, 2001, the troops have been engaged in Afghanistan and Iraq. Operation Enduring Freedom and Operation Iraqi Freedom have drawn upon the bravery of the men and women of service. Mounting casualties have placed pressure on the government to seek a peaceful solution to the conflict.

The U.S. military says that it has a steady level of recruiting interest and can maintain the forces necessary for a strong military posture. In 2003, there were over 1.1 million people enlisted in the Reserves and National Guard. More than 157,000 people in these trained forces have been called upon for duty in Iraq and Afghanistan.

While some service members risk their lives on the front line, others work back home in relief operations, including the 39,000 active members in the Coast Guard as of 2005. When Hurricane Katrina devastated New Orleans, men and women of the military helped to keep the peace and restore order in the aftermath.

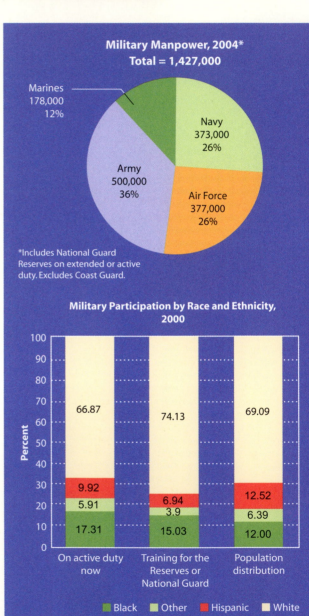

Military Manpower, 2004*
Total = 1,427,000

Marines 178,000 12%
Navy 373,000 26%
Army 500,000 36%
Air Force 377,000 26%

*Includes National Guard Reserves on extended or active duty. Excludes Coast Guard.

Military Participation by Race and Ethnicity, 2000

	On active duty now	Training for the Reserves or National Guard	Population distribution
White	66.87	74.13	69.09
Hispanic	9.92	6.94	12.52
Other	5.91	3.9	6.39
Black	17.31	15.03	12.00

■ Black   ■ Other   ■ Hispanic   ■ White

A disproportionately high number of blacks are on active duty or training for the Reserves or National Guard. While blacks only make up 12 percent of the population, they represent over 17 percent of active duty personnel and over 15 percent of those in military training. Hispanics, on the other hand, are underrepresented.

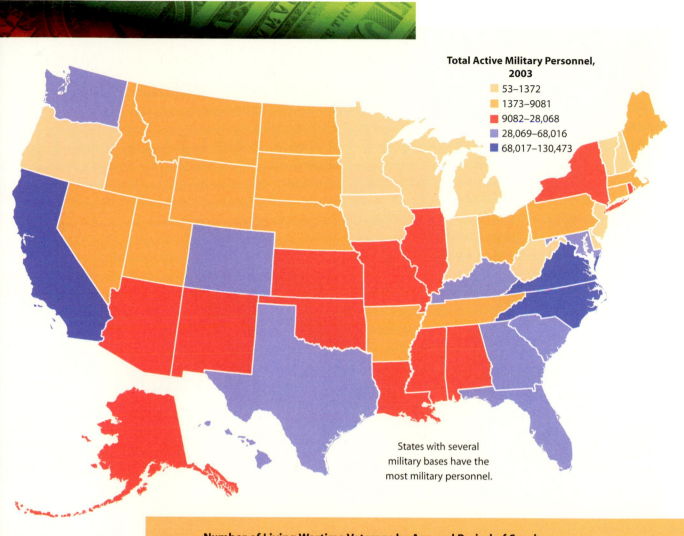

Total Active Military Personnel, 2003

- 53–1372
- 1373–9081
- 9082–28,068
- 28,069–68,016
- 68,017–130,473

States with several military bases have the most military personnel.

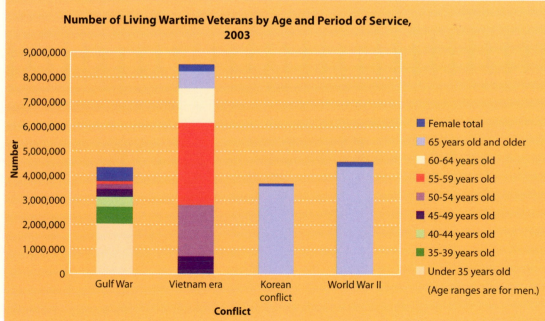

Number of Living Wartime Veterans by Age and Period of Service, 2003

Number

- Female total
- 65 years old and older
- 60-64 years old
- 55-59 years old
- 50-54 years old
- 45-49 years old
- 40-44 years old
- 35-39 years old
- Under 35 years old

(Age ranges are for men.)

Conflict: Gulf War, Vietnam era, Korean conflict, World War II

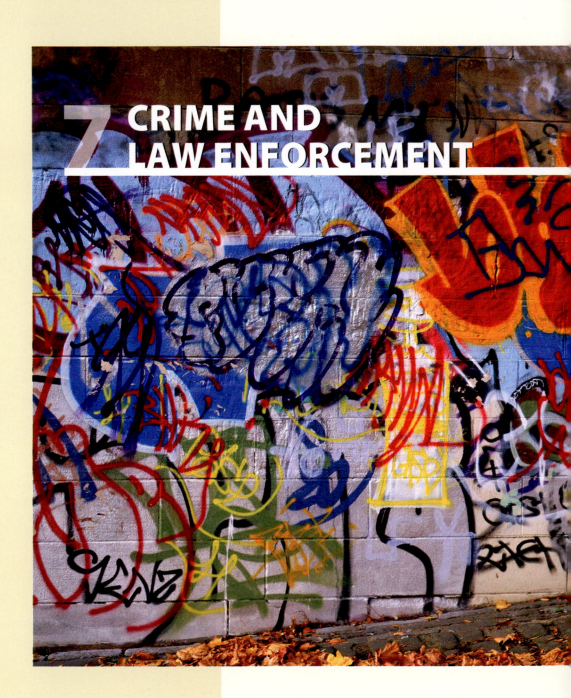

7 CRIME AND LAW ENFORCEMENT

Criminal Activity

I n 2003, over 1.1 million law enforcement officials worked to protect Americans from criminal activity. The total cost for police functions increased from only $165 per capita in 1982 to over $286 per capita in 2003. The larger financial investment may have contributed to a decrease in the crime rate. The 2004 crime rate was at the lowest level ever recorded. According to the FBI, nationwide there were an estimated 1,367,009 violent crimes.

When violent crimes—including rape, robbery, aggravated and simple assault, and homicide—started to escalate in the early 1990s, Congress responded by passing the Violent Crime Control and Law Enforcement Act of 1994. While there may be other reasons for a decline in violence, crime rates did begin to drop off in the mid to late 1990s and continued to fall through 2004. By 1996, crime rates had dropped to mid-1980s levels. In only 10 years from 1994 to 2004, violent crime rates dropped from 51.2 victimizations per 1,000 people age 12 and over to only 21.1. The reduced rate of violent crimes represents improvements in safety, especially in major cities.

Law enforcement officials were able to identify the circumstances surrounding about 65 percent of murder cases in 2004, but the circumstances surrounding murder remained unknown for the rest of the cases. Where murder circumstances were known, arguments were the most common cause and accounted for about 44 percent of murders.

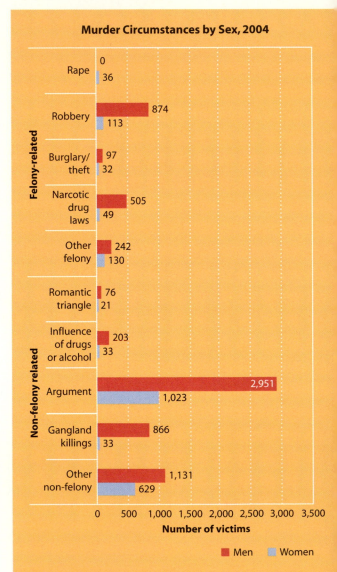

Murders often occur in conjunction with or as a result of other illegal activity. The chart shows the number of murder victims and the contributing event leading to their deaths.

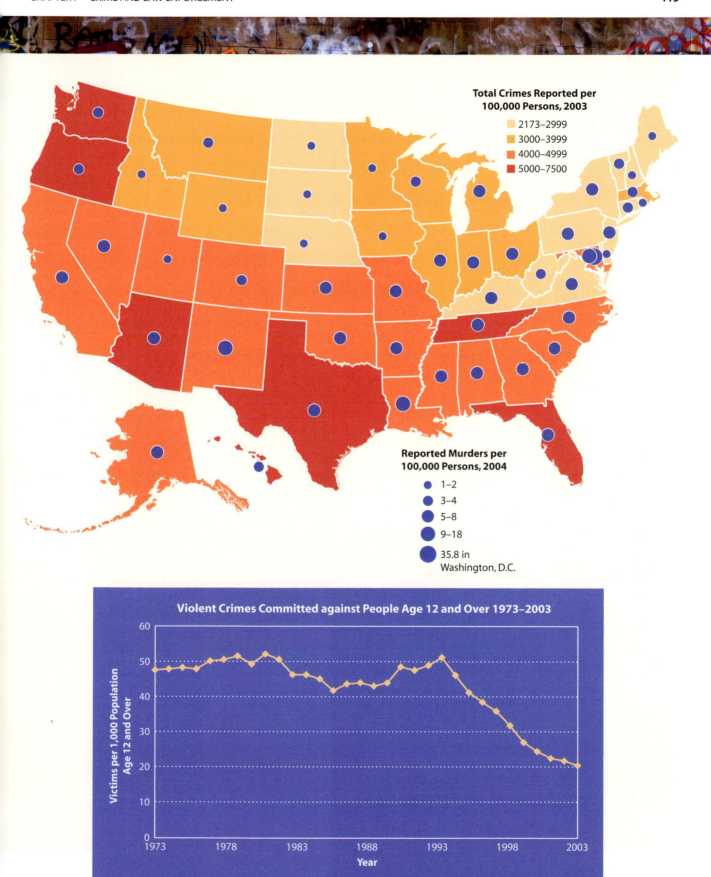

**Total Crimes Reported per
100,000 Persons, 2003**

2173–2999
3000–3999
4000–4999
5000–7500

**Reported Murders per
100,000 Persons, 2004**

1–2
3–4
5–8
9–18
35.8 in
Washington, D.C.

Violent Crimes Committed against People Age 12 and Over 1973–2003

Victims per 1,000 Population Age 12 and Over

Year

Criminal Activity

The FBI defines a hate crime as "a criminal offense committed against a person, property, or society that is motivated, in whole or in part, by the offender's bias against a race, religion, disability, sexual orientation, or ethnicity/national origin." In 2004, 7,649 hate crimes were reported, the majority of which were cases of vandalism (2,812), intimidation (2,267), or misdemeanor assault (1,448).

Because of their subjective classification, rates of hate crimes reported may differ from one area to the next. Although hate crimes appear least prevalent in the South, the low rates may have more to do with classification standards than actual differences in criminal activity.

Use of electronic media and an increasingly depersonalized society has made access to private personal information easier. Identity theft has become a concern for many Americans. In fact, during just a six-month period in 2004, 3.6 million households (three percent of all households) learned that they had become victims of some form of identity fraud.

While fraud against the individual can devastate lives, corporate fraud poses a serious and wide-reaching economic risk. High profile cases like the Enron and WorldCom scandals in 2001 brought attention to white-collar crime and its offenders.

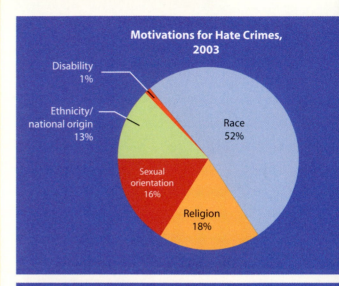

Motivations for Hate Crimes, 2003

- Disability 1%
- Ethnicity/national origin 13%
- Race 52%
- Sexual orientation 16%
- Religion 18%

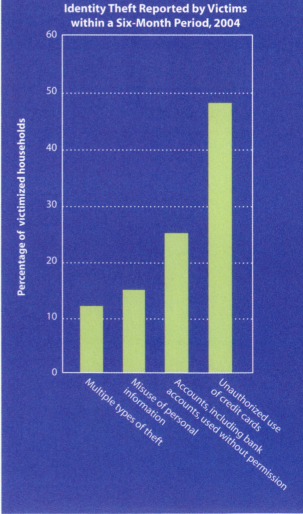

Identity Theft Reported by Victims within a Six-Month Period, 2004

Percentage of victimized households

- Multiple types of theft
- Misuse of personal information
- Accounts, including bank accounts, used without permission
- Unauthorized use of credit cards

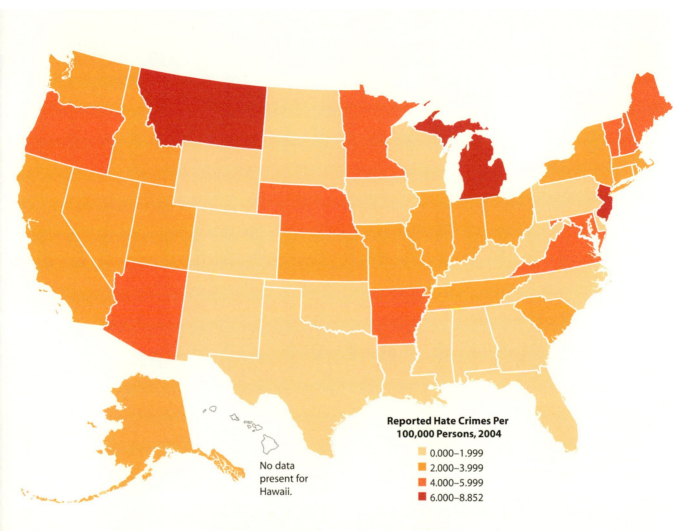

Reported Hate Crimes Per
100,000 Persons, 2004

- 0.000–1.999
- 2.000–3.999
- 4.000–5.999
- 6.000–8.852

No data
present for
Hawaii.

The estimated total value of motor vehicles stolen in 2004 was $7.6 billion.

Doing Time: Prisoners and Incarceration

The United States has a greater percentage of its citizens in correctional facilities than any other developed nation in the world. In 2004, over 2.1 million persons were in corrective custody. Of these inmates, 66 percent were held in federal and state prisons; most of the remaining inmates were held in local jails and private prisons.

The racial composition of the prison population is not proportional to the composition of the United States population as a whole. Of inmates with sentences of one year or more in 2004, black men were represented at almost seven times the rate of whites and almost three times that of Hispanics. A similar imbalance exists in gender. In both jails and prisons, more than 90 percent of prisoners are men.

Though the incarceration rate has risen steadily in the last decade, from 6.01 per 1,000 persons in 1995 to 7.24 per 1,000 persons in 2004, capacity rates have decreased. In 2004, state prisons were operating at an average of 99 percent of their capacity, down from 114 percent in 1995.

In addition to other common problems, HIV infection rates are higher in prisons than in the general population. In 1995, one in every three prisoner deaths was a result of HIV/AIDS. By 2003, only one in every 16 prisoner deaths was a result of HIV/AIDS. Although infection rates declined between 2001 and 2003, HIV infection remained a problem. For example, 7.6 percent of New York state's prison population was HIV positive at the end of 2003.

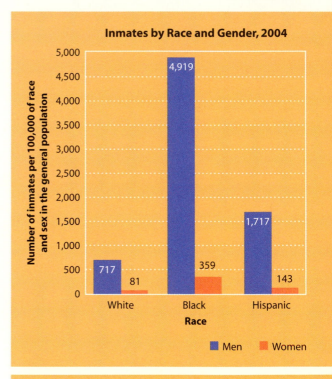

Inmates by Race and Gender, 2004

HIV in Prisoners, 1998–2003

Year end	Number of HIV positive inmates	Percentage of inmate population testing HIV positive
1998	25,680	2.2%
1999	25,807	2.1%
2000	25,333	2.0%
2001	24,147	1.9%
2002	23,864	1.9%
2003	23,659	1.9%

More than a fifth (5,000) of all inmates known to be HIV positive in 2003 were in New York. Florida, however, had the greatest increase, with 264 more HIV-positive inmates than 2002. During that same year, 268 prisoners held in state prisons and 14 prisoners in federal prisons died from AIDS-related causes. The rate of confirmed AIDS cases in the prison population (0.51 percent) is more than three times that of the general population (0.15 percent).

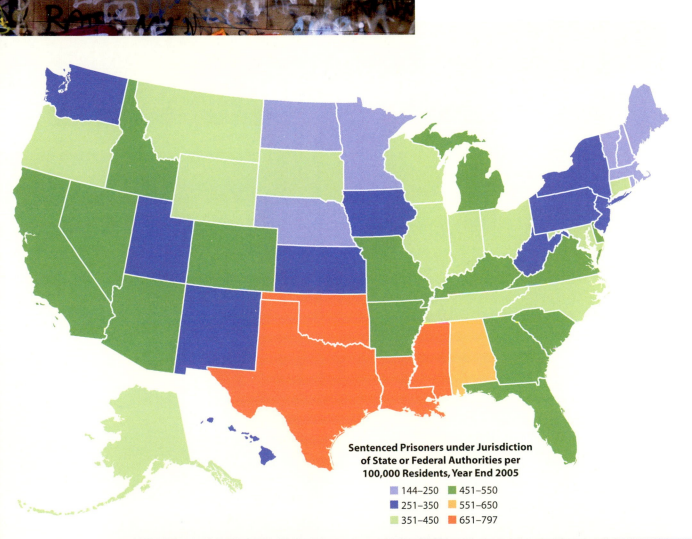

Sentenced Prisoners under Jurisdiction
of State or Federal Authorities per
100,000 Residents, Year End 2005

- 144–250
- 251–350
- 351–450
- 451–550
- 551–650
- 651–797

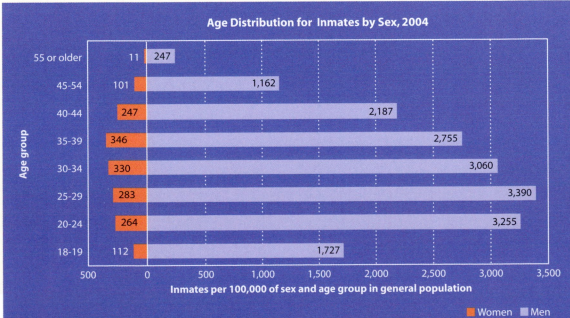

Age Distribution for Inmates by Sex, 2004

Age group	Women	Men
55 or older	11	247
45-54	101	1,162
40-44	247	2,187
35-39	346	2,755
30-34	330	3,060
25-29	283	3,390
20-24	264	3,255
18-19	112	1,727

Inmates per 100,000 of sex and age group in general population

■ Women ■ Men

The High Price of Vice:
Alcohol, Drug Abuse, and Gambling

In 2004, 14.5 percent of people 12 and older had used an illicit drug within the past year. Additionally, there were over 17 million alcoholics or alcohol abusers in the United States. The CDC reports that illicit drug use contributed to 19,698 deaths in 2000.

Drug and alcohol abuse contribute to a range of serious social problems. Of those arrested for violent crimes, including homicide, theft, and assault, over 50 percent are reported to be under the influence of drugs.

For both alcohol and drug use, many people needing treatment do not receive it because they are not ready to stop using. Of the 6 million people who were dependent on or abused illicit drugs in 2002, and did not receive treatment, 94 percent did not perceive a need for treatment. Similarly, a very large percentage (95.5) of the 17 million individuals with alcohol dependence or abuse problems not receiving treatment perceived no need for treatment. For those who are ready to stop using, cost remains the most common reason for not receiving treatment.

Nearly 7.5 millions Americans in 1997 were problem or pathological gamblers. Gambling addictions have the potential to devastate families and can lead to financial ruin and job loss. The National Gambling Impact Study Commission found that high levels of alcohol and drug use often appear in those with addictive gambling behaviors; indeed, the incidence of substance abuse among pathological gamblers ranges from 25 to 63 percent.

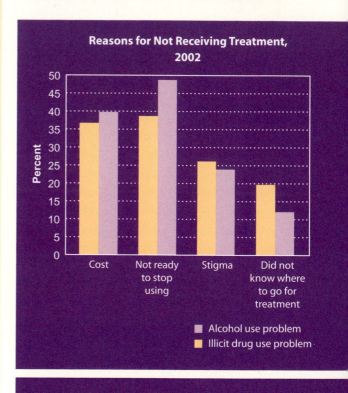

Reasons for Not Receiving Treatment, 2002

■ Alcohol use problem
■ Illicit drug use problem

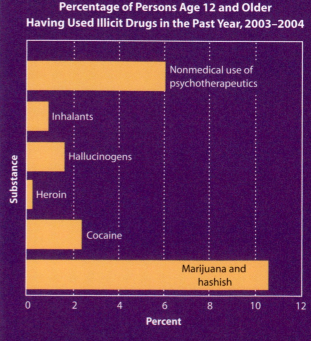

Percentage of Persons Age 12 and Older Having Used Illicit Drugs in the Past Year, 2003–2004

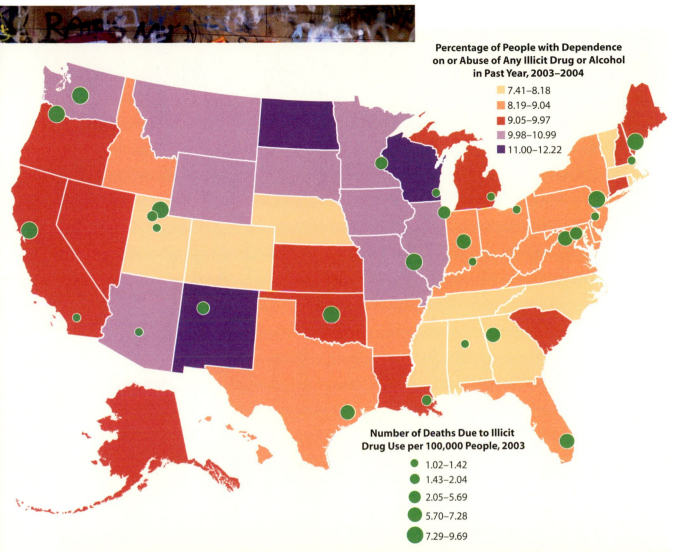

Percentage of People with Dependence on or Abuse of Any Illicit Drug or Alcohol in Past Year, 2003–2004

- 7.41–8.18
- 8.19–9.04
- 9.05–9.97
- 9.98–10.99
- 11.00–12.22

Number of Deaths Due to Illicit Drug Use per 100,000 People, 2003

- 1.02–1.42
- 1.43–2.04
- 2.05–5.69
- 5.70–7.28
- 7.29–9.69

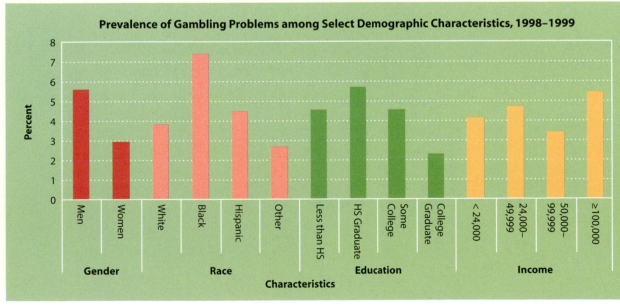

Prevalence of Gambling Problems among Select Demographic Characteristics, 1998–1999

Percent (y-axis: 0 to 8)

Characteristics:

Gender: Men, Women
Race: White, Black, Hispanic, Other
Education: Less than HS, HS Graduate, Some College, College Graduate
Income: < 24,000, 24,000–49,999, 50,000–99,999, ≥ 100,000

Risky Business: Teenage Substance Abuse

Drug, alcohol, and tobacco use among American teenagers remains a serious concern. Despite declining rates of use in recent years, by the time of graduation from high school in 2004, three of every four graduates had drunk alcohol, and over 50 percent had used drugs.

Among eighth-graders, 44 percent had consumed alcohol in their lifetime, while 30.2 percent had used an illegal drug. The percentage of high school sophomores using drugs had declined from previous years across all categories except two: the use of heroin without a needle, and cocaine. More high school seniors, however, reported using cocaine, crack, sedatives, tranquilizers, and alcohol, with three of five having been drunk in their lifetime.

Aside from alcohol and tobacco use, the drugs of choice for eighth-graders were inhalants, while high school students abused marijuana more than any other controlled substance. Alcohol abuse was the greatest problem among these age groups.

Teens are more likely to drink alcohol or use drugs if living in a household without both parents. For example, while 71.7 percent of teens living in households with both parents reported never having used drugs in 2003, only 64.6 percent of teens living in households with one parent, and 54.9 percent of teens living in households with neither parent, reported never having using drugs.

While only 54.7 percent of white teens and 54.6 percent of Hispanic teens reported never having drunk alcohol, alcohol avoidance was less troublesome for Asian teens (73.8 percent) and black teens (64.3 percent).

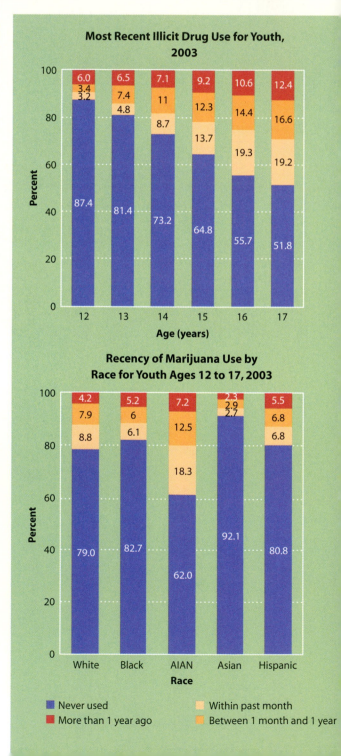

Most Recent Illicit Drug Use for Youth, 2003

Recency of Marijuana Use by Race for Youth Ages 12 to 17, 2003

■ Never used   □ Within past month
■ More than 1 year ago   ■ Between 1 month and 1 year

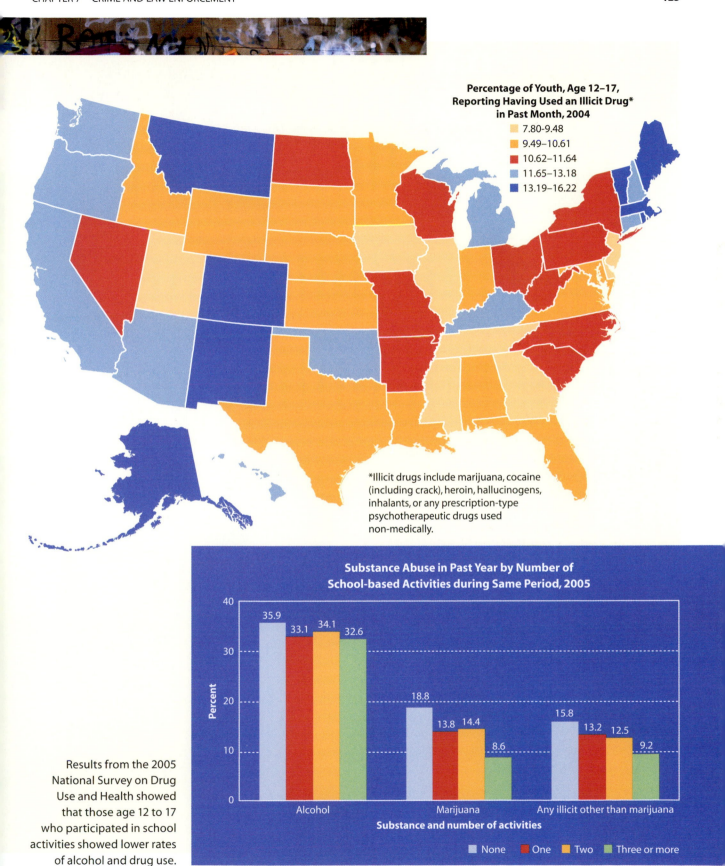

Percentage of Youth, Age 12–17, Reporting Having Used an Illicit Drug* in Past Month, 2004

- 7.80–9.48
- 9.49–10.61
- 10.62–11.64
- 11.65–13.18
- 13.19–16.22

*Illicit drugs include marijuana, cocaine (including crack), heroin, hallucinogens, inhalants, or any prescription-type psychotherapeutic drugs used non-medically.

Substance Abuse in Past Year by Number of School-based Activities during Same Period, 2005

Percent

Alcohol	Marijuana	Any illicit other than marijuana
35.9	18.8	15.8
33.1	13.8	13.2
34.1	14.4	12.5
32.6	8.6	9.2

Substance and number of activities

☐ None   ■ One   ■ Two   ■ Three or more

Results from the 2005 National Survey on Drug Use and Health showed that those age 12 to 17 who participated in school activities showed lower rates of alcohol and drug use.

Children and Crime: Juvenile Delinquency

In the 1990s, alarmingly high levels of juvenile crime prompted serious efforts to curb violent youth behavior. Between 1995 and 2002, juvenile crime declined, after peaking in 1994. Data show that rates are at one of the lowest levels in 20 years. While some believe that an epidemic has subsided, others fear that if law enforcement officials get too relaxed, youth crime will increase once again.

The death penalty is a controversial method of punishment for all ages and especially for youthful offenders. In 2003, 15 states specified minimum age limitations for imposing the death penalty. Additionally, eight states technically reserved the right to use capital punishment for youth offenders by imposing no minimum age limit for capital punishment. As of 2004, Kansas and Vermont had the lowest specified limitation for allowing death sentences. Offenders of only 10 years of age could receive the death penalty in these two states. In 2003, 67 of the 3,117 people on death row were age 17 or younger at the time of their arrest.

In 2004, 15.8 percent of all persons arrested were under the age of 18. Total juvenile arrests decreased 1.7 percent from the previous year. Property crimes remained the most common form of delinquency among people under age 18. Of all juvenile arrests, 20.7 percent were associated with property crime. Juveniles accounted for 50.2 percent of all arson arrests in 2004 and 37.9 percent of all vandalism arrests. Eight percent of all homicide arrests were juveniles. The number of male juveniles convicted of homicide was ten times higher than the number of female juveniles convicted.

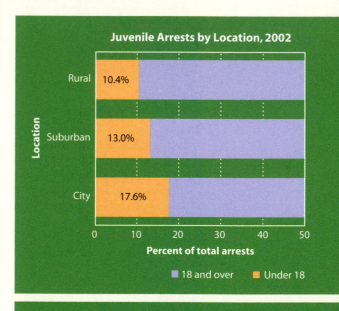

Juvenile Arrests by Location, 2002

Rural: 10.4%
Suburban: 13.0%
City: 17.6%

Percent of total arrests

■ 18 and over   ■ Under 18

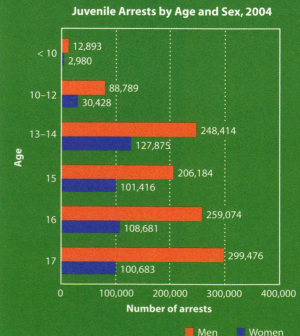

Juvenile Arrests by Age and Sex, 2004

Age	Men	Women
< 10	12,893	2,980
10–12	88,789	30,428
13–14	248,414	127,875
15	206,184	101,416
16	259,074	108,681
17	299,476	100,683

Number of arrests

■ Men   ■ Women

Females accounted for 29.9 percent of juvenile arrests, remaining the minority in all offenses except prostitution and running away from home.

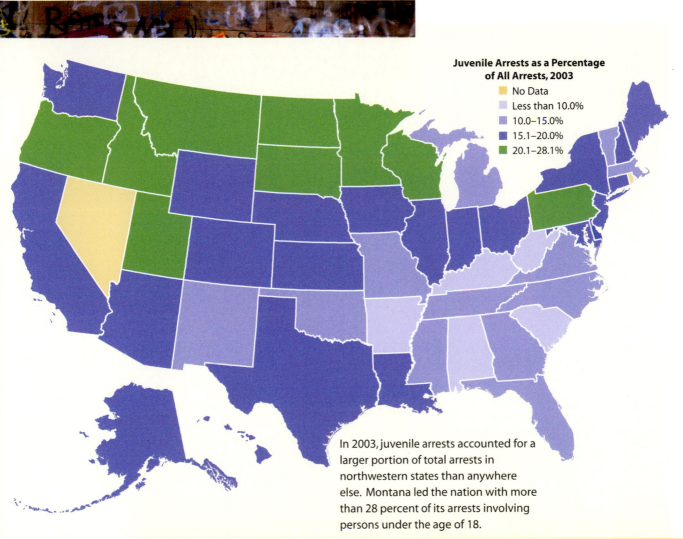

Juvenile Arrests as a Percentage of All Arrests, 2003

- No Data
- Less than 10.0%
- 10.0–15.0%
- 15.1–20.0%
- 20.1–28.1%

In 2003, juvenile arrests accounted for a larger portion of total arrests in northwestern states than anywhere else. Montana led the nation with more than 28 percent of its arrests involving persons under the age of 18.

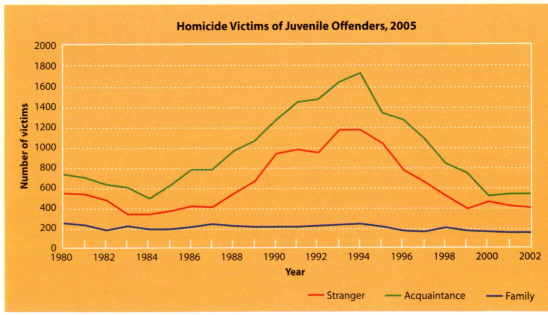

Homicide Victims of Juvenile Offenders, 2005

— Stranger   — Acquaintance   — Family

The Youngest Crime Victims

n 2004, at least 1,806,070 cases of child maltreatment were reported and investigated. Of all cases, 62.4 percent involved neglect, 17.5 percent involved physical abuse, 9.7 percent involved sexual abuse, and 7.0 percent involved psychological abuse. Rates of child maltreatment decreased with age: 16 in 1,000 children age 0 to 3 were victims of maltreatment, whereas for children age 16 to 17, the rate dropped to 6 in 1,000.

Approximately 1,500 children died as a result of maltreatment in 2004. More than 80 percent of abuse fatalities were young children. Forty-five percent were less than a year old. More than one third of these deaths were a result of child neglect.

Of all murder victims in 2004, 9.6 percent were under age 18. Among child murder victims, 68 percent were boys and 32 percent were girls. Examined by race, 50.5 percent of murder victims under 18 were white and 45.3 percent were black.

Weapon type involved in child deaths differed by the age of the victim. For children under the age of five, personal weapons, such as hands, fists, and feet, were most commonly used. For all children age five and over, firearms were used most often.

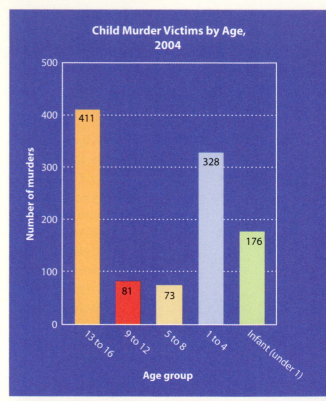

Child Murder Victims by Age, 2004

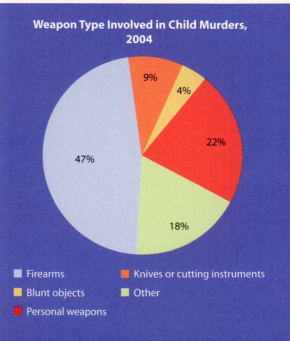

Weapon Type Involved in Child Murders, 2004

- Firearms
- Blunt objects
- Personal weapons
- Knives or cutting instruments
- Other

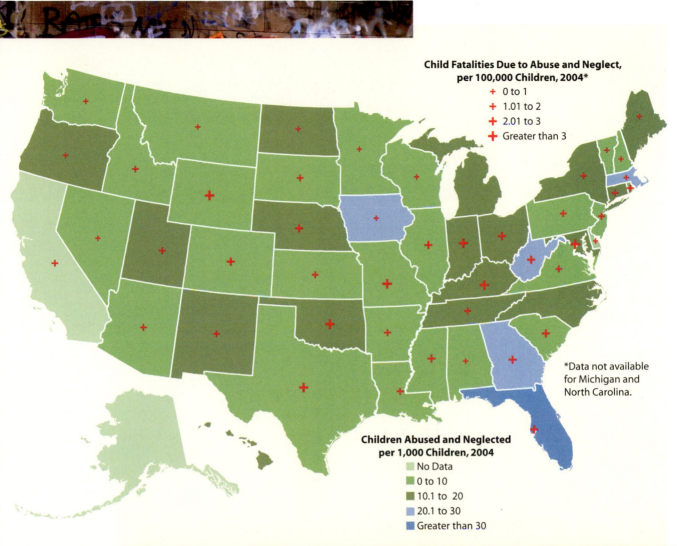

Child Fatalities Due to Abuse and Neglect, per 100,000 Children, 2004*

+ 0 to 1
+ 1.01 to 2
+ 2.01 to 3
+ Greater than 3

*Data not available for Michigan and North Carolina.

Children Abused and Neglected per 1,000 Children, 2004

- No Data
- 0 to 10
- 10.1 to 20
- 20.1 to 30
- Greater than 30

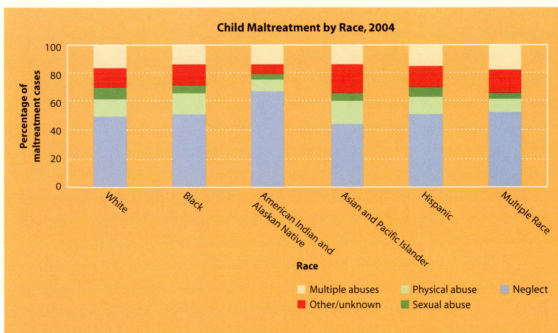

Child Maltreatment by Race, 2004

Percentage of maltreatment cases

Race: White, Black, American Indian and Alaskan Native, Asian and Pacific Islander, Hispanic, Multiple Race

- Multiple abuses
- Physical abuse
- Neglect
- Other/unknown
- Sexual abuse

8 NATURAL RESOURCES AND THE ENVIRONMENT

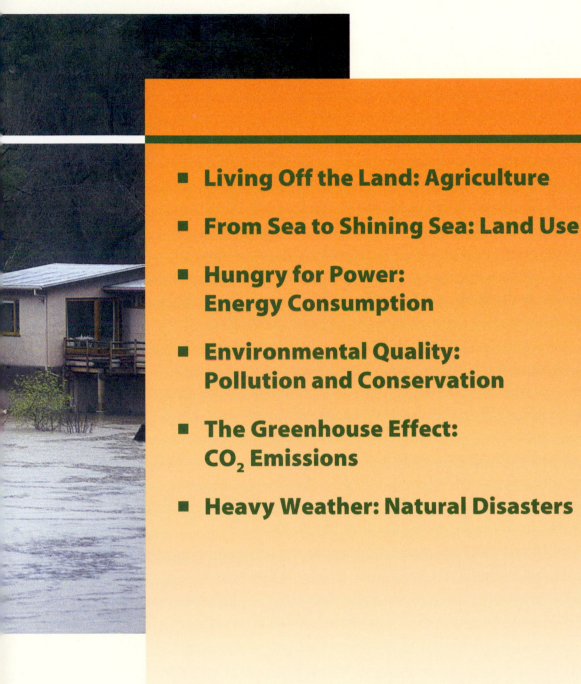

- **Living Off the Land: Agriculture**

- **From Sea to Shining Sea: Land Use**

- **Hungry for Power:**
  Energy Consumption

- **Environmental Quality:**
  Pollution and Conservation

- **The Greenhouse Effect:**
  CO_2 Emissions

- **Heavy Weather: Natural Disasters**

Living Off the Land: Agriculture

Since World War II, the United States has become a suburban nation where housing subdivisions and regional shopping districts replace less intensive land uses such as agriculture. Crop yields are increasing across the nation, but often as a result of an increased use of chemicals (fertilizers, pesticides, etc.).

Although some claim there is no net farmland loss in the United States, the U.S. Department of Agriculture data show that the percentage of farmland has declined: a three percent loss from 1982 to 1997. Farmland preservation advocates suggest that the percentage of land dedicated to agricultural activity is remaining constant only because more marginal areas, such as wetlands and low-productivity lands, are being converted to agriculture.

America's agricultural heritage is disappearing as farmers get older and younger generations fail to carry on family traditions. In 2002, the average age of the American farmer was 55.3, an increase of nearly 5 years since 1982. The age distribution of farmers is quite different from that of the entire nation; 35 percent of the country was aged 15 to 34, while only 9 percent of farmers were under 35.

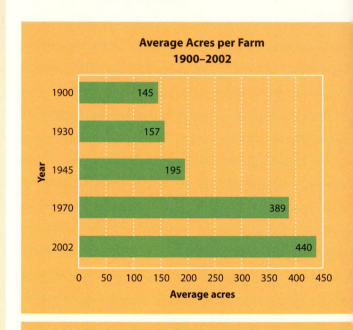

Average Acres per Farm 1900–2002

Year	Average acres
1900	145
1930	157
1945	195
1970	389
2002	440

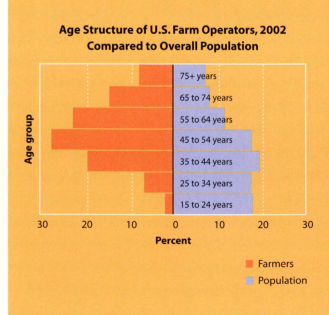

Age Structure of U.S. Farm Operators, 2002 Compared to Overall Population

Age group:
- 75+ years
- 65 to 74 years
- 55 to 64 years
- 45 to 54 years
- 35 to 44 years
- 25 to 34 years
- 15 to 24 years

Percent

■ Farmers
■ Population

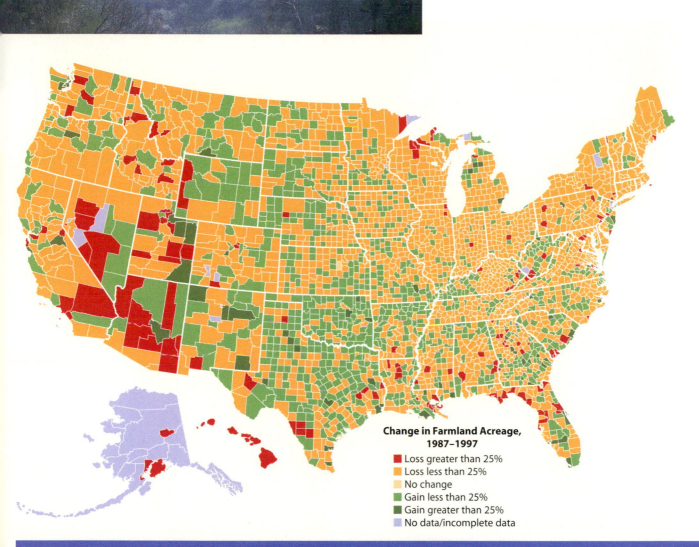

Change in Farmland Acreage, 1987–1997

- 🟥 Loss greater than 25%
- 🟧 Loss less than 25%
- 🟨 No change
- 🟩 Gain less than 25%
- 🟩 Gain greater than 25%
- 🟪 No data/incomplete data

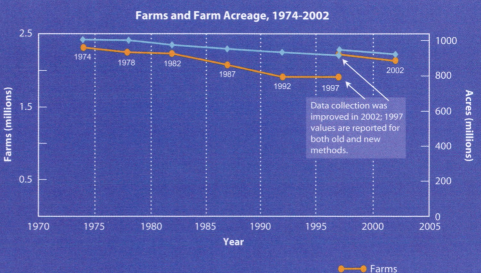

Though the number of farms has decreased, the average acreage per farm has been increasing due to a decline in small family farms and an increase in larger farms. Large farms, those with 500 acres and more, have increased while smaller farms with less than 500 acres have been decreasing. Between 1935 and 1997, farms with over 500 acres increased from 4 to 18 percent of all farms.

Farms and Farm Acreage, 1974-2002

Farms (millions) / Acres (millions)

1974   1978   1982   1987   1992   1997   2002

Data collection was improved in 2002; 1997 values are reported for both old and new methods.

Year

- Farms
- Land in farms

From Sea to Shining Sea: Land Use

Between 1850 and 1900, nearly 200 million acres of forests were destroyed. Despite possible encroachment from increasing populations, U.S. forests have been relatively stable over the last century. Four main threats to forests include fires, invasive species, loss of open space, and unmanaged recreation.

Parks and forest areas provide an essential habitat for wildlife, and also serve as recreational resources for outdoor adventurers. In 2001, 82 million U.S. residents participated in outdoor wildlife-related recreation, including activities such as fishing, hunting, and wildlife-watching. Nature enthusiasts spent over $108 billion on their excursions that year. Only 39 percent of people in the United States participated in these types of activities, but rates differed by state.

In comparison with other forms of land use, development is the most lasting form of habitat loss. Large cities are major sources of pollution; however, in terms of land use, city clusters actually help to preserve habitat. Suburbanization, on the other hand, results in widespread destruction of natural landscapes.

The continental United States has about 107.7 million acres of wetlands, accounting for about 5 percent of land area. Thousands of plants and animals depend on wetland habitats for survival, including 46 percent of all endangered species in the country. Despite the loss of 50 percent of the wetlands in the last several hundred years, there have been recent gains in wetlands areas due to recognition of their importance and resulting restoration initiatives.

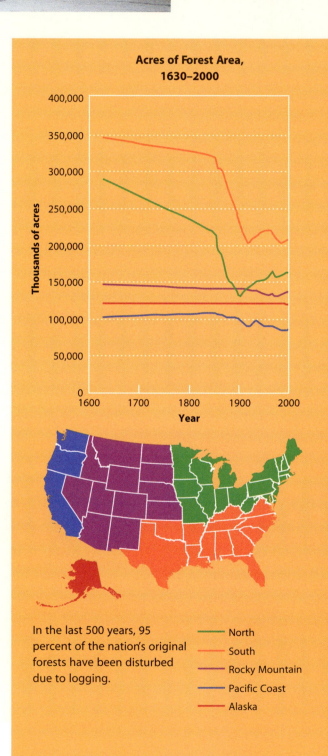

Acres of Forest Area, 1630–2000

Thousands of acres (y-axis: 0 to 400,000)
Year (x-axis: 1600 to 2000)

In the last 500 years, 95 percent of the nation's original forests have been disturbed due to logging.

— North
— South
— Rocky Mountain
— Pacific Coast
— Alaska

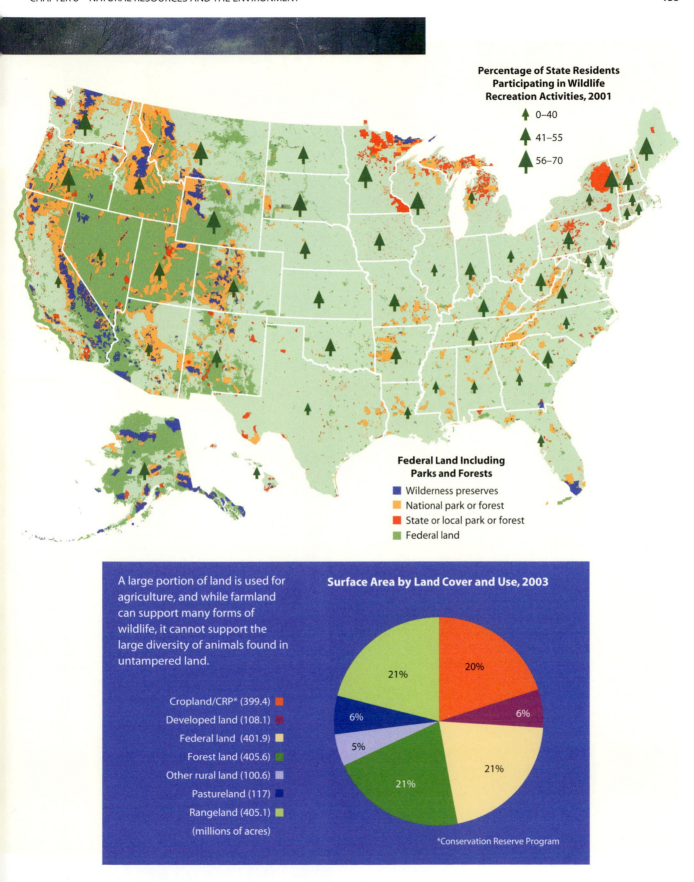

Percentage of State Residents Participating in Wildlife Recreation Activities, 2001

0–40

41–55

56–70

Federal Land Including Parks and Forests

■ Wilderness preserves

■ National park or forest

■ State or local park or forest

■ Federal land

A large portion of land is used for agriculture, and while farmland can support many forms of wildlife, it cannot support the large diversity of animals found in untampered land.

Surface Area by Land Cover and Use, 2003

Cropland/CRP* (399.4)
Developed land (108.1)
Federal land (401.9)
Forest land (405.6)
Other rural land (100.6)
Pastureland (117)
Rangeland (405.1)
(millions of acres)

20%

6%

21%

21%

5%

6%

21%

*Conservation Reserve Program

Hungry for Power: Energy Consumption

The United States consumes more energy than any other country in the world. While the population makes up less than 5 percent of the world's total population, about 25 percent of all energy consumption happens in the United States.

In 2001, the per capita use was 338 million Btu (British Thermal Unit). In Alaska, energy use per person was almost 3.5 times higher. Per capita expenditures topped out at $4,702 in Wyoming due to high energy consumption. Florida, on the other hand, had the lowest per capita expenditures at $1,932. Even though energy prices per unit were higher in Florida than in Wyoming, low energy use kept the per capita expenditures in Florida to a minimum.

In 2004, 86 percent of energy used was produced by the burning of fossil fuels, including coal, oil, and gas. Unfortunately, scientists have become increasingly confident that the burning of fossil fuels is a leading cause of climate change. In 1991, nuclear power production surpassed that of renewable energy, and by 2004, generated eight percent of the energy consumed. Renewables—naturally replenishing energy sources such as biomass, water, solar, and wind power—produced six percent of energy used in 2004. Dammed water is the largest source of renewable energy and supplies most of the power generated in the Pacific Northwest.

On average, heating consumes about 50 percent of residential energy. One-fourth is used for lighting and appliances. The remaining fourth is used for other demands such as air conditioning, refrigeration, and water heating.

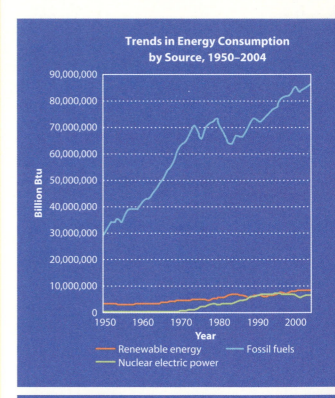

Trends in Energy Consumption by Source, 1950–2004

While households with more people tend to use more energy, the per capita use decreases with an increase in household size. Single-person households are the most inefficient in terms of energy expenditures.

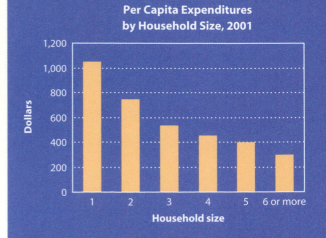

Per Capita Expenditures by Household Size, 2001

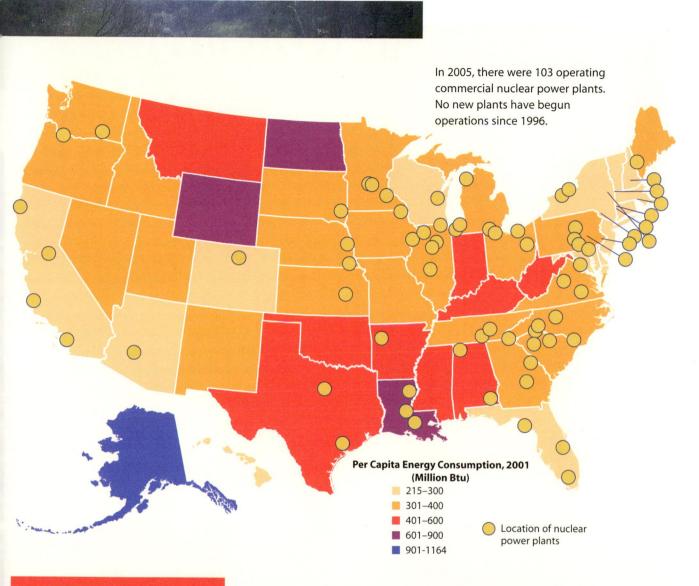

In 2005, there were 103 operating commercial nuclear power plants. No new plants have begun operations since 1996.

Per Capita Energy Consumption, 2001 (Million Btu)
- 215–300
- 301–400
- 401–600
- 601–900
- 901-1164
- ○ Location of nuclear power plants

3,413 Btu = 1 kilowatt hour

Transportation is a major drain on energy. Almost 60 percent of energy for transportation is used to fuel personal vehicles. The remaining 40 percent fuels other vehicles such as large trucks, buses, trains, and airplanes.

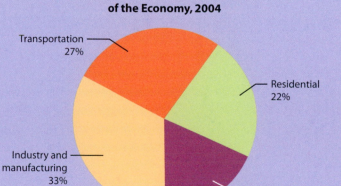

Energy Distribution among Sectors of the Economy, 2004

- Transportation 27%
- Residential 22%
- Commercial 18%
- Industry and manufacturing 33%

Environmental Quality: Pollution and Conservation

In 1960, only six percent of municipal solid waste, or "garbage," was recycled. As concern increased about the condition of the environment, recycling rates began to rise. By 2003, almost a third of all waste was recovered through recycling and composting, noticeably reducing the potential amount of discarded waste that year. Despite the success of recycling programs, the amount of garbage humans throw away continues to increase and waste generation remains an important concern. In 2003, over 236 million tons of garbage were thrown away; 72 million tons were recovered.

The main compounds that contribute to acid rain are sulfur dioxide (SO_2) and the various nitrogen oxide compounds (NO_x). Two-thirds of SO_2 emissions and one-fourth of NO_x emissions result from the burning of fossil fuels in the production of electric power. Acid rain causes damage to soil and wildlife, negatively affects human health, and has a variety of other unpleasant impacts.

The Superfund Program was established in 1980 to identify and clean abandoned hazardous waste sites after years of unregulated and careless industrial dumping of chemical waste. The current National Priority List (NPL) includes over 1,200 sites throughout the United States. Once the Environmental Protection Agency determines that an NPL site no longer poses a threat to human health or the environment, the sites can be deleted from the list. Over 300 sites have been removed from the list, but new sites continue to be proposed.

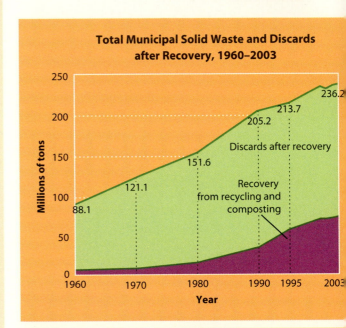

Total Municipal Solid Waste and Discards after Recovery, 1960–2003

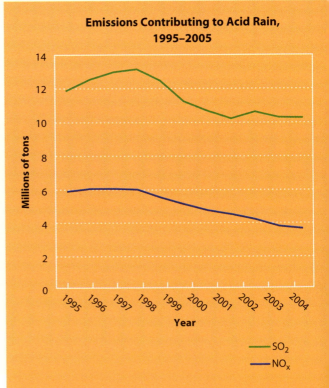

Emissions Contributing to Acid Rain, 1995–2005

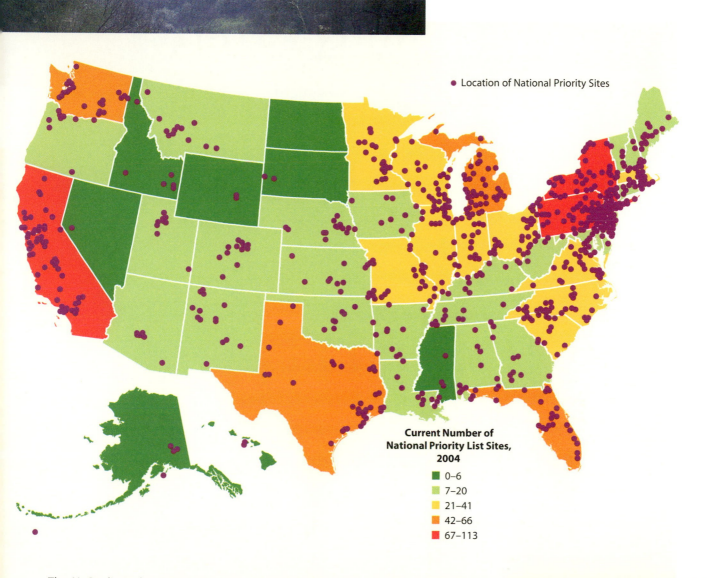

Location of National Priority Sites

Current Number of National Priority List Sites, 2004

- 0–6
- 7–20
- 21–41
- 42–66
- 67–113

The Air Quality Index (AQI) is the system used to rate the level of pollution in the air. The national air quality standard is 100, and anything below is generally thought to be acceptable. Higher numbers represent heavier concentrations of pollutants in the air and indicate increased health risks.

In 2004, the three metropolitan areas spending the most days with an AQI above 100 were all in California. Los Angeles (65 days) and Riverside–San Bernardino (88 days) trailed behind Bakersfield, which spent 103 days, nearly a third of the year, with an AQI rating above 100, making it the metropolitan area with the most hazardous air quality. While Riverside–San Bernardino still ranks high, air quality in the city has improved since the early 1990s. In 1992, the AQI in the city was above 100 for 172 days!

Twenty-six metropolitan areas had no days with an AQI above 100 in 2004. While air quality in industrial areas might be expected to be worse than surrounding areas, often the areas downwind suffer the most severe consequences of industrial air pollution.

The Air Quality Index (AQI)

Range	Description
0–50	Good
51–100	Moderate
101–150	Unhealthy for sensitive groups
151–200	Unhealthy
201–300	Very unhealthy
301–500	Hazardous

The Greenhouse Effect: CO$_2$ Emissions

The United States emits more carbon dioxide (CO$_2$) into the atmosphere every year than any other country in the world. Despite years of uncertainty, mounting evidence has largely brought scientists to a consensus on the topic of climate change and the risks it poses to human life and all life. While CO$_2$ is naturally occurring and essential to life on earth, continued increases in the amount of CO$_2$ in the atmosphere may have consequences that are only beginning to be understood.

The Kyoto Protocol is an international treaty with signatures from over 160 countries with the aim to reduce greenhouse gas emissions below 1990 levels by 2012. As of early 2007 the United States had not ratified the treaty.

The commercial and industrial sectors accounted for 46 percent of CO$_2$ emissions in 2004; the transportation sector accounted for 33 percent of CO$_2$ emissions. About 21 percent of emissions in the United States was from residential homes.

Individuals can help reduce CO$_2$ emissions by limiting in-home energy use with simple measures such as turning off unneeded lights and appliances. Reducing drive time and using recycled paper products are other easy ways to limit one's personal impact. The purchase of carbon futures has become another means by which individuals can attempt to neutralize their carbon-producing activities. Money spent on carbon offsets is used to invest in carbon sequestration and clean energy projects.

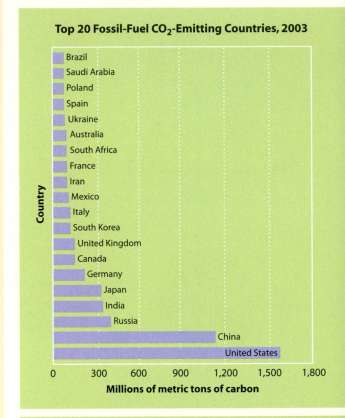

Top 20 Fossil-Fuel CO$_2$-Emitting Countries, 2003

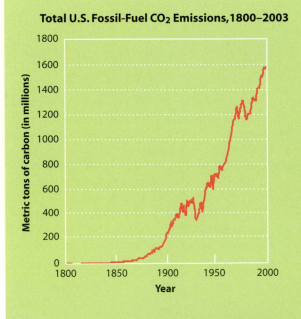

Total U.S. Fossil-Fuel CO$_2$ Emissions, 1800–2003

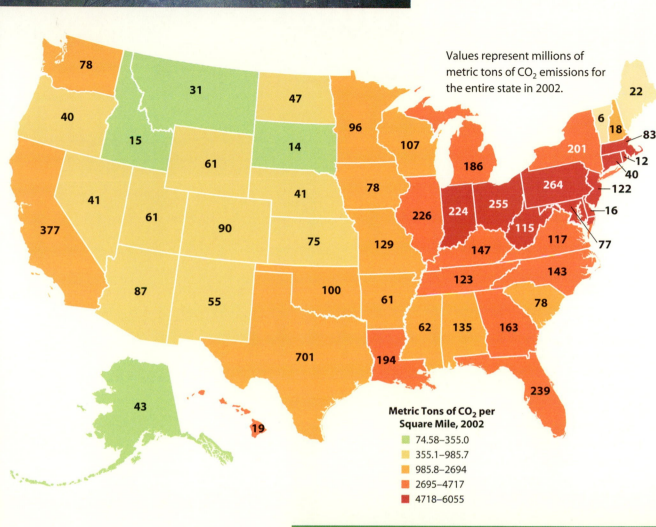

Values represent millions of metric tons of CO_2 emissions for the entire state in 2002.

Metric Tons of CO_2 per Square Mile, 2002

- 74.58–355.0
- 355.1–985.7
- 985.8–2694
- 2695–4717
- 4718–6055

Carbon sequestration involves the capture and conversion of CO_2 from the atmosphere. Trees and forests are vital CO_2 sinks: preventing deforestation and increasing reforestation efforts will slow the rate of warming. Traditional carbon sequestration projects include forest preservation, tree planting, and urban forestry. The urgency caused by this climate change has led to research on new and innovative ways of storing CO_2 that would otherwise remain in the atmosphere.

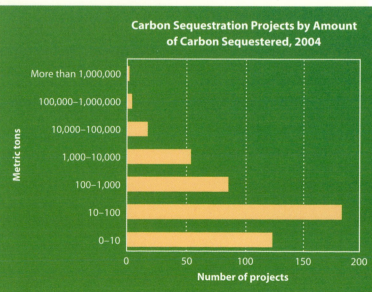

Carbon Sequestration Projects by Amount of Carbon Sequestered, 2004

Metric tons (y-axis):
- More than 1,000,000
- 100,000–1,000,000
- 10,000–100,000
- 1,000–10,000
- 100–1,000
- 10–100
- 0–10

Number of projects (x-axis): 0, 50, 100, 150, 200

Heavy Weather: Natural Disasters

Natural disasters do not strike uniformly. Some years, natural disasters are much more severe than others. A single year's events can only offer a snapshot of one year's impact of natural disasters. Therefore looking at the average yearly impact of natural disasters can show a much more realistic picture.

Natural disasters are wreaking economic havoc. Because of population growth, more people are now living in harm's way. More than 50 percent of the U.S. population lives within 50 miles of coastline, putting a large portion of the population in the way of potential hurricanes, tropical storms, or storm surge. The value of coastline property is also much higher on average, contributing to the high economic costs of natural disasters. Also, high population densities and the infrastructure in large cities make the costs of any single disaster more extensive. A single major earthquake could cause extreme damage in a large city. A powerful tornado tearing through a metropolitan area could mean billions of dollars in damage. Between 2000 and 2004, the United States suffered almost $65 billion in property and crop damage from natural disasters and severe weather events.

Over 1,000 tornados occur annually and can occur anywhere at anytime of the year. The peak season for tornados is March through the early months of summer. Tornados are most common in the Great Plains, often referred to as "Tornado Alley." Between 2000 and 2004, 225 people died in tornados and 4,075 were injured. That's an average of 45 deaths and 815 injuries per year due to tornados. Mobile homes are notoriously dangerous places to be during tornados.

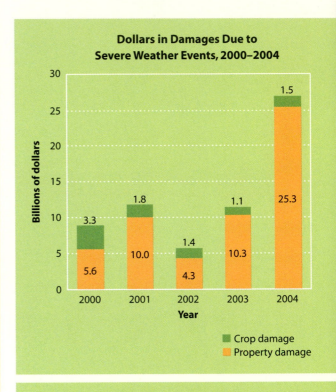

Dollars in Damages Due to Severe Weather Events, 2000–2004

Billions of dollars (y-axis)

- 2000: Property damage 5.6, Crop damage 3.3
- 2001: Property damage 10.0, Crop damage 1.8
- 2002: Property damage 4.3, Crop damage 1.4
- 2003: Property damage 10.3, Crop damage 1.1
- 2004: Property damage 25.3, Crop damage 1.5

■ Crop damage
■ Property damage

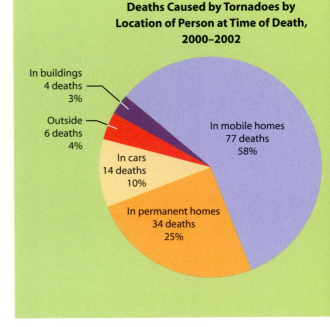

Deaths Caused by Tornadoes by Location of Person at Time of Death, 2000–2002

- In buildings: 4 deaths, 3%
- Outside: 6 deaths, 4%
- In cars: 14 deaths, 10%
- In permanent homes: 34 deaths, 25%
- In mobile homes: 77 deaths, 58%

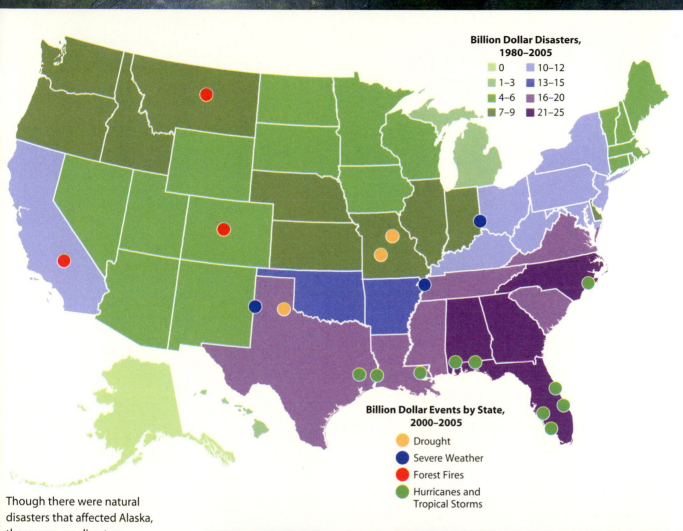

Billion Dollar Disasters, 1980–2005

- 0
- 1–3
- 4–6
- 7–9
- 10–12
- 13–15
- 16–20
- 21–25

Billion Dollar Events by State, 2000–2005

- Drought
- Severe Weather
- Forest Fires
- Hurricanes and Tropical Storms

Though there were natural disasters that affected Alaska, there were no disasters causing over $1 billion in damage between 1980 and 2005.

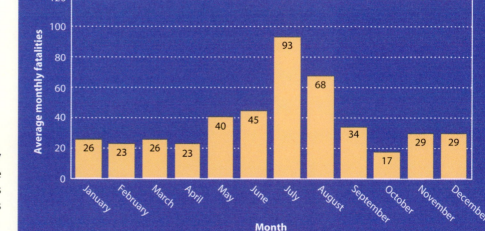

Average Fatalitites Due to Severe Weather Events by Month, 2000–2004

Month	Average monthly fatalities
January	26
February	23
March	26
April	23
May	40
June	45
July	93
August	68
September	34
October	17
November	29
December	29

Between 2000 and 2004, 2,267 deaths resulted from extreme weather events. More deaths occur in the summer months than in the winter months.

Heavy Weather: Natural Disasters

The largest earthquake on record in United States history occurred in Alaska in 1964. That earthquake measured 9.2 on the Richter Scale. Earthquakes happen daily throughout the world, especially along fault lines, but those below 3.0 are most common and are usually not felt. In December 2004, the world witnessed the enormous deadly force that can be generated by an earthquake when one registering over 9.0 off the coast of Sumatra in Indonesia generated a tsunami that killed over 170,000 people.

Between 1995 and 2005, nine hurricane seasons were classified as above normal for hurricane activity; seven of these nine were classified as hyperactive. During this time, there was an annual average of 15 named hurricanes or tropical storms: 8.5 were hurricanes and four of these hurricanes were considered major. Hurricanes are expected to increase in intensity and frequency as climate change warms the ocean waters. However scientists have also identified natural 20 to 40 year cycles of increased hurricane activity.

Hurricane Katrina in 2005 was the most costly natural disaster ever to hit the United States, the most deadly since 1928, and the strongest storm to impact the U.S. coast in over 100 years. The official death toll mounted to over 1,800 fatalities and total damages were estimated to be about $125 billion. Over 250,000 people were displaced. In 2007, some areas of New Orleans were still uninhabitable.

Though natural disasters cannot be prevented, devastation caused by them can be limited with proper planning and risk analysis. The future surely holds its fair share of disasters. Early warning and preparation for nature's wrath will save lives and minimize costs.

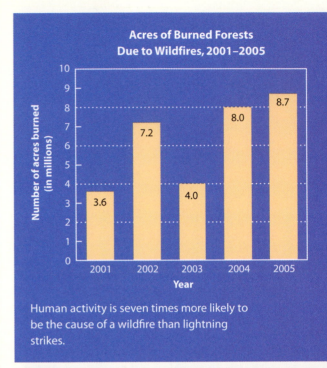

Human activity is seven times more likely to be the cause of a wildfire than lightning strikes.

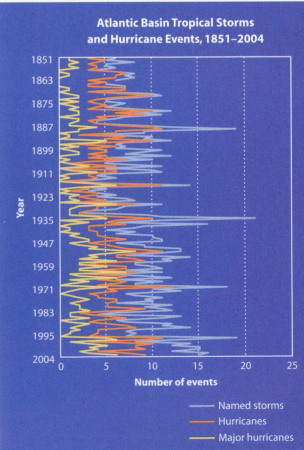

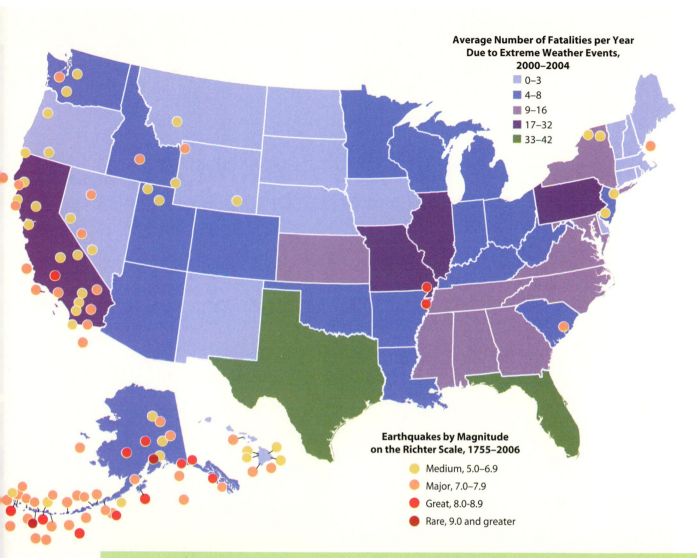

Average Number of Fatalities per Year Due to Extreme Weather Events, 2000–2004

- 0–3
- 4–8
- 9–16
- 17–32
- 33–42

Earthquakes by Magnitude on the Richter Scale, 1755–2006

- Medium, 5.0–6.9
- Major, 7.0–7.9
- Great, 8.0-8.9
- Rare, 9.0 and greater

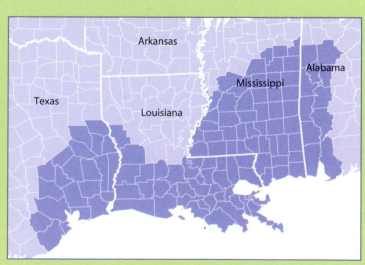

Breeches in the levees caused widespread and devastating flooding in New Orleans in the days after Hurricane Katrina had passed.

Counties in dark blue were eligible to receive individual and public assistance (IPA) based on disaster declarations by the Federal Emergency Management Agency (FEMA) in association with Hurricane Katrina and Hurricane Rita, October 2005.

Arkansas

Alabama

Mississippi

Texas

Louisiana

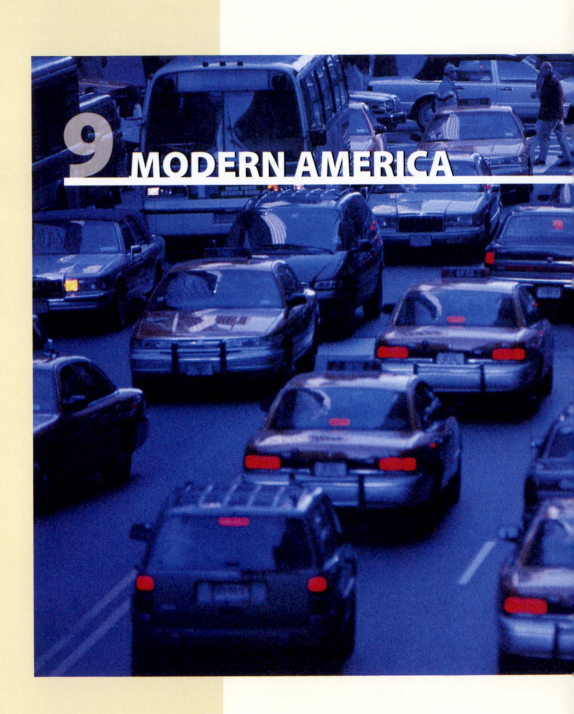

9 MODERN AMERICA

- **Stuck in Traffic:**
  Commuting and Roadway Congestion

- **Planes, Trains, and Buses:**
  Mass Transportation

- **Wired America:**
  Computers and Usage

- **On the Air: Broadcast Media**

Stuck in Traffic:
Commuting and Roadway Congestion

In 2005, 109 million people (88.4 percent of workers) used an automobile to get to work. Ninety percent of them drove to work alone. The number of cars on the road headed to and from work increased by approximately 18 million vehicles between 1993 and 2005. In 2003, people spent an average of 100 hours stuck in traffic while commuting to and from work. That is over four days spent sitting in a car!

Traffic congestion is greater in large metropolitan areas than in smaller ones. Rush hour tends to be worse both in intensity and duration. The Roadway Congestion Index (RCI) is a measure of vehicle travel density on major roadways in a metropolitan area. An RCI exceeding 1.0 indicates an undesirable congestion level on the freeways and street systems during the peak driving times. An RCI of 0.99 or below is deemed acceptable. Every one of the largest metropolitan areas had an RCI greater than 1.0.

The costs of traffic backups are not only in wasted time and productivity. Traffic backups also cost drivers, on average, $422 in wasted fuel per year. Congestion also takes a toll on the environment by increasing the amount of pollution emitted from standing vehicles.

Bottlenecks, traffic incidents, and work zones account for about 75 percent of traffic congestion. Bad weather, poor signal timing, and special events are also major causes of traffic congestion.

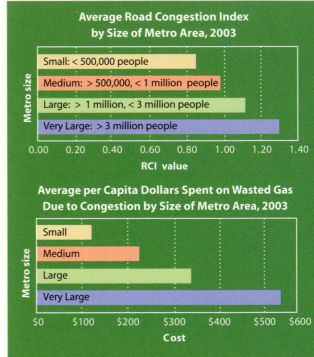

Average Road Congestion Index by Size of Metro Area, 2003

Metro size:
- Small: < 500,000 people
- Medium: > 500,000, < 1 million people
- Large: > 1 million, < 3 million people
- Very Large: > 3 million people

RCI value (0.00 – 1.40)

Average per Capita Dollars Spent on Wasted Gas Due to Congestion by Size of Metro Area, 2003

Metro size:
- Small
- Medium
- Large
- Very Large

Cost ($0 – $600)

Ranking of the Top 10 Most Congested Metro Areas with Populations Over 3 Million, 2003

Rank	City	Annual roadway congestion index	Per capita cost of wasted fuel
1	LA–Long Beach–Santa Ana, CA	1.57	$855
2	San Francisco–Oakland, CA	1.42	$631
3	Chicago, IL–IN	1.39	$526
4	Washington, DC–VA–MD	1.37	$577
5	Atlanta, GA	1.36	$584
6	Houston, TX	1.33	$609
7	Miami, FL	1.31	$487
8	Detroit, MI	1.27	$499
9	Phoenix, AZ	1.23	$431
10	Dallas–Fort Worth–Arlington, TX	1.19	$592

Boston, New York, and Philadelphia ranked 11th, 12th, and 13th respectively.

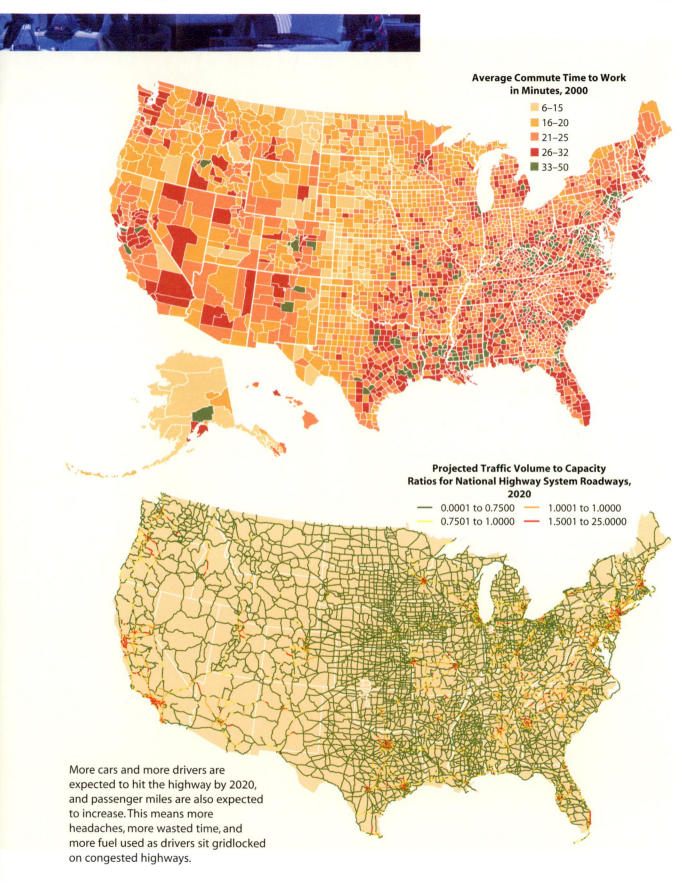

Average Commute Time to Work in Minutes, 2000

- 6–15
- 16–20
- 21–25
- 26–32
- 33–50

Projected Traffic Volume to Capacity Ratios for National Highway System Roadways, 2020

- 0.0001 to 0.7500
- 0.7501 to 1.0000
- 1.0001 to 1.0000
- 1.5001 to 25.0000

More cars and more drivers are expected to hit the highway by 2020, and passenger miles are also expected to increase. This means more headaches, more wasted time, and more fuel used as drivers sit gridlocked on congested highways.

Planes, Trains, and Buses: Mass Transportation

In 2005, people in the U.S. took more than 9.7 billion trips using public transportation. With exception of a slight drop in ridership in 2002 and 2003, numbers of trips have been on the rise since 1997. In fact, between 1995 and 2005, trips using public transit systems increased by over 25 percent. However, these numbers are still much lower than the peak of 23.4 billion rides in 1946.

For short trips, public transportation was the choice of nearly six million U.S. workers in 2000. As expected, New York City had the highest percentage (29 percent) of workers using public transportation. Just over half of all transit trips were taken for the purpose of going to work.

For all public transit trips, buses were the most common mode of transportation, with a total of 21.4 billion passenger-miles traveled in 2004.

With rising prices at the gas pump, many Americans have turned to public transit. Bus transit cost 19 cents per mile, on average. Commuter rail was the least expensive major method of transit, averaging 15 cents per mile in 2002.

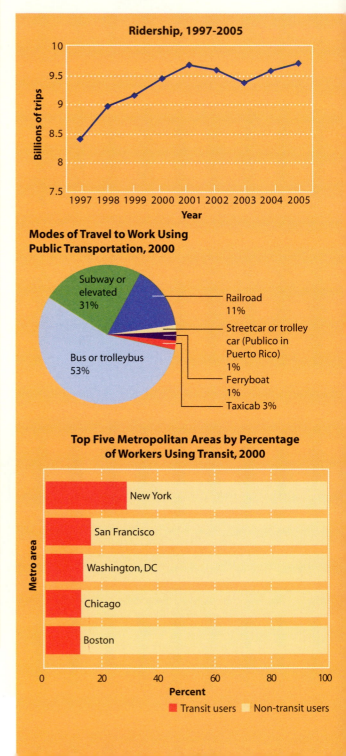

Ridership, 1997-2005

Modes of Travel to Work Using Public Transportation, 2000

Subway or elevated 31%
Bus or trolleybus 53%
Railroad 11%
Streetcar or trolley car (Publico in Puerto Rico) 1%
Ferryboat 1%
Taxicab 3%

Top Five Metropolitan Areas by Percentage of Workers Using Transit, 2000

New York
San Francisco
Washington, DC
Chicago
Boston

Transit users   Non-transit users

Top U.S. Airports
by Passenger Volume, 2002

3-5 million   15-20 million
5-10 million   More than 20 million
10-15 million

For American travelers, the airlines remain a popular transportation option. The airlines
served nearly 575 million passengers in 2002. Thirty-seven million of these travelers passed
through the nation's busiest airport, Hartsfield International in Atlanta, Georgia.

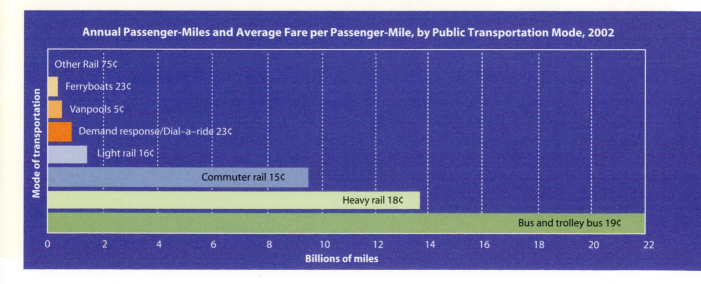

Annual Passenger-Miles and Average Fare per Passenger-Mile, by Public Transportation Mode, 2002

Other Rail 75¢
Ferryboats 23¢
Vanpools 5¢
Demand response/Dial–a–ride 23¢
Light rail 16¢
Commuter rail 15¢
Heavy rail 18¢
Bus and trolley bus 19¢

Mode of transportation

Billions of miles

Wired America: Computers and Usage

In only a few decades, personal computers have advanced from finicky tools only slightly more powerful than simple calculators, yet costing thousands of dollars, into the pervasive and versatile machines we can purchase today for only a few hundred dollars. Although most consumers use their computers mainly for word processing and Web browsing, the low prices have encouraged consumers to continue purchasing new systems, whether necessary or not. The Environmental Protection Agency has estimated that as many as 500 million personal computers were discarded between 2000 and 2007 as a result.

The widespread availability of home computers with Internet access has spurred the creation of new uses, such as for online shopping, for telephone service, and for business meetings. Electronic commerce (eCommerce), for example, allows computer users to shop for goods and services through Web-based portals without ever having to leave home. For the third quarter of 2006, eCommerce accounted for $27.5 billion in retail sales, which corresponded to 2.8 percent of total retail sales ($990 billion). The increase in eCommerce has been substantial; for the third quarter in 2005, eCommerce represented 2.4 percent ($22.7 billion) of the total sales, and as recently as late 2000, online sales accounted for less than 1.0 percent of total retail sales.

Cyber "storefronts" have quickly become crucial for most retailers, especially mail-order businesses and others with catalogs. eCommerce contributed 35.5 percent of the catalog industry's sales revenue.

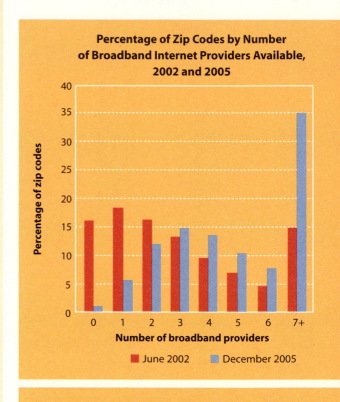

Percentage of Zip Codes by Number of Broadband Internet Providers Available, 2002 and 2005

Percentage of zip codes (y-axis) vs Number of broadband providers (x-axis: 0, 1, 2, 3, 4, 5, 6, 7+)

■ June 2002   ■ December 2005

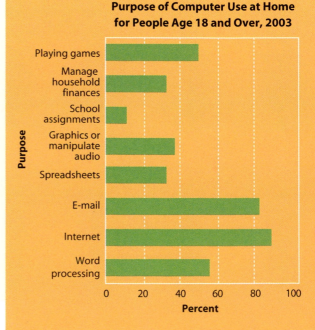

Purpose of Computer Use at Home for People Age 18 and Over, 2003

Purpose (y-axis): Playing games, Manage household finances, School assignments, Graphics or manipulate audio, Spreadsheets, E-mail, Internet, Word processing

Percent (x-axis: 0, 20, 40, 60, 80, 100)

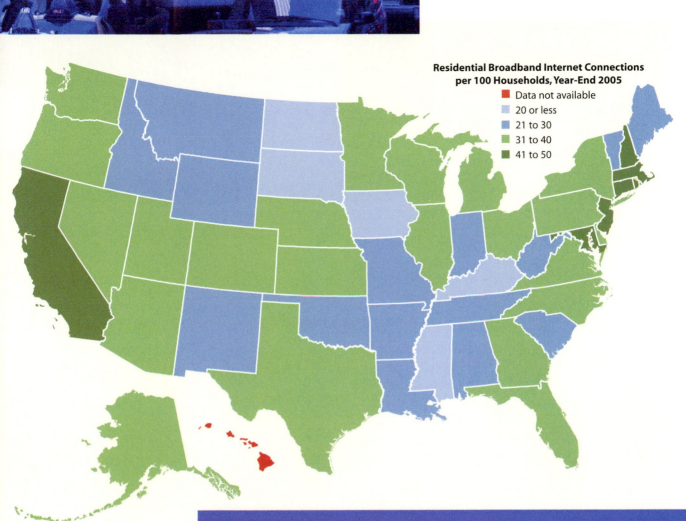

Residential Broadband Internet Connections
per 100 Households, Year-End 2005
- Data not available
- 20 or less
- 21 to 30
- 31 to 40
- 41 to 50

The availability of computers and Internet access in homes varies across the country and is associated with characteristics such as age, race, family income, and education. For many, such technology would be welcomed if not for the expense. As computers have become an essential tool in education and many careers, individuals with limited technical experience are less likely to obtain higher paying jobs when entering the work force. The result is a growing economic gap between those who can afford access to current technologies and those who cannot.

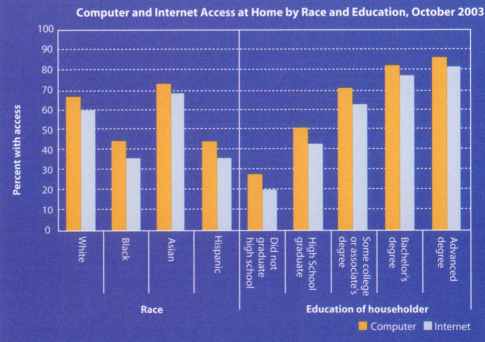

Computer and Internet Access at Home by Race and Education, October 2003

Percent with access

Race: White, Black, Asian, Hispanic

Education of householder: Did not graduate high school, High School graduate, Some college or associate's degree, Bachelor's degree, Advanced degree

Computer   Internet

On the Air: Broadcast Media

Every day, millions of people tune to their favorite radio stations during the daily commute. They tune in for news, weather, traffic, commentary, and of course, music. After work, many people spend time watching their favorite television programs. Watching television has become one of America's pastimes.

Recent innovations, including digital satellite television, TiVo, satellite radio, and portable digital music players, are quickly changing the viewing and listening habits of Americans. Still, the average American was projected to spend an average of almost 1,900 hours watching television and another 1,100 hours listening to the radio in 2007. Of the 1,900 hours spent watching television, almost 800 hours were projected to be spent watching broadcast television. That averages out to over five hours watching television each day, of which more than two hours will be spent watching broadcast television.

Starting February 18, 2009, the familiar analog television signals will cease being broadcast in the final stage of the transition to digital television. The transition, however, began in the 1990s, when some stations started broadcasting both analog and digital signals. By 2006, all broadcast markets had at least one digital signal. By March 2007, regulations required that all televisions be manufactured with digital tuners. For those who have already purchased analog-only sets, the government will offer rebates so that households can purchase digital–analog converter boxes.

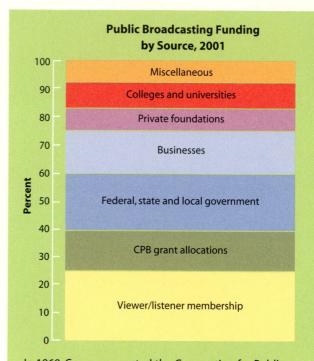

Public Broadcasting Funding by Source, 2001

Percent

- Miscellaneous
- Colleges and universities
- Private foundations
- Businesses
- Federal, state and local government
- CPB grant allocations
- Viewer/listener membership

In 1969, Congress created the Corporation for Public Broadcasting (CPB) to manage grant funding to support the nation's non-commercial radio and television stations. These grant allocations tend to be greater (on a per capita basis) in the northern states, with the highest values occurring in Washington, DC (home of NPR) and Virginia (home of PBS). Membership pledges accounted for the greatest portion (26 percent) of public broadcasting operating funds in 2001.

The nation's 356 public television stations reach 99 percent of American homes, while 790 public radio stations can be heard in 93 percent of homes. Perhaps one of the most recognizable public broadcasting shows is Sesame Street, which in 2001, at the ripe old age of 33, still drew an audience of 7.5 million people each week.

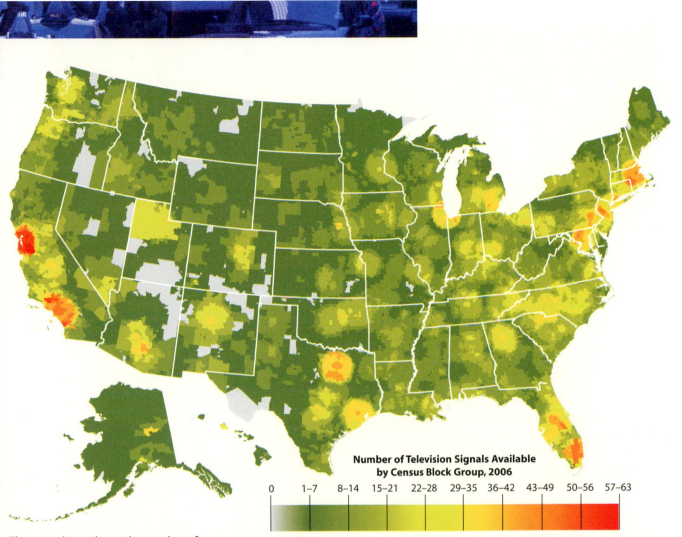

Number of Television Signals Available by Census Block Group, 2006

| 0 | 1–7 | 8–14 | 15–21 | 22–28 | 29–35 | 36–42 | 43–49 | 50–56 | 57–63 |

The map above shows the number of broadcast television signals (both analog and digital) available at any given point in the country. Some broadcasted stations may be counted twice—once for an analog and again for digital. In addition to the network stations, some areas also receive signals broadcasted by the local government, colleges, or other institutions.

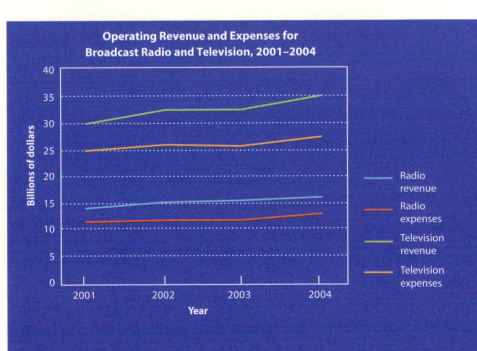

Operating Revenue and Expenses for Broadcast Radio and Television, 2001–2004

Billions of dollars

Year

Radio revenue
Radio expenses
Television revenue
Television expenses

SOURCES

CHAPTER 1: OUR DYNAMIC POPULACE

Adding and Subtracting: Regional Population Change

Census 1990, Summary Tape File 1, U.S. Census Bureau. |Census 2000, Summary File 1, U.S. Census Bureau. | Hobbs, F., & Stoops, N. (2002, November). *Demographic trends in the 20th century* (U.S. Census Bureau Series, Census 2000 Special Reports, CENSR-4). Washington, DC: U.S. Government Printing Office. | National Oceanic and Atmospheric Administration. (2005, March). *Population trends along the coastal United States: 1980-2008*. Washington, DC: U.S. Government Printing Office. | National Technical Information Service. *The population of states and counties of the United States: 1790 to 1990*. Washington, DC: Author. | Population Estimates Program, 2005, U.S. Census Bureau. | U.S. Census Bureau. *1990 population and housing unit counts: United States*. Washington, DC: Author.

The Newest Americans: Immigration

American Community Survey 2003, U.S. Census Bureau. | Census 2000, Summary File 3, U.S. Census Bureau. | Census 2000, Summary File 4, U.S. Census Bureau. | Department of Homeland Security. (2005). *Yearbook of immigration statistics: 2004*. Washington, DC: Author. | Department of Homeland Security. (2006). *Yearbook of immigration statistics: 2005*. Washington, DC: Author. | Passel, J. (2006, March). *The size and characteristics of the unauthorized migrant population in the U.S.* Washington, DC: Pew Hispanic Center.

Pulling Up Stakes: Migration and Mobility

Census 2000, Summary File 1, U.S. Census Bureau. | Census 2000, Summary File 3, U.S. Census Bureau. | Current Population Survey 2004, U.S. Census Bureau. | Schachter, J., Franklin, R., & Perry, M. (2003, August). *Census 2000 special reports: Migration and geographic mobility in metropolitan and nonmetropolitan America: 1995 to 2000* (U.S. Census Bureau Series CENSR-9). Washington, DC: U.S. Government Printing Office. | Schachter, J. (2004, March). *Geographic mobility: 2002 to 2003* (U.S. Census Bureau Series, Current Population Reports, P20-549). Washington, DC: U.S. Government Printing Office. | U.S. Census Bureau. (2005). *Geographical mobility/migration*. Washington, DC: Author. | U.S. Census Bureau. Migration for the population 5 years and over for the United States, regions, states, counties, New England minor civil divisions, metropolitan areas, and Puerto Rico: 2000. *Census 2000: special tabulations*. Washington, DC: Author.

Generations Young and Old: Age Distribution

U.S. Census Bureau, Statistical Abstract of the United States, 2003. | Meyer, J. (2001, October). *Age: 2000* (U.S. Census Bureau Series, Census 2000 Brief, C2KBR/01-12). Washington, DC: U.S. Government Printing Office. | Census 2000, Summary File 1, U.S. Census Bureau. | U.S Census Bureau. (2001, May). Nation's Median Age Highest Ever, But 65-and-Over Population's Growth Lags. *U.S Census Bureau Press Release*.

The Baby Factor: Fertility and Birth Rates

The Henry J. Kaiser Family Foundation. *Kaiser Statehealthfacts.org: 50 State Comparisons*. | U.S. Census (2002). *Fertility of American Women Current Population Survey*. | Martin, J. A. (2005). Births: Final Data for 2003. *National Vital Statistics Reports, 54,* 98. | U.S Census Bureau. *Adopted Children and Stepchildren: 2000.* | National Center for Health Statistics. (2005). *Health, United States, 2005*. Hyattsville, MD: Author. | National Center for Health Statistics. National Vital Statistics System, Birth File.

Witnesses to a Century: Americans 65 and Older

American Community Survey 2004, U.S. Census Bureau. | Census 2000, Summary File 1, U.S. Census Bureau. | Census 2000, Summary File 3, U.S. Census Bureau. | Current Population Survey 2003, U.S. Census Bureau. | Federal Interagency Forum on Aging-Related Statistics. (2004). *Population: Older Americans 2004: Key indicators of well-being*. Washinton, DC: Author. | Gist, Y., & Hetzel, L. (2004, December). *We the people: Aging in the United States* (U.S. Census Bureau Series, Census 2000 Special Reports, CENSR-19). Washington, DC: U.S. Government Printing Office. | He, W., & Schachter, J. (2003, August). *Internal migration of the older population: 1995 to 2000* (U.S. Census Bureau Series, Census 2000 Special Reports, CENSR-10). Washington, DC: U.S. Government Printing Office. | He, W., Sengupta, M., Velkoff, V., & Debarros, K. (2005, December). *65+ in the United States: 2005* (U.S. Census Bureau Series, Current Population Reports, P23-209). Washington, DC: U.S. Government Printing Office. | Population Estimates Program, 2005, U.S. Census Bureau. | Population Projections Program, 2005, US. Census Bureau.

Life Expectancy and Mortality

Census 2000, Summary File 1, U.S. Census Bureau. | National Center for Health Statistics. (2003). *National vital statistics system, mortality file.* Hyattsville, MD: Author. | National Center for Health Statistics. (2005). *Health, United States, 2005*. Washington, DC: U.S. Government Printing Office.

Urban and Rural Living

Census 2000, Five-Percent Public Use Microdata Series, U.S. Census Bureau. | Census 2000, Summary File 1, U.S. Census Bureau. | Census 2000, Summary File 2, U.S. Census Bureau. | Census 2000, Summary File 3, U.S. Census Bureau. | Census 2000, Summary File 4, U.S. Census Bureau. | *National File—2000 Urbanized Areas* [Mapping data file]. Washington, DC: U.S. Census Bureau.

Marriage and Divorce

Kreider, R. (2005, February). *Number, timing, and duration of marriages and divorces: 2001* (U.S. Census Bureau Series, Current Population Reports—Household Economic Studies, P70-97). Washington, DC: U.S. Government Printing Office. | U.S. Census Bureau. (2004, November). *"Stay-at-home" parents top 5 million* (U.S. Census Bureau Series, Census Bureau Press Releases, CB04-230). Washington, DC: Author. | National Center for Health Statistics. CDC. (2001, May 24). Forty-three percent of first marriages break-up within 15 years. *National Center for Health Statistics Press Release.* | Current Population Survey, Annual Social and Economic Supplement, 2005. U.S. Census Bureau. | Census 2000. U.S. Census Bureau. *Sex by Marital Status by Age for the Population 15 years and Over.* | National Center for Health Statistics. Vital Statistics Reports. *Marriages and Divorces—Number and Rate by State: 1990 to 2004.*

Blood, Marriage, or Adoption: Family Structure

U.S. Census Bureau. CPS. (2004, November 30). Stay-at-Home Parents Top 5 Million, Census Bureau Reports. *U.S. Census Bureau Press Release.* | U.S. Census Bureau, Population Division, Fertility & Family Statistics Branch. (2004). *America's Families and Living Arrangements: 2004.* Washington, DC: | American Community Survey 2004, U.S. Census Bureau. | Census 2000, Summary File 1, U.S Census Bureau. | American Community Survey 2005, U.S Census Bureau. *Median Family Income in the Past 12 Months (in 2005 Inflation-Adjusted Dollars) by Family Type by Presence of own Children under 18 years.*

CHAPTER 2: RACE, ETHNICITY, AND MINORITY STATUS

Racial Groups and Inequalities

American Community Survey 2004, U.S. Census Bureau. | Census 2000, Summary File 1, U.S. Census Bureau. | Current Population Survey 2005, U.S. Census Bureau. | Population Projections Program 2006, U.S. Census Bureau.

White Ancestry

Brittingham, A., & de la Cruz, G.P. (2004, June). *Ancestry: 2000* (U.S. Census Bureau Series, Census 2000 Brief, C2KBR-35). Washington, DC: U.S. Government Printing Office. | Census 2000, Summary File 3, U.S. Census Bureau. | Department of Homeland Security. (2006). *Yearbook of immigration statistics: 2005.* Washington, DC: Author. | Grieco, E. (2001, August). *The white population: 2000* (U.S. Census Bureau Series, Census 2000 Brief, C2KBR/01-4). Washington, DC: U.S. Government Printing Office. | Population Estimates Program, 2005, U.S. Census Bureau. | Population Projections Program, 2005, US. Census Bureau.

Black Americans

Census 2000, Summary File 1, U.S. Census Bureau. | McKinnon, J. (2001, August). *The black population: 2000* (U.S. Census Bureau Series, Census 2000 Brief, C2KBR/01-5). Washington, DC: U.S. Government Printing Office. | McKinnon, J.D., & Bennett, C.E. (2005, August). *We the people: Blacks in the United States* (U.S. Census Bureau Series, Census 2000 Special Reports, CENSR-25). Washington, DC: U.S. Government Printing Office.

Hispanic Americans

Census 2000, Summary File 1, U.S. Census Bureau. | Census 2000, Summary File 3, U.S. Census Bureau. | Census 2000, Summary File 4, U.S. Census Bureau. | Current Population Survey 2003, U.S. Census Bureau. | Guzmán, B. (2001, May). *The Hispanic Population* (U.S. Census Bureau Series, Census 2000 Brief, C2KBR/01-3). Washington, DC: U.S. Government Printing Office. | Ramirez, R.R. (2004, December). *We the people: Hispanics in the United States* (U.S. Census Bureau Series, Census 2000 Special Reports, CENSR-18). Washington, DC: U.S. Government Printing Office. | Passel, J. (2006, March). *The size and characteristics of the unauthorized migrant population in the U.S.* Washington, DC: Pew Hispanic Center. | Population Estimates Program, 2005, US. Census Bureau. | Population Projections Program, 2005, US. Census Bureau.

Asians and Pacific Islanders

Barnes, J.S., & Bennett, C.E. (2002, February). *The Asian population: 2000* (U.S. Census Bureau Series, Census 2000 Brief, C2KBR/01-16).Washington, DC: U.S. Government Printing Office. | Census 2000, Summary File 1, U.S. Census Bureau. | Census 2000, Summary File 3, U.S. Census Bureau. | Population Estimates Program, 2005, US. Census Bureau. | Reeves, T.J., & Bennett, C.E. (2004, December). *We the people: Asians in the United States* (U.S. Census Bureau Series, Census 2000 Special Reports, CENSR-17). Washington, DC: U.S. Government Printing Office.

American Indians and Alaskan Natives

American Community Survey 2005, U.S. Census Bureau. | Census 2000, Summary File 1, U.S. Census Bureau. | Census 2000, Summary File 2, U.S. Census Bureau. | Census 2000, Summary File 3, U.S. Census Bureau. | Census 2000, Summary File 4, U.S. Census Bureau. | *National File—2000 Urbanized Areas* [Mapping data file]. Washington, DC: U.S. Census Bureau. | Ogunwole, S.U. (2002, February). *The American Indian and Alaska Native population: 2000* (U.S. Census Bureau Series, Census 2000 Brief, C2KBR/01-15). Washington, DC: U.S. Government Printing Office. | Ogunwole, S.U. (2006, February). *We the people: American Indians and Alaska Natives in the United States* (U.S. Census Bureau Series, Census 2000 Special Reports, CENSR-28). Washington, DC: U.S. Government Printing Office. | Population Estimates Program, 2005, U.S. Census Bureau.

Our Segregated Cities

Census 2000, Summary File 1, U.S. Census Bureau. | Iceland, J., Weinberg, D.H., & Steinmetz, E. (2002, August). *Racial and Ethnic Residential Segregation in the United States: 1980-2000* (U.S. Census Bureau, Census 2000 Special Reports, CENSR-3). Washington, DC: U.S. Government Printing Office. | Iceland, J. (2004, December). *The multigroup entropy index: (Also known as Theil's H or the information theory index).* Washington, DC: U.S. Census Bureau. | *Housing patterns in places: 2000—Residential-pattern indicators for 1980, 1990, and 2000—Multi-group entropy index* [Data file]. Washington, DC: U.S. Census Bureau. | *Housing patterns in metropolitan areas: 2000—Black or African American* [Data file]. Washington, DC: U.S. Census Bureau. | Population Estimates Program, 2005, US. Census Bureau. | Population Estimates Program, 2006, US. Census Bureau.

Gay, Lesbian, and Bisexual Americans

Simmons, T., & O'Connell, M. (2003, February). *Married-couple and unmarried-partner households: 2000* (U.S. Census Bureau Series, Census 2000 Special Reports, CENSR-5). Washington, DC: U.S. Government Printing Office. | Massachusetts Department of Education. (2003). *Massachusetts High School Students and Sexual Orientation Results of the 2003 Youth Risk Behavior Survey.* Boston, MA: Author. | U.S. Department of Health and Human Services. (2000). *Gay and Lesbian Adoptive Parents: Resources for Professionals and Parents.* Washington, DC: Child Welfare Information Gateway.

CHAPTER 3: WEALTH, INCOME, AND OPPORTUNITY

Chasing the American Dream

Census 2000, Five-Percent Public Use Microdata Series, U.S. Census Bureau. | Census 2000, Summary File 1, U.S. Census Bureau. | Census 2000, Summary File 3, U.S. Census Bureau. | Survey of Business Owners 2002, U.S. Census Bureau. | Survey of Minority- and Women-Owned Business Enterprises 1997, U.S. Census Bureau.

Over Our Heads: Consumer Debt

Board of Governors of the Federal Reserve System, unpublished data. | American Community Survey 2005, U.S. Census Bureau.

| Census 2000, Summary File 3, U.S. Census Bureau. | Bucks, B. K., Kennickell, K. B., & Moore, K. B. (2006). *"Recent Changes in U.S. Family Finances: Evidence from the 2001 and 2004 Survey of Consumer Finances*. Federal Reserve Bulletin.

The Persistence of Poverty
American Community Survey 2005, U.S. Census Bureau. | Bhandari, S., & Gifford, E. (2003, August). *Children with health insurance: 2001* (U.S. Census Bureau Series, Consumer Income, P60-224). Washington, DC: U.S. Government Printing Office. | Census 2000, Five-Percent Public Use Microdata Series, U.S. Census Bureau. | Census 2000, Summary File 3, U.S. Census Bureau. | Census 2000, Summary File 4, U.S. Census Bureau. | DeNavas-Walt, C., Procter, B.D., & Lee, C.H. (2006, August). *Income, poverty, and health insurance coverage in the United States: 2005* (U.S. Census Bureau Series, Current Population Reports—Consumer Income, P60-231). Washington, DC: U.S. Government Printing Office.

Educational Attainment and Life Chances
American Community Survey 2004, U.S. Census Bureau. | Census 2000, Summary File 3, U.S. Census Bureau.

Unfinished Business: High School and College Dropouts
American Community Survey 2004, U.S. Census Bureau. | Census 2000, Five-Percent Public Use Microdata Series, U.S. Census Bureau. | Census 2000, Summary File 3, U.S. Census Bureau. | Current Population Surveys 1920-2003, U.S. Census Bureau. | Laird, J., Lew, S., DeBell, M., & Chapman, C. (2006). *Dropout rates in the United States: 2002 and 2003* (NCES 2006-062). U.S. Department of Education. Washington, DC: National Center for Education Statistics. | National Center for Education Statistics. (2005). *Digest of education statistics, 2004* (NCES 2006-005). U.S. Department of Education. Washington, DC: Author.

Alternatives to Public Education
National Center for Education Statistics. *Reasons for Homeschooling*, 1999. | Broughman, S. T., & Pugh, K. (2004). *Characteristics of Private Schools in the United States: Results From the 2001-2002 Private School Universe Survey* (Rep.). Washington DC: U.S. Department of Education, Institute of Education Sciences. | Princiotta, D., & Bielick, S. (2006). *Homeschooling in the United States: 2003* (Rep.). Washington DC: U.S. Department of Education Institute of Education Sciences.

CHAPTER 4: THE ECONOMY AND WORKPLACE

Earning Our Keep: The American Workforce
Summary Statistics by 2002 NAICS United States. Washington, DC: U.S Census Bureau. | *Career Guide to Industries, Overview and Outlook* (2006.). Washington DC: U.S. Bureau of Labor Statistics. | U.S. Census Bureau. Statistical Abstract of the United States, 2006. | American Community Survey 2005, U.S. Census Bureau. | Census 2000, Summary File 3, U.S. Census Bureau. | U.S Census Bureau, Foreign Trade Division. (2007). *U.S. Trade in Goods and Services—Balance of Payments (BOP) Basis*. Washington, DC. | American Community Survey 2004, U.S. Census Bureau. | 2002 Economic Census, U.S. Census Bureau. | Denavas-Walt, C., Procter, B. D., & Lee, C. H. (2005). *Income, Poverty, and Health Insurance Coverage in the United States: 2004*. Washington DC: U.S Census Bureau. | U.S. Census Bureau, Company Statistics Division, Economic Census Branch. (2005). *2002 Survey of Business Owners Preliminary estimates of Business Ownership by Gender, Hispanic or Latino Origin, and Race: 2002. Washington DC*.

Working Overtime: Labor Conditions
Census 2000, Summary File 3, U.S. Census Bureau. | Fatal and Nonfatal Injuries, and Selected Illnesses and Conditions. *Worker Health Chartbook 2004*. (2004). National Institute for Occupational Safety and Health. | Bureau of Labor Statistics. USDL.(2003, March 27). Lost-Worktime Injuries and Illnesses: Characteristics and Resulting Days Away from Work, 2001. *U.S. Department of Labor Press Release*. | Bureau of Labor Statistics, U.S. Department of Labor. | Bureau of Labor Statistics, 2002.

The State of the Unions: Organized Labor
Bureau of Labor Statistics. USDL. (2007, January 25). Union Members Summary. *Bureau of Labor Statistics Press Release*. | Union Sourcebook 1947-1983; U.S. Bureau of Labor Statistics.

Equal Opportunity Employment: Diversity in the Workplace
(2004, Summer). *Occupational Outlook Quarterly*. | *Diversity in the Finance Industry* (Rep.). (2006). Washington DC: The U.S. Equal Employment Opportunity Commission. | *Diversity in the Media: A Chart Book for Selected Industries* (Rep.). (2004). Washington DC: U.S. Equal Employment Opportunity Commission. | *Diversity in Law Firms* (Rep.). (2003). Washington DC: U.S. Equal Employment Opportunity Commission. | The U.S. Equal Employment Opportunity Commission. *Occupational Employment in Private Industry by Race/Ethic Group/Sex and by Industry, United States, 2003*. | Bureau of Labor Statistics, U.S Department of Labor. | The U.S. Equal Employment Opportunity Commission. (2005, December 8). New Gallup Poll on Employment Discrimination Shows Progress, problems 40 Years after founding of EEOC. *The U.S. Equal Employment Opportunity Commission Press Release*. | The U.S. Equal Employment Opportunity Commission. *Enforcement Statistics and Litigation*. | Population Estimates Program, 2006, U.S. Census Bureau. |

The Workplace Gender Gap
American Community Survey 2004, U.S. Census Bureau. | Census 2000, Summary File 3, U.S. Census Bureau.

CHAPTER 5: HEALTH AND WELLNESS

Health Insurance: The Haves and the Have-Nots
Current Population Surveys 1988-2006, U.S. Census Bureau. | DeNavas-Walt, C., Procter, B.D., & Lee, C.H. (2005, August). *Income, poverty, and health insurance coverage in the United States: 2004* (U.S. Census Bureau Series, Current Population Reports—Consumer Income, P60-229). Washington, DC: U.S. Government Printing Office. | Population Projections Program, 2006, US. Census Bureau.

Living on the Edge: Behavioral Risk Factors
Health, United States, 2005, Centers for Disease Control and Prevention, National Center for Health Statistics, National Health Interview Survey, family core and sample adult questionnaires. | National Survey on Drug Use and Health, 2002.

The Threat of Pandemic Disease
Centers for Disease Control and Prevention. (1998). Prevention and control of influenza: Recommendations of the Advisory Committee on Immunization Practices (ACIP). *MMWR Morb*

Mortal Wkly, 47(RR-6): 1-26. | Congressional Budget Office. (2006, May). *A potential influenza pandemic: An update on possible macroeconomic effects and policy issues*. Washington, DC: Author. | Glezen, P.W. (1996). Emerging infections: pandemic influenza. *Epidemiol Rev, 18*, 64-76.| Meltzer, M.I., Cox, N.J., & Fukuda, K. (1999). The economic impact of pandemic influenza in the United States: Priorities for intervention. *Emerging Infectious Diseases, 5*(5), 659-671.

A Matter of Life and Death: Cancer
American Cancer Society. (2006). *Cancer Facts & Figures—2006*. Atlanta, GA: Author. | Census 2000, Summary File 3, U.S. Census Bureau. | Ries, L.A.G., Melbert, D., Krapcho, M., Mariotto, A, Miller, B.A., Feuer, E.J., et al. (2006). *SEER Cancer Statistics Review, 1975-2003*. Bethesda, MD: National Cancer Institute.

Sexually Transmitted Diseases
Centers for Disease Control and Prevention. (2006, November). *Sexually Transmitted Disease Surveillance, 2005*. Atlanta, GA: U.S. Department of Health and Human Services. | Fleming, D.T., McQuillan, G.M., Johnson, R.E., Nahmias, A.J., Aral, S.O., Lee, F.K., St. Louis, M.E. (1997). Herpes simplex virus type 2 in the United States, 1976 to 1994. *NEJM, 16*, 1105-1111. | National Center for Health Statistics. (2005). *Health, United States, 2005*. Washington, DC: U.S. Government Printing Office. | Warnecke, R. (ed). (1995). *Health survey research methods conference proceedings*. Conference on Health Survey Research Methods, Breckenridge, CO.

Battling the Epidemic: AIDS in America
Centers for Disease Control and Prevention. (2002). *HIV/AIDS surveillance report 2002*. Atlanta, GA: U.S. Department of Health and Human Services. | National Alliance of State and Territorial AIDS Directors. (2006). *Centers for Disease Control and Prevention HIV/AIDS funding by state*. Unpublished Data. | Population Estimates Program for 2002. (2004). U.S. Census Bureau.

Americans with Disabilities
American Community Survey 2004, U.S. Census Bureau. | Census 2000, Summary File 3, U.S. Census Bureau. | National Center for Health Statistics. (2005). *Health, United States, 2005*. Washington, DC: U.S. Government Printing Office. | Office of Special Education and Rehabilitative Services. (2005). *Report of children with disabilities receiving special education Part B, Individuals with Disabilities Act* (OMB: 1820-0043). Washington, DC: Author. | U.S. Census Bureau. (2006, July). *Americans with Disabilities Act: July 26* (U.S. Census Bureau Series, Facts for Features, CB06-FF.10-2). Washington, DC: Author. | Waldrop, J., & Stern, S.M. (2003, March). *Disability status: 2000* (U.S. Census Bureau Series, Census 2000 Brief, C2KBR-17). Washington, DC: U.S. Government Printing Office. | Wang, Q. (2005, July). *Disability and American families: 2000* (U.S. Census Bureau Series, Census 2000 Special Reports, CENSR-23). Washington, DC: U.S. Government Printing Office.

Mental Health and Disability
American Community Survey 2004, U.S. Census Bureau. | Census 2000, Summary File 3, U.S. Census Bureau. | Centers for Disease Control and Prevention. (2006). *National Ambulatory Medical Care Survey: 2004 Summary*. Atlanta, GA: Author. | National Center for Health Statistics. (2005). *Health, United States, 2005*. Washington, DC: U.S. Government Printing Office.

| National Institute of Mental Health. (2006). *The numbers count: Mental disorders in America*. Bethesda, MD: Author. | Substance Abuse and Mental Health Services Administration. (2000). *Mental health, United States, 2000*. Rockville, MD: Author. | U.S. Census Bureau. (2006, July). *Americans with Disabilities Act: July 26* (U.S. Census Bureau Series, Facts for Features, CB06-FF.10-2). Washington, DC: Author. | U.S. Department of Health and Human Services. (1999). *Mental health: A report of the Surgeon General—executive summary*. Rockville, MD: Author. | Waldrop, J., & Stern, S.M. (2003, March). *Disability status: 2000* (U.S. Census Bureau Series, Census 2000 Brief, C2KBR-17). Washington, DC: U.S. Government Printing Office. | Wang, Q. (2005, July). *Disability and American families: 2000* (U.S. Census Bureau Series, Census 2000 Special Reports, CENSR-23). Washington, DC: U.S. Government Printing Office.

CHAPTER 6: POLITICS AND GOVERNMENT

The Federal Purse: Government Spending
Consolidated Federal Funds (Rep.). (2005). Washington DC: U.S. Census Bureau. | Census 2000, Summary File 1, U.S. Census Bureau. | Office of Management and Budget, Department of Defense. | U.S. Census Bureau. (2006, April 3). National Spending Per Student Rises to $8,287. *U.S. Census Bureau Press Release*. | U.S Department of Treasury. *Fact Sheet on Economics of Taxation*. | Congressional Budget Office; Office of Management and Budget. *Revenues, Outlays, Surpluses, Deficits, and Debt Held by the Public, 1962 to 2006*. | *Federal Debt: Answers to Frequently Asked Questions*. (2004). Washington DC: United States Government Accountability Office. | *Federal Aid to States for Fiscal Year 2004* (Rep.). (2006). Washington DC: U.S. Census Bureau.

Exercising Your Right: Voter Participation
U.S. Census Bureau, Population Division, Education & Social Stratification Branch. *Voting and Registration in the Election of November 2004*. | U.S. Census Bureau. Statistical Abstract of the United States: 2006. | 2004 Senatorial Election Data Sources.

Diversity in Government
Joint Center for Political and Economic Studies. (2001). *Black Elected Officials: A Statistical Summary 2001*. Washington, DC: Author. | Library of Congress. (2005). Congressional Research Service. | Senate Historical Office. (2006). *Ethnic Diversity in the Senate*. Washington, DC: U.S. Senate. | <http://www.senate.gov/artandhistory/history/common/briefing/minority_senators.htm> accessed on February 6, 2007. | U.S. House of Representatives, "House Press Gallery," <http://www.house.gov/daily/hpg.htm> (as of January 17, 2006)

Defending the Nation: The Military
U.S. Census Bureau, Statistical Abstract of the United States: 2006 | U.S. Department of Defense. (2006). *Operation Iraqi Freedom U.S. Casualty List*. U.S. Department of Defense website: http://www.defenselink.mil/news/casualty.pdf . | Census 2000, 5% PUMS, U.S.

CHAPTER 7: CRIME AND LAW ENFORCEMENT

Criminal Activity
Federal Bureau of Investigation. *Uniform Crime Reports: Crime in the United States, 2004*. | Federal Bureau of Investigation.

Uniform Crime Reports 1995-2004. | Bureau of Justice Statistics. (2007, April 18). Justice Expenditure and Employment (Rep.). (2006). Washington DC: U.S. Department of Justice. | Bureau of Justice Statistics. (2006, September 10). | FBI, Uniform Crime Reports, prepared by the National Archive of Criminal Justice Data.

Doing Time: Prisoners and Incarceration
Bureau of Justice Statistics. (2004, June). Data collections for the Prison Rape Elimination Act of 2003. Washington, DC: Author. | Harrison, P.M., & Beck, A.J. (2005, April). Prisoner and jail inmates at midyear 2004 (NCJ 208801). Washington, DC: Bureau of Justice Statistics. | Harrison, P.M., & Beck, A.J. (2005, October). Prisoners in 2004 (NCJ 210677). Washington, DC: Bureau of Justice Statistics. | Harrison, P.M., & Beck, A.J. (2006, November). Prisoners in 2005 (NCJ 215092). Washington, DC: Bureau of Justice Statistics. | Marauschak, L.M. (2005, September). HIV in prisons, 2003 (NCJ 210344). Washington, DC: Bureau of Justice Statistics.

The High Price of Vice: Alcohol, Drug Abuse, and Gambling
Spiess, M. (2003). Drug Policy Information Clearinghouse Fact Sheet Rockville, Maryland: ONDCP Drug Policy Information Clearinghouse. | Problem and Pathological Gambling (Rep.). National Gambling Impact Commission. | National Institute of Drug Abuse. (2005, February 2). | SAMHSA, Office of Applied Studies, National Survey on Drug Use and Health, 2003 and 2004. | National Problem Gambling Awareness Week. (2007, March). | American Gaming Association. (2003). | SAMHSA, Office of Applied Studies, National Survey on Drug Use and Health, 2003 and 2004. | SAMHSA, Drug Abuse Warning Network 2003 (09/2004 update). | The NSDUH Report (Rep.). (2005). Office of Applied Studies, Substance Abuse and Mental Health Services Administration.| Crime in the United States 2004 (2006). Department of Justice, Federal Bureau of Investigation. | The NSDUH Report (Rep.). (2003). Office of Applied Studies, Substance Abuse and Mental Health Services Administration.

Risky Business: Teenage Substance Abuse
National Center for Health Statistics. (2005). Health, United States, 2005. Washington, DC: U.S. Government Printing Office. | Substance Abuse & Mental Health Services Administration. (2005). National survey on drug use and health, 2004. Rockville, MD: Author. | Substance Abuse & Mental Health Services Administration. (2006). National survey on drug use and health, 2005. Rockville, MD: Author.

Children and Crime: Juvenile Delinquency
Federal Bureau of Investigation. Uniform Crime Reports: Crime in the United States, 2003. | Federal Bureau of Investigation. Uniform Crime Reports: Crime in the United States, 2004. | Juvenile Offenders and Victims: 2006 National Report OJJDP, March 2006. | Federal Bureau of Investigation. Uniform Crime Reports: Crime in the United States, 2002. | OJJDP Statistical Briefing Book. Online. Available: http://ojjdp.ncjrs.gov/ojstatbb/structure_process/qa04105.asp?qaDate=2004. Released on March 27, 2006. | Juvenile Offenders and Victims: 2006 National Report, OJJDP, March 2006.

The Youngest Crime Victims
U.S. Department of Health and Human Services. (2004). Administration on Children, Youth and Families. Child Maltreatment, Washington, DC: U.S. Government Printing Office, 2006. | Federal Bureau of Investigation. Uniform Crime Reports: Crime in the United States, 2003. | U.S. Department of Health and Human Services. (2006).Administration on Children, Youth and Families. Child Maltreatment 2004, Washington, DC: U.S. Government Printing Office.

CHAPTER 8: NATURAL RESOURCES AND THE ENVIRONMENT

Living Off the Land: Agriculture
2002 Census of Agriculture; US Census Bureau 2002 Population. | U.S. Department of Agriculture, Census of Agriculture, 2002. | U.S. Department of Agriculture Economic Research Service. Average acres per farm by census region, 1900-2002. | U.S. Department of Agriculture, Economic Research Service. Distribution of farms by acreage class, 1880-1997.

From Sea to Shining Sea: Land Use
National Park Service. [Map data files]. | U.S. Environmental Protection Agency. | U.S. Bureau of Land Management. (2006, November 21). National Landscape Conservation System Summary Tables. | Public Land Statistics. (Rep.). (2004). U.S. Department of the Interior, Bureau of Land Management. | U.S. Department of the Interior, Fish and Wildlife Service. Endangered Species Habitat Conservation Planning. | U.S. Department of Agriculture, Forest Service. National Wilderness Areas by State. | Data Report: A Supplement to the National Report on Sustainable Forests, 2003. (Rep.). (2004, May). U.S. Department of Agriculture. | U.S. Department of Agriculture, Natural Resources Conservation Service. (2001, May 7). Broad Land Cover/Use, by State, 1997. | U.S. Department of the Interior, Fish and Wildlife Department. (2005, November). Species Information Threatened and Endangered Animals and Plants. | U.S. Department of Agriculture, Natural Resources Conservation Service. (2000, December). State Rankings by Acreage and Rate of Non-Federated Land Developed. | 2003 Report on Sustainable Forests. (Rep.). (2003). U.S. Department of Agriculture, Forest Service. | U.S. Department of Agriculture. (2002). National Resources Inventory, Land Use. | U.S. Department of the Interior, Fish and Wildlife Service and U.S. Department of Commerce, U.S. Census Bureau. 2001 National Survey of Fishing, Hunting, and Wildlife-Associated Recreation. | U.S. Department of the Interior, Fish and Wildlife Service. National Wetlands Inventory, Why Map Wetlands?

Hungry for Power: Energy Consumption
U.S. Department of Energy, Energy Information Administration. Table S3. Energy Consumption Estimates by Source, 2004. State Energy Consumption, Price, and Expenditure Estimates, 2004. | U.S. Department of Energy, Energy Information Administration. (2007, June 1). State Energy Consumption, Price, and Expenditure Estimates, 2004. | Annual Energy Review, 2005. (Rep.). (2006, July 27). Energy Information Administration. | U.S. Department of Energy, Energy Information Administration. (2006, May). Nuclear Power Generation. | U.S. Department of Energy, Energy Information Administration. Table 1.3. Energy Consumption by Source, 1949-2005. | U.S. Department of Energy, Energy Information Administration. (2006, October). Energy INFOcard: United States. | U.S. Department of Energy, Energy Information Administration. (2001). Table CE1-5.1u. Total Energy Consumption and Expenditures by Household Member and Demographics, 2001. Residential Energy Consumption Survey:

Household Energy Consumption and Expenditures Tables. | U.S. Department of Energy, Energy Information Administration. (2006, July 26). *Energy Overview.* | U.S. Department of Energy, Energy Information Administration. (2006, October). *Energy INFOcard: Uses of Energy.* | U.S. Department of Energy, Energy Information Administration. (2006, October). *Energy INFOcard: Transportation Energy Use.*

Environmental Quality: Pollution and Conservation
Environmental Protection Agency. (2006). *Clean Air Markets Data and Maps.* Accessed at http://cfpub.epa.gov/gdm/ | *2005, Annual Performance and Progress Report: Air Quality in National Parks.* (2005, December 6). Department of the Interior, National Park Service. | U.S. Department of the Interior, National Park Service. (2005). *Air Quality Trends in National Parks, 1995-2004.* | U.S. Department of the Interior, Environmental Protection Agency. (2003, August). *Air Quality Index: A Guide to Air Quality and Your Health.* | U.S. Department of the Interior, Environmental Protection Agency. (2007, June 12). *Air Quality Monitoring Information.* | Environmental Protection Agency. (2005). Municipal Solid Waste in the U.S., 2001 Facts and Figures Executive Summary, EPA 530-F-05-003, pp. 1-16 |U.S. Department of the Interior, Environmental Protection Agency. (2006, July 3). *Locate Superfund Sites.*

The Greenhouse Effect: CO$_2$ Emissions
U.S. Department of the Interior, Environmental Protection Agency. (2006, April 15). *Inventory of U.S. Greenhouse Gas Emissions and Sinks: 1990-2004.* | Energy Information Administration. (1996, July). *Voluntary reporting of greenhouse gases, 1995* (DOE/EIA-0608). Washington, DC: Author. | Klein, Daniel E. (2006, January). *Overview of the Carbon Sequestration Project Database.* (Rep.). McLean, VA: U.S Department of Energy. | U.S. Department of the Interior, Environmental Protection Agency. (2006, October 19). *State Greenhouse Gas Inventories.* | U.S. Department of the Interior, Energy Information Administration. (2005, December). *Emissions of Greenhouse Gases in the United States, 2004.* Table C3. Summary of State Energy-related Carbon Dioxide Emissions, 1990-2001. | U.S. Department of Energy, Carbon Dioxide Information Analysis Center. (2004, August). *Estimates of Annual Fossil-Fuel CO$_2$ Emitted for Each State in the U.S.A. and the District of Columbia for Each Year from 1960 Through 2000.* | U.S. Department of the Interior, Environmental Protection Agency. *CO$_2$ Emissions from Fossil Fuel Combustion Million Metric Tons CO$_2$ (MMTCO$_2$).* | U.S. Department of Energy, Carbon Dioxide Information Analysis Center. *National Fossil-Fuel CO$_2$ Emissions.* | Marland, Gregg, Tom Boden, and Robert J. Andres. *National CO$_2$ Emissions from Fossil-Fuel Burning, Cement Manufacture, and Gas Flaring: 1751-2003.* (Rep.). Oakland, TN: U.S. Department of Energy, Carbon Dioxide Information Analysis Center.

Heavy Weather: Natural Disasters
U.S. Department of Commerce, National Oceanic and Atmospheric Administration, National Weather Service, Office of Climate, Water, and Weather Services. (2007, March 16). *Natural Hazard Statistics.* | U.S. Department of Commerce, National Oceanic and Atmospheric Administration, National Geophysical Data Center. *The Significant Earthquake Database.* | Graumann, Axel, Tamara Houston, Jay Lawrimore, David Levinson, Neal Lott, Sam McCown, Scott Stephens, and David Wuertz. *Hurricane Katrina: A Climatological Perspective*

(preliminary report). (Rep.). (2005, August 29). Asheville, NC: National Oceanic and Atmospheric Administration, National Climactic Data Center. | U.S. Department of Commerce, National Oceanic and Atmospheric Administration, National Weather Service, Climate Prediction Center. (2007, May 22). NOAA: 2007 Atlantic Hurricane Season Outlook. *National Oceanic and Atmospheric Administration Press Release.* | National Interagency Fire Center. *Wildland Fire Statistics.* | U.S. Department of Commerce, National Oceanic and Atmospheric Administration, Atlantic Oceanographic and Meteorological Laboratory, Hurricane Research Division. *Tropical cyclones in the Atlantic basin, 1944-2006.* | U.S. Department of Commerce, National Oceanic and Atmospheric Administration. (2003, March 5). *Mobile Homes and Vehicles Deadly in Tornadoes.*

CHAPTER 9: MODERN AMERICA

Stuck in Traffic: Commuting and Roadway Congestion
Census 2000, Summary File 3, U.S. Census Bureau. | 2000 Census, Means of Transportation to Work, U.S. Census Bureau. | American Community Survey. (2005, March 30). Americans Spend More Than 100 Hours Commuting to. *American Community Survey Press Release.* | *Traffic Congestion and Reliability: Trends and Advanced Strategies for Congestion Mitigation* (Rep.). (2005). United States Department of Transportation - Federal Highway Administration. | Bureau of Transportation Statistics. National Transportation Statistics. | U.S. Department of Housing and Urban Development. *American Housing Survey for the United States*: 2005 (Washington, DC: 2006) | Texas Transportation Institute, The 2005 Annual Urban Mobility Report (College Station, TX: 2005) | 2000 Census, Means of Transportation to Work, U.S. Census Bureau. | APTA, Americans in Transit, 1992, Characteristics of Transit Riders. | APTA, Federal Transit Administration National Transit Database. | U.S. Department of Transportation. Bureau of Transportation Statistics, Office of Airline Information,Washington, DC 2003. | American Public Transportation Association. (2006, April 4). Public Transportation Ridership Up In 2005. *American Public Transportation Association Press Release.* | American Public Transportation Association. *Public Transportation Ridership Statistics.*

Planes, Trains, and Buses: Mass Transportation
2000 Census, Means of Transportation to Work, U.S. Census Bureau. | APTA, Americans in Transit, 1992, Characteristics of Transit Riders. | APTA, Federal Transit Administration National Transit Database. | U.S. Department of Transportation. Bureau of Transportation Statistics, Office of Airline Information,Washington, DC 2003. | American Public Transportation Association. (2006, April 4). Public Transportation Ridership Up In 2005. *American Public Transportation Association Press Release.* | American Public Transportation Association. *Public Transportation Ridership Statistics.*

Wired America: Computers and Usage
Current Population Survey 2003, U.S. Census Bureau. | Day, J.C., Janus, A., & Davis, J. *Computer and Internet use in the United States: 2003* (U.S. Census Bureau Series, Current Population Reports, P23-208). Washington, DC: U.S. Government Printing Office. | Federal Communications Commission, Wireline Competition Bureau. (2006, July). *High-speed services for Internet*

access: Status as of December 31, 2005. Washington, DC: Author. | Population Estimates Program for 2005, U.S. Census Bureau. | U.S. Census Bureau. (2006, May). *E-stats, 2004 e-commerce multi-sector report*. Washington, DC: Author. | U.S. Census Bureau. (2006, November). *Quarterly retail e-commerce sales: 3ʳᵈ quarter 2006* (CB06-167). Washington, DC: Author.

On the Air: Broadcast Media
Federal Communications Commission. (2006, September). *National File—Television Broadcast Signal Coverage* [Mapping data file]. Washington, DC: Author. | U.S. Census Bureau. (2005, December). *2004 service annual survey, information sector services*. Washington, DC: Author. | Veronis Suhler Stevenson. (2006). *Communications industry forecast & report*. New York, NY: Author.

INDEX

Note: Page numbers followed by the letter *m* indicate maps.